D0620814

Selected Letters of
THEODORE ROETHKE

SELECTED

LETTERS OF

THEODORE

ROETHKE

EDITED WITH AN INTRODUCTION BY

Ralph J. Mills, Jr.

UNIVERSITY OF WASHINGTON PRESS
Seattle & London

"His Words" (from "The Dying Man"), copyright © 1956
by The Atlantic Monthly Corporation,
from *The Collected Poems of Theodore Roethke.*
Reprinted by permission of Doubleday and Company, Inc.

Copyright © 1968 by Beatrice Roethke
as administratrix of the estate of Theodore Roethke
Library of Congress Catalog Card Number 68-11045
Manufactured by the Colonial Press Inc., Clinton, Mass,
Printed in the United States of America
All rights reserved

I wake to sleep, and take my waking slow.
I learn by going where I have to go.

THEODORE ROETHKE, from "The Waking"

Acknowledgments

THIS book was made possible through a generous grant from the Bloedel Foundation of Seattle which enabled Beatrice Roethke, the poet's widow, to collect and sort the large number of letters from which this selection was made. I am deeply indebted to Mrs. Roethke for her kind invitation to edit this book and for the enormous amount of patient work she has done on the correspondence. She has been of such help that she must really be called a coeditor. Likewise, I owe an immense debt of gratitude to the University of Washington Library, particularly to its Manuscripts Section and to Mrs. Kari F. Inglis for providing Xeroxed copies of the letters and for a great deal of help with chronology and other details. Thanks are due the University Research Board of the Graduate College of the University of Illinois for awarding me a Faculty Fellowship for the summer of 1966 and a traveling grant the same year to facilitate work on this volume.

I should also like to extend my warmest thanks to the following individuals for various kinds of valuable assistance: Robert Bly, James Wright, Henry Rago, and Peter Viereck (for making available to me some uncollected letters); Herschel Baker; Mrs. John Berryman; Mrs. Dorothee Bowie; John Ciardi; Franklin Folsom; George Hendrick; Rolfe Humphries; Mrs. James P. Kelly; Stanley Kunitz; John Frederick Nims; Robert Ogle; Anthony Ostroff;

David Randall (of the Lilly Library of Indiana University); Miss June Roethke; Robert Rosenthal and Mrs. Janet Lowrey (of the University of Chicago Library); Karl Shapiro; Jacob Steinberg; Miss Katharine Stokes; and Mrs. Elizabeth Wright. Throughout my work, I have had the essential help provided by John Matheson's bibliography of Roethke.

One of the greatest debts I have to acknowledge here goes beyond the particulars of this book. To Richard Ellmann and Nathan A. Scott, Jr., teachers and friends of long standing, I should like to extend my deepest gratitude, for their continued interest, advice, judgment, and encouragement over a number of years.

RALPH J. MILLS, JR.

University of Illinois
at Chicago Circle
December, 1967

Contents

Illustrations

Introduction

SINCE his sudden death on August 1, 1963, at the age of fifty-five, Theodore Roethke has continued to increase in magnitude and force as a living poetic voice. This growth has been evident in various ways: in the developing critical recognition of his stature as a poet of the first importance—which has come tardily to him as to other fine poets of his generation; in the acknowledgment by contemporary poets of the high esteem in which they hold his work —though he started to win such approval even before the publication of his initial book; in the appeal he has for the young, whether writers themselves or simply readers. Roethke's poetic voice, brought to full strength by the posthumous publication of *The Far Field* (1964) and the *Collected Poems* (1966), is the voice of the total self, nothing withheld, moving through and articulating the whole range of the poet's experience, from his origins to the threshold of death, and touching, often terrifyingly, the areas of madness and of mystical perception.

There are, however, other Roethke voices to be found—prose voices we will have to call them by comparison with the qualities of the poetry, but nonetheless voices having their own genuine character and frequently complementing the poems. Certain of these prose voices can no longer be heard (though we do have recordings and the magnificent film *In a Dark Time,* made in the poet's last year, in which we can see and hear him talk about poetry and read it): these are the voices of the poet in conversation with friends and fellow poets, or in the classroom with his students. Some of this will doubtless eventually come to us in memoirs, essays, biographies, and autobiographies; some of it, too, will be felt only indirectly as it influences the thought and art of those with whom Roethke had personal communication.

Besides these speaking voices in the changing air of human contacts, there are the prose pieces on paper—criticism and writings about the craft of poetry and the poet's life in relation to it (these pieces have been gathered separately);[1] the notebooks, with their abundance of materials, lines, stanzas, drafts, ideas, images, and so forth, which lie behind, generate, or coalesce into the shapes of poems; the letters, which emerge from and are concerned with many aspects of the poet's living, both as an individual and an artist. Portions of the large body of notebooks have been sensitively and skillfully edited by the poet David Wagoner and have appeared in periodicals; more comprehensive editing of them in book form will surely follow. The notebooks should offer a rewarding view of Roethke's career from a purely aesthetic standpoint. Students of his work will be able to see where many poems originated and learn something of the operations of Roethke's imagination.

The letters present a wider and, of necessity, less concentrated perspective on Roethke. Those included here count as only a small part of the ones he wrote and have been selected (with the exception of those to James Wright, Peter Viereck, and Henry Rago) from the large collection in the University of Washington Library to illustrate particularly his career as poet. Other letters are still outstanding; some undoubtedly have been lost and some destroyed.

Roethke was not, to begin with, a devoted letter writer, as relatively few poets would seem to be these days; and once or twice he went so far in letters as to lament the fact that he was compelled to write them. Yet, time consuming as it was (in addition to the demands of teaching and other daily tasks, plus the requirements of his art), we find him putting pen to paper again and again—occasionally with gregarious enthusiasm and generally in a manner

---

[1] In *On the Poet and His Craft: Selected Prose of Theodore Roethke*, ed. by Ralph J. Mills, Jr. (Seattle: University of Washington Press, 1965).

that reflects one side or another of the man. He had many correspondents—not all of them represented in the present volume—
but a considerable number were poets themselves, academic
friends or colleagues, editors, students or former students, and
some were lady friends or "loves." (In this last category it is well
to remember that Roethke was a long-time bachelor and did not
marry until 1953.) Many of the letters are of what might be termed
a business nature and have little if any interest for the reader of a
selective book, though they may be of value to the specialist or
biographer. As one would guess, letters written to different persons during the same period of time occasionally repeat things or
overlap one another; still others—and in this group I include a
large proportion of the available "love" letters—are really hur-
ried and often random notes about special details of a day, or a
job, or whatever, coupled with rather repetitious declarations of
affection, so that they seemed too insubstantial to print, especially
when other letters provided a larger impression of the identical
part of his life.

Along with the letters in this selection, I have printed several
poems, the majority of them dating from the earlier years of
Roethke's literary life. These include unpublished poems and
early versions of poems which later appeared in magazines or
books, or both. I have also included poems which Roethke did
not see fit to reprint after their journal publication. While no
masterpiece is hidden among them, their omission would distort
the letters; for Roethke was constantly enclosing poems with his
letters and asking those poets and critics whose accomplishments
he respected—Louise Bogan, Stanley Kunitz, Rolfe Humphries,
William Carlos Williams, and Kenneth Burke are chief among
them—to judge his work by their own, usually severe, standards.
Obviously, this practice does not mean that he always submitted
to the judgments of others; but he was willing to reconsider poems
in the light of different responses, as well as trust to his own sense
of imaginative rightness (which he probably came to do more and
more when composing the experimental poems of the "Praise to
the End!" sequence in the 1940's, though he consulted with Kenneth Burke about them). Unfortunately, it has been impossible
to publish all the poems not otherwise readily available which ac-
companied letters because in many instances they have been lost

or disposed of and cannot be identified from the texts of the letters themselves. Poems mentioned or discussed that can be found easily in Roethke's various books or in the new *Collected Poems* have not been reprinted, but the reader has been referred in a footnote to the proper page in the latter edition. Over and above the poems printed following the letters with which they were originally sent (or appear to have been sent), there is yet another group of pieces whose recipients are usually known but which cannot be attached with certainty to individual letters. Such poems appear occasionally throughout the text and are inserted near letters of the same date. Whenever possible they are also printed in proximity to letters by Roethke to the recipient of the poems—if the recipient is known.

Reading through the letters gathered here, one discovers that each decade, roughly speaking, has its own emphases. In the 1930's Roethke appeared in his correspondence as what he then was, the apprentice poet who had yet to publish a first book, though he was, visibly, through the decade working toward a significant one. The poet John Holmes, a friend and admirer, at one point drew up a proposed table of contents for the collection; Stanley Kunitz provided the final title, *Open House*. In one attempt at book publication, Roethke submitted a manuscript to the competition for the Yale Series of Younger Poets, but without success; meanwhile he continued to send out poems and to have them accepted and printed in an impressive variety of journals. Along with these poetic endeavors, and their indication of Roethke's deep-seated need for recognition (which continued long after he had attained that recognition, but must not be mistaken for a mere shallow kind of vanity even in its bluntest expressions), went the struggle through the depression years to make a living wage by teaching and other jobs. In a letter to William Mather Lewis, president of Lafayette College, written in December, 1934, to help secure his position for the next academic year, Roethke specified the tasks he had been performing for the college in addition to his teaching: these included the school's publicity work and the job of tennis coach.

Years later, in 1958, Roethke looked back on the exhaustion of that period in a letter warning a young poet, his former student James Wright, of the consequences of such fatigue. For in the autumn of 1935, while teaching his first (and only) term at Michigan State, Roethke crossed the "threshold" of mental breakdown, from which he was to suffer recurrently throughout the remainder of his life. I do not propose to discuss these illnesses here, nor am I competent to do so. In any case, they are matters better handled by his biographers or by those with authority to speak on the subject. That such breakdowns did take place, however, will be evident from time to time in the letters written during hospitalization, some of them readily indicative of the "high," extravagant, or euphoric phases of the manic cycle of elation and depression of which Roethke was the victim. Yet we should be aware that in these instances, no matter how much of an overstatement (sometimes a comic or satiric one) a letter might contain, there is mixed with it the expression of an authentic perception, judgment, attitude, or desire. Letters composed in the later years of his life disclose the psychiatric treatment he occasionally underwent in the apparently unsuccessful attempt to root out hidden neuroses and heal covert wounds. The extremely sensitive states in which he often found himself are revealed in a letter of November, 1958, to Princess Marguerite Caetani about the French poet René Char, with whom he discovered a deeply felt bond.

With his move to Bennington in 1943, Roethke's letters changed. His life, too, had changed: *Open House* had received excellent reviews from such tough judges as W. H. Auden, Yvor Winters, Louise Bogan, and Rolfe Humphries; and he had moved to a very different sort of college. At about this point he apparently began the venture into daring poetic experimentation with the interior life of childhood and the evolution of the self which carried through his next two books, *The Lost Son and Other Poems* (1948) and *Praise to the End!* (1951). Numerous letters to Kenneth Burke, who was a Bennington colleague and later wrote a brilliant critical essay on the poems, at this time and after Roethke's move to Seattle, make plain the poet's belief in his new work as a real imaginative breakthrough—which, in fact, it proved to be. If Roethke said a good deal about these pieces, it was still not his habit to provide exegeses of his symbolism or to discuss his methods of composition. Nonetheless, what he did say is illuminating; and the strenuous efforts he had to put forth to get the poems accepted, understood, and appreciated for their ac-

complishment may seem surprising in an age purportedly dedicated to bold artistic innovation.

On January 22, 1948, he wrote a long letter (later to become
the basis for his epistolary essay "Open Letter") to Babette
Deutsch, explaining his aims in "The Lost Son" and filling in
some background material on the childhood sequence. It is worth-
while remarking how Roethke, here as elsewhere, stressed the
point that his poems were *not* bookish, that their experience did
not derive from reading but from his own life:

> In doing these, I have worked intuitively all the time. I've read
> almost no psychology. Several people have made the point that
> they [the poems] are at once a personal history and a history of
> the race itself. (That sounds high falutin'; but that's what they
> said.) I can make no claims, of course, one way or another. They
> *are* written to be heard; and they were written out of suffering,
> and are mine, by God.

And some years later, when approached by a student of these
poems, Roethke again insisted on how little psychology he had
read. It would appear that only toward the end of his life did he
intend to read systematically in the areas of philosophy and re-
ligion that interested him; at any rate, in 1959 he was awarded a
two-year grant from the Ford Foundation for the purpose of reading such subjects. Like Dylan Thomas, who was often mistakenly
thought to keep volumes of Freud handy when he wrote his poems,
Roethke probably gathered most of his knowledge of psychoana-
lytic theories indirectly, from the general intellectual atmosphere
of our time.

In 1947 Roethke took a position in the English department at
the University of Washington in Seattle, where he remained except for several trips abroad until his death. His selected poems,
The Waking, published in 1953, brought him the Pulitzer Prize
and the beginnings of a larger public reputation, though Stanley
Kunitz has noted that Roethke continued wryly to speak of himself as "the oldest younger poet" in America. The same year he
married Beatrice O'Connell, and with her the poet took the first
of three trips to Europe. During his stay at the University of
Washington, Roethke had established firmly what was obvious
early in the letters: that he was an enormously gifted teacher,

proud and dedicated in this work, and frequently exhausted by the demands it made upon him. A year before his death, the university created its only honorary post for him, Poet in Residence.

The letters from the last decade of his life, 1953 to 1963, show the same urges were on Roethke: the incessant wish for recognition, in spite of the honors accorded *Words for the Wind;* the unfailing exploratory drive in his art, the will to development and change so clearly in evidence in the "North American Sequence" poems of *The Far Field.* That volume was several years in the making and is often referred to in the letters under a title later discarded, *Dance On, Dance On, Dance On.* Occasionally, Roethke spoke of this as his last book—certainly not in the sense of failing artistic powers, for he was at the top of his form in these poems— perhaps with prophetic insight and because his health was not always good. Allen Tate has remarked that Roethke could write poetry in which he foresaw, and indeed experienced symbolically or vicariously, his own death. And that observation has nowhere more application than in some of the latest pieces, such as "Infirmity":

> Things without hands take hands: there is no choice,—
> Eternity's not easily come by.
> When opposites come suddenly in place,
> I teach my eyes to hear, my ears to see
> How body from spirit slowly does unwind
> Until we are pure spirit at the end.

Or "The Decision":

> Rising or falling's all one discipline!
> The line of my horizon's growing thin!
> Which is the way? I cry to the dread black,
> The shifting shade, the cinders at my back.
> Which is the way? I ask, and turn to go,
> As a man turns to face on-coming snow.

The question asked in the stanza above echoes, and now with a more profound and final resonance, that voice of the child protagonist in "The Lost Son" a decade and a half before:

> Tell me:
> Which is the way I take;

> Out of what door do I go,
> Where and to whom?

    All of Roethke's poetry involves search, transformation, the continuous process of becoming, in technique and style obviously, and also in vision, in the depth and intensity of experience he pursued. The letters are, of course, a by-product of that searching, the main energy of which is invariably directed into the poems. But however limited or fragmentary letters may be, they can at moments bring us close to the person of Theodore Roethke in a way that only correspondence or diaries can. A sense of the man within and behind the poetry attracts us as our appreciation and awareness of the excellence of his art increases. Roethke has already won a place for himself among the finest American poets; and I believe the letters that follow will provide the growing number of his readers with some meaningful glimpses of the person and the life from which his poems emerged.

> I heard a dying man
> Say to his gathered kin,
> "My soul's hung out to dry,
> Like a fresh-salted skin;
> I doubt I'll use it again.
>
> "What's done is yet to come;
> The flesh deserts the bone,
> But a kiss widens the rose;
> I know, as the dying know,
> Eternity is Now.
>
> "A man sees, as he dies,
> Death's possibilities;
> My heart sways with the world.
> I am that final thing,
> A man learning to sing."
>   —"His Words"

R.J.M., JR.

A Note on the Editing

MOST of the letters included in this volume were prepared from Xerox copies of the originals made available to the editor by the University of Washington Library from their Theodore Roethke collection. The letter to Henry Rago was prepared from a Xerox copy made available from the collection of Mr. Rago's papers at the Lilly Library of Indiana University. In most instances the original manuscripts were used in preparing the letters to James Wright, Peter Viereck, and the editor.

Most of the letters are handwritten. Roethke mentions in an early letter that he does not type; and during the 1930's and early 1940's typed letters and poetry manuscripts were done for him by his sister, June Roethke, or by friends. More typed letters do appear in the last fifteen or so years of his life, but many of these were dictated to or copied by secretaries. In any event, Roethke continued to write letters longhand as well. (It should be noted here that the letters to Kenneth Burke were typed for the Roethke collection from handwritten originals, and only the typescripts were consulted.)

Roethke did not always date his letters or specify the place from which they were sent; but frequently the postmark or internal evidence has made it possible to determine that information, which is printed in brackets at the top of the letter in such cases.

As I have tried to indicate in the introduction, the present selection of letters is based rather rigorously on their relation to
Roethke as a practicing poet and to his opinions about his art, as
well as to his career and the teaching of poetry. Since this book
does not constitute a collected edition but a very selective body of
correspondence by a contemporary poet only a few years dead, I
have tried to avoid an elaborate editorial apparatus. My aim has
been to provide a volume which—like *On the Poet and His Craft*
—can serve as a companion to Roethke's poetry and shed some
further light on it. However, I have made an effort to give the
reader identifications and annotations wherever they might be
needed. For many readers a number of these footnotes will be unnecessary, and may even appear superfluous; but I believe it is
wiser to err in this direction than to be too sparing of such details.
In some cases, identifications—titles of poems enclosed or full
names and occupations of persons—simply could not be made.
Throughout the text, I have tried to supply the required information without detracting from the letters themselves.

With the exception of a few persons so well known that it would
be absurd to comment on them, I have identified each of Roethke's
correspondents the first time a letter to him or her appears. The
correspondents are sometimes identified by posts or jobs held at
the time the letter was written; these may have changed in later
years.

One or two peculiarities of the letters remain to be mentioned.
Roethke frequently ended a sentence with a series of periods or
dots, as ". . . ." These have been left in the text but should not be
mistaken for an ellipsis to indicate an editorial deletion, which is
always bracketed. Another of his habits was to draw a line beneath
a paragraph as if to indicate a transition in thought or the conclusion of a certain part of a letter. These lines do not denote any
omissions. When I have omitted a complete paragraph or several
paragraphs, the deletion is noted by a full line of ellipses. In the
matter of spelling, I have usually corrected occasional minor er-
rors without any indication in the text.

R. J. M., JR.

A Brief Roethke Chronology

1908	Born May 25 in Saginaw, Michigan.
1929	Received A.B. from University of Michigan.
1930–31	Did graduate study at Harvard; was encouraged by Robert Hillyer to send out his poems.
1931–35	Taught at Lafayette College.
1935	Taught from end of September until mid-November at Michigan State University; had first breakdown in November; in hospital and sanitarium until January, 1936; not given job back at Michigan State.
1936	Received M.A. from University of Michigan. In fall of this year began teaching at Pennsylvania State College and remained there until 1943.
1941	*Open House,* first book, published.
1943	Began teaching at Bennington College; stayed on staff until 1946.
1945	Guggenheim fellowship.
1947	Began teaching at the University of Washington, where he remained until his death.
1948	*The Lost Son and Other Poems.*
1950	Second Guggenheim fellowship.
1951	*Praise to the End!*
1953	Married to Beatrice O'Connell in January; from

March until August in Europe (Italy, Paris, London). *The Waking: Poems 1933–1953* published (received Pulitzer Prize in spring of 1954).

1955–56   Fulbright lecturer in Italy. Travels included Spain, France, Austria, and England. Returned to United States in August, 1956.

1957   Beatrice Roethke ill with tuberculosis, in sanitarium January till May. In spring bought house at 3802 East John Street, Seattle.

1958   *Words for the Wind* (National Book Award, Bollingen Prize, several other awards). English edition, published the previous fall, was Christmas choice of the Poetry Book Society.

1959   Awarded two-year Ford Foundation grant.

1960   Made Honored Alumnus, Arthur Hill High School, Saginaw, Michigan, in May. Traveled to Europe in June: Antwerp, Paris, Brittany; in July to Dublin, then Inishbofin. Roethke entered hospital at Ballinisloe for a month in August. October: to London for the winter.

1961   March: returned to the United States. *I Am! Says the Lamb*. Award of the Golden Plate, Academy of Achievement (Monterey, California).

1962   Made Honorary Member of Poetry Society of America; awarded Honorary Doctor of Letters, University of Michigan; given only honorary title at the University of Washington, "Poet in Residence."

1963   *Party at the Zoo* (for children); *Sequence, Sometimes Metaphysical*. Died suddenly on Bainbridge Island, Washington, August 1.

1964   *The Far Field* (National Book Award).

1966   *Collected Poems*.

Selected Letters of
THEODORE ROETHKE

1931-37

To Harriet Monroe[1]

Easton, Pennsylvania
November 19, 1931

My dear Miss Monroe:—Could I be assured, in just this one instance, that you yourself pass judgment on these poems? [2]

It has been some time since I have submitted anything to your office. When I first began to write verse, I was much discouraged by your immediate and impersonal rejections. Recent acceptances, however, by such magazines as *The New Republic, The Commonweal, The Sewanee Review* have led me to hope that perhaps I do write a poem occasionally. The enclosed poems represent the work of many months. For this reason, if for no other, may I be pardoned for making this request?

Please do not be prejudicial on account of the letterhead. This is my first year of teaching.

Sincerely,
Theodore Roethke

[1] Poet and founding editor of *Poetry*.
[2] Probably "Bound" and "Fugitive," published in *Poetry* (September, 1932).

3

[EDITOR'S NOTE: *This poem not assignable to a specific letter. The present poem was untitled in typescript, but published as "The Conqueror" in* Commonweal *(Oct. 7, 1931).*]

Be proud to live alone.

Be proud to live alone.
Be murdered and undone,

But do not seek escape
In visionary shape,

Nor make disunion
A partner to your own.

Be brave and do not keep
A guardian for your sleep.

Preserve your promised word
As bright as any sword,

Your lively mirrors chaste
Uncheckered to the last.

Erase the shape of doom
From the walls of your room.

Constrain the willing blood
To virtue's platitude.

Live valiantly to find
Felicity in mind,

Perfection in the pain
That mortifies the brain.

To Harriet Monroe

Easton, Pennsylvania
February 5, 1931 [*1932*][1]

My dear Miss Monroe:—I can say truly that I am proud to have your magazine accept my little pieces.

I have not replied sooner because I have been trying to

[1] Early in the year Roethke occasionally uses the previous year for his dating.

strengthen the two poems your letter said "might tempt us but for weak lines." I hope they are satisfactory. In "Exhortation" I have tried to increase the number of inner rhyme effects: sudden-sodden, in addition to bleak-blank.[2]

You may title the negative tree poem anything you like—"Negative Tree," perhaps?

You ask for autobiographical details. I was born in Saginaw, Michigan, which has always been my permanent home. The address is 1725 Gratiot Avenue. I was educated at the University of Michigan and Harvard University.

No one is more aware than I of the defects of my present technique, especially, as you say, its frequent "effect of dryness." I hope to think more metaphorically, to add colour and warmth to my style.

Sincerely,
Theodore Roethke

To Dorothy Gordon[1]

Saginaw, Michigan
July 20, 1933

My dear Mrs. Gordon: I cannot begin conventionally by saying that I find thanking you difficult, for I do not; so if my words are empty and fatuous, it is simply evidence of my usual stupidity. But in these days of blatant self-promotion, it seems wonderful indeed that someone should spend so much time and energy helping a struggling pot-poet whom she has never seen! At its best, helping any creative artist is the highest form of philanthropy; in this case, unfortunately, the cause is not so noble—which is all the more reason for gratitude. I can say, then, in all sincerity that I am profoundly grateful for your kindness to me. I have, moreover, a kind of sublime faith that you will bring me good luck. Lord knows, I need it!

In one sense I feel that I know you rather well already, for

---

[2] Cannot identify second poem.

[1] Wife of a businessman, Mrs. Gordon lived in England and marketed Roethke's poems to various periodicals there.

John[2] has mentioned you frequently in the past two years. Yet to my provincial mind, living in such a remote and splendid world as London gives you an air of unreality. It's like writing to some-one in Mars, or to Santa Claus!

I myself have been spending a curious summer. For three weeks I've been down at a friend's country place, near which his father is attempting to develop a model rural community.[3] Chesterton[4] is always referring to the projects of Mad Millionaires in the Middle West but this one would startle even him in some respects. Yet the Permanent Secretary of Cambridgeshire said, after trav-elling extensively in this country, that the experiment was the most interesting thing he'd seen in America. Well, to come to the point, I am to spend the rest of the summer writing a monograph on the subject for its sponsor. God forbid that I don't emerge from it all—a sociologist!

I am sending under special cover the first volume of Harold Lewis Cook,[5] a young American poet. Cook is quite traditional and has a warm mellow style which at its best is very good. For me the most exciting recent American poet is Stanley Kunitz whose volume[6] I'll send along when I can secure a decent copy.

But enough of this naive prattling.

I should be very happy to have any word from you, if you ever feel inclined to write.

Sincerely,
Theodore Roethke

To Dorothy Gordon

Easton, Pennsylvania
September 26, 1933

Dear Dorothy Gordon: This is a belated note to acknowledge your delightful letter.

I've been exceedingly busy in the last month finishing the mono-

---

2 The poet John Holmes.
3 The Hartland, Michigan, project.
4 G. K. Chesterton.
5 *Spell Against Death* (1933).
6 *Intellectual Things* (1930).

graphs I was writing,[1] getting started here at Lafayette College. In addition to everything else, I've been sick most of the time. So I've really had little time for anything important—such as writing verse or answering your very charming letter.

You ask about what magazines to submit poems.[2] Well, any that you think are worth publishing in. It isn't the money, of course, for that's usually negligible anyhow; but there's no use publishing where an appearance will do more harm than good. Don't send anything to *New Verse,* for I subscribe to the magazine, and the editor Grigson[3] has sent me a note or two.

You spoke about sending six copies of poems. Do you mean of the poems you already have? (I'm very stupid here, because I've mislaid your letter.) I don't have a typewriter, you see, but I'll get some typed and send them on. I have some other poems which I'd like you to try.

But what about postage and stamps which you must use? Wouldn't it be better if you could let me know how much that's costing you? It's only business, you know.

Lord, this is an awful letter, but I've been harried no end of late. My stomach linings have been ruined by alcohol, I guess.

What have I been reading? Aldous Huxley, for one thing. I'm quite behind the fashion here, I know; but I'm working up a writing course for this fall. I do think he's quite witty and learned. His faults are so obvious that they don't bother me so much. I remember I. A. Richards saying that Huxley was very good second-rate, that he got much of his best stuff from repeating conversations of his brilliant friends.

How dull this all is,—but it's a dull day.

I hope some editor has been foolish enough to take something.

Theodore Roethke

Lord, what a boor I am! What a way to end a letter! But I'm in an awful period of self-disgust. I seem to have lost my self-respect.

[1] Monographs about the Hartland Area project. See letter to Mrs. Gordon of July 20, 1933.

[2] That is, to what English magazines should Mrs. Gordon submit Roethke's poems.

[3] Geoffrey Grigson.

To Rolfe Humphries[1]

[*Mailed September 28, 1933*]
Written weeks ago—

Dear Rolfe: I must tell you about an unknown admirer of yours. I was having lunch with Leo Kirshbaum, an English instructor in the engineering school at Ann Arbor. He was trying to ride me for going left when the question of writing in *The New Masses* came up. Then he said "I will admit that I read one hell of a swell review of John Clare in *The New Masses* by a guy named Rolfe Humphries. I don't care much about Clare, but this was a damned good piece of writing, etc., etc." Kirshbaum is one of the few able young guys they have at A[2].[2] He writes bad poetry, but did a fairly good job running a little sheet called *Contemporary* (student writing mostly) out there.

Thanks for the words to Cowley.[3] I don't know how much of an authority I am, but I'd like to get a chance to kick some of these pretentious little pots in the behind. I mean like Grigson.

Got job at Michigan State. Beat out two Harvard Ph.D.'s.

Louise[4] is sore at me, I guess.

Write me c/o Dept. of English, Michigan State College, East Lansing.

Ted

To Dorothy Gordon

[*1933*]

Dear Dorothy Gordon: It's curious how we may be deeply affected by a chance remark. Your letter of last summer came to me after a hair-brained week-end trip involving a drive of over a thousand

---

1 American poet and translator.
2 Roethke's abbreviation of Ann Arbor.
3 Malcolm Cowley, then book review editor of the *New Republic*.
4 The poet Louise Bogan

miles. I lost the letter almost immediately (as I almost always do) but I remember your saying something about wishing I were in London so we could sit down and have some tea with rum and talk. I almost sent you a cable saying I wished so too!

But I must hasten to apologize for encroaching on your territory: I sent three poems to *The Adelphi* and they took two of them. I'm enclosing copies.[1] The reason I did this is that they'd taken a piece of mine before—published April last—sent from my Michigan address. I thought it wouldn't be sensible to be popping up all over the globe.

I'm also enclosing poems "This Various Light" (which I wrote some time ago and still think one of my best pieces, although nobody else does) and a little religious poem.[2] If you like, you may send them somewhere. Also a poem "Todes Stück" [3] which I submit for your opinion. In it, I've tried hard to get condensation, surprise, real progression in the figures. At the moment, it is "out" in this country, so please don't submit it to an editor.

––––––––––

I'm sorry you are depressed. I am too. My mother has been ill and has lost almost all her money. My sister has had to leave school. And in this job I have, I'm just pouring my blood on the sands. I'm a good teacher, so I'm told, but there is no future here.

But here I'm groaning all this to you—

––––––––––

Hasn't John been doing wonderfully well this last year? He's really getting himself a national reputation.

Do write to me when you feel so inclined, won't you? And please don't worry about "bothering" me. Lord knows, I'm just a reckless and stupid (most of the time) boy who has to work hard and who weakly resorts to alcohol for peace of mind. But what I mean to say is this: that in your little notes there seems to be present a

---

[1] The two poems published in *The Adelphi* (September, 1934) were "Autumnal" (later section III of "The Coming of the Cold"), *CP*, p. 15, and "To My Sister," *CP*, p. 5. (All citations to the *Collected Poems* [New York: Doubleday, 1966] are abbreviated *CP*.)

[2] "This Various Light" and "Prepare Thyself for Change," printed below. Both poems appeared in *American Poetry Journal* (November, 1934).

[3] Later printed in *Open House* as "Death Piece." *CP*, p. 4.

warmth, a humanness, a tenderness that is one of the rarest feminine qualities. Do you mind my saying that?

Theodore Roethke

P.S. I hope you can push that light poem. I've worried about it for a long time, but *I* like it. That blasphemous little piece about the eye[4] has never been submitted anywhere. I'll leave it to your own judgment.

This Various Light

This light is the very flush of spring; it is innocent and warm;
It is gentle as celestial rain; it is mellow as gold;
Its pure effulgence may unbind the form
Of a blossoming tree; it may quicken the fallow mould.

This light is various and strange; its luminous hue
May transmute the bleakest dust to silver snow;
Its radiance may be caught within a pool, a bead of dew;
It may contract to the sheerest point; it may arch to a bow.

This light is heaven's transcendent boon, a beam
Of infinite calm; it will never cease;
It will illuminate forever the aether-stream;
This light will lead me to eventual peace.

Theodore Roethke

Prepare thyself for change,
The ever-strange,
The soul's immortal range.

His Word, bright as a flame,
Will quickly tame
Thy gross-compacted frame.

Corruptive machine of lust
Is deftly thrust
Beneath the level dust.

But soul, immortal, white,
Lifts into Light
In unbewildered flight.

[4] "Prayer." *CP,* p. 8.

To Dorothy Gordon

[May 6, 1934]

Dear Dorothy: In my last letter to you, I believe that I said I was enclosing the two poems *The Adelphi* had taken. In my excitement, I forgot to put them in. Well, here they are. One is the original manuscript, which is all I have left.[1] Perhaps the changes I made will interest you.

You know, I hope very much that you can get someone to print that piece "This Various Light."[2] I've always thought it one of the best I've ever done, but few people seem to understand. What I'm trying to say is that light—so various and strange in its nature —is, after all, the supreme gift of God—(Imagine my being religious!) But I wrote it after reading Vaughan one time.

There's a terrific blurb about John in a magazine called *The Poetry Journal*. He is compared to Blake, Keats; his diction has "the stark simplicity of Wordsworth." Such a spiel I haven't heard about anyone in years.

Ted Roethke

[Words and passages in parentheses were crossed out by the poet.]

O my sister remember the stars the tears the trains
The woods in spring the leaves the scented lanes
Recall the gradual dark the snow's unmeasured fall
The naked fields the clouds' immaculate folds
Recount each childhood pleasure: the skies of azure
The pageantry of wings the eyes' bright treasures
(Remember too the loins from whence you sprung the limbs
Within the grave before you have his love)
Keep faith with present joys refuse to choose
Defer the vice of flesh the irrevocable choice
(Rejoice in narrow thighs in)
Cherish the (wintry) eyes (the buds of breasts) the proud incredible
     poise

[1] "To My Sister." This version printed below. The other poem was "Autumnal." *CP*, pp. 5, 15.
[2] See preceding letter to Dorothy Gordon.

(Rejoice in narrow thighs in proud incredible poise)
Walk boldly my sister but do not deign (go) to give
(And spill no precious blood) Remain secure from pain preserve (thy
 heart) thy hate thy heart (thy hate)

To DOROTHY GORDON

[*Easton, Pennsylvania*]
[*Probably February, 1934*]

Dear Dorothy: I wrote these first two pages the night before last.
Yesterday morning your grand letter and the poems arrived. I
was pleased no end. That "You came and quacked beside me in
the wood" was priceless. And the brandy-to-whiskey, too.[1]

I'll try to answer your questions.

Of course I like to read criticism—favourable or unfavourable.
(Note English spelling in deference to you.) I'm sufficiently sure
of myself not to be upset by what people say. Of course, there are
certain critics in this country and friends whose criticism I value
and who can worry me by not liking poems; but I feel, frankly,
that despite my little production I am beyond the poet-taster stage.

In this case, I am rather amused. Apparently, this man has one
of those biased, salty, vigorous minds.[2] But whatever I am, I don't
think I am confused or vague, do you? But I was glad to read
what he said, and I hope we can sell him something.

You ask about me. I'll be quite shameless and tell you. For one
thing, I'm not the delicate fellow my verse would lead you to
think: I am six feet two and weigh two hundred and ten. Blonde
with grey-green eyes. (Oh God, this sounds like an answer to a
lonely hearts column—my excuse is that I'm drinking some of the
worst whiskey in America right now—some rye from the remote
fastnesses of New Jersey. I've been trying to go on the wagon
of late, and I'm succeeding pretty well.)

---

[1] The quotation is from Rupert Brooke's "The Voice" (a passage Mrs.
Gordon remembered and liked); the "brandy-to-whiskey" refers to a passage
in J. C. Powys' *Glastonbury Romance* in which a character has brandy in a
flask and then, inconsistently, in a couple of pages, whiskey.

[2] Presumably J. C. Squire of the *London Mercury*, who rejected some of
Roethke's poems submitted by Mrs. Gordon.

But forgive all this.

I'd love to see your room. I've never had a nice room. I've always lived in a complete disorder even at home, with books and papers strewn all over. I'm writing now from my room *in the freshman dormitory*. It's a corner room on the ground floor. From one window you can look down at the town; from the other you can see a lawn (now covered with snow) and tennis courts surrounded by high bushes. It isn't unpleasant, but the room's a mess. There is a steel book shelf, a bed, a chair filled with books, a dresser piled with books & papers, a desk covered with junk. A fur coat hangs on a moulding in the wall—I can't get it in the closet. There are books on the window ledges. That's all there is—there aren't any pictures, any curtains, any rugs.

About poetry—I fear I must take you to task. I was reading Rupert Brooke last summer again—with pleasure. But there are too many echoes in him for [my] taste. He's very good—but not tough enough.

I can't understand why you don't like Stephen Spender. "I Think Continually" and "In 1929" and "Oh young men or young comrades" are fine poems to my mind.

I'm tired of all this Eliot-Pound worship. Eliot's a good poet, but there are others.

Do you know the American poets Elinor Wylie, Louise Bogan, or Léonie Adams? I think you'd like their work.

Of course I like music. I don't know much about the moderns—Schöenberg, Carpenter, etc. My most recent excitement is the Beethoven interpretations by Schnabel,[3] the German. He is in this country now. His recordings are released by the Beethoven society. You must make an effort to hear them.

You make me depressed talking about your London. I've always thought I'd love it, despite its bigness, and dullness, and poor theatres.

I met Clemence Dane[4] a few weeks ago. She was here for a lecture and three of us were assigned to take care of her. She was very nice to me. She asked me to send her some of my verse, although I never mentioned that I wrote. Wait—that can be mis-

[3] Artur Schnabel, Austrian-born pianist and composer.
[4] British novelist, dramatist, and poet.

construed. She turned to me suddenly and said "Do you write?" The other two answered for me.

This is the longest letter I've ever written anyone. So please answer it right away.

Ted Roethke

To Dorothy Gordon

[*Easton, Pennsylvania*]
[*May, 1934*]

Dear Dorothy: I have been hoping that I'd hear from you, although I know that you wrote last. And what a puzzling letter it was! I couldn't quite figure out whether deep in your heart of hearts you thought what I write is lousy or whether you were perplexed or what. But no matter.

I've been doing a lot of silly things just to keep from starving. Publicity among other things. And coaching the tennis team. You see this job is not permanent and I'm trying to make myself as useful as possible because there are hundreds of college teachers out of work.

Lord how tiresome this is! But here's the point: If I could only publish in several more places between now and next November, I *might* get a really decent, permanent position and I would get time for some really important work. So if you could push some of that stuff, it would be a great help. Don't you think that "This Various Light" would go somewhere? And that piece "Exhortation"? Has Orage[1] seen that light piece? But here I'm violating your rule of no business in the body of the letter, so I'll put it on another paper. I do hate to be pestering you like a snivelling peasant, but it is so important that I hang on for a while, especially since my mother has been cleaned out. (This isn't sob stuff—I just want you to understand.)

You see, last week poems of mine appeared in *The Atlantic* and *The Nation*. This created quite a stir in our little academic circle.[2]

---

[1] A. R. Orage, editor of *The New English Weekly*.

[2] "The Genius," *Atlantic Monthly* (May, 1934); "Death Piece," *Nation,* (May 2, 1934). *CP,* p. 4.

Your letter really made me very mad at the time. I tore it up. But I wanted very much to see you and talk to you. I think we might get along. Either that or have an awful row.

I was going up to Boston spring vacation to see John, but I was very ill the whole time with an infected tooth.

A while ago I went down to Washington with the tennis team. The cherry blossoms were still in bloom. There's a strange kind of excitement in the capital. People seem to realize that they're in the midst of a social revolution, but exactly what's happening no one really knows.

Forgive me for being so dull, won't you? I'm harried and depressed.

Ted

Business

(1) I *can't* think of a title for that "Prepare thyself for change." I'm poor at titles. Do they really matter? Call it "The Change," perhaps. Incidentally, Padraic Colum,[3] who was here on a lecture tour, liked that piece. I met him at a party and sent him some stuff later. He was very decent. Also I met Clemence Dane.

(2) What magazines have seen that first batch of six? *Week-End Review, The Listener, The Saturday Review, Twentieth Century, The Spectator, The Nation and Atheneum? The Observer, The English Review, The Times, The Bermondsey Book, New Statesman*

(3) Do you think "G. K.'s Weekly" might use that "Prepare thyself" piece?

(4) Here's a religious piece I wrote a long time ago:

> Receive this child, O Lord of All Control!
> Accen

Hell, I can't remember it.

(5) If you are tired of sending any pieces around, let me know for I have one or two leads here about some of them.

(6) Do you know those rhyme sheet and broadside series of *The Poetry Bookshop*? Is it possible to submit poems for those series? Or do they select the work? I mean, if they approved a poem, would they print it if I paid for the artist and the printing? I

---

[3] Irish poet and dramatist.

have a piece, printed in *Adelphi* for April 1933[4] which I think they'd like.

To Rolfe Humphries

[Probably 1934]

Dear Rolfe: That review of F. Frost[1] was certainly a hair-raiser. I always feel hesitant about saying someone's influencing somebody else because sometimes I see a metaphor that I think is mine in someone else's work—in stuff I've never seen before, etc., etc.

But you certainly caught that girl with her pants down. Those were all terrific steals.

I think you're rapidly becoming the critical sensation of the year. I know people who don't give a damn about poetry who follow your reviews.

———

I don't know when my bum has been dragging closer to the terrain. It seems to me that nowadays when you're a young buck you have to eat more than your share of dung.

But I'm so damned tired of guys who aren't on the up and up.

———

Look, will you come up and talk to my boys sometime? I could get together some intelligent kids. And you spoke of Louise Bogan —could she be enticed sometime? Or did I ask that before?

———

Hell, it seems that I don't have any peace of mind anymore. Less than 1% of my time is spent in doing anything of any significance.

———

Forgive me for all this childish and cowardly sobbing.

———

I see old Mike Gold[2] gave P. Engle some good kicks in *New Masses.*

———

[4] "The Buds Now Stretch."

[1] Frances Frost's *Woman of the Earth,* reviewed by Humphries in *Poetry* (October, 1934).

[2] Michael Gold was a left-wing writer and critic. Roethke is apparently referring to his remarks about Paul Engle's book of poems, *American Song* (1934).

There are some pretty good English books—or what ought to be pretty good—coming out. Spender has essays on poets, and C. Day Lewis has a book of essays.

———

A gal in England [3] tells me those *New Verse* editors praise her work and then try to get her to pay for publication in their sheet. I believe her absolutely. She's the wife of a Standard Oil official, no twittery culture-yearner.

Ted

To A. J. M. Smith[1]

Hartland, Michigan
July 14, 1934

My dear Sir: Rolfe Humphries mentioned to me the fact that you were teaching in East Lansing and suggested that I try to look you up. It seemed a good idea: hence this note.

Usually I get to Lansing in the summer and we might, if you find it convenient, have lunch or a few drinks together. Very likely you are up in Canada at the present time, but perhaps not.

In case you wish to find out whether you are dealing with another jackass or pot poet, I might say that I was born in these parts, am twenty-six, am fairly simple-minded, and have published in *The Nation,* May (5)? '34, *The Atlantic,* May '34, *The Adelphi,* April '33, *The New Republic,* Jan. 20 (?), '32, *The Sat. Rev. of Lit. The Commonweal, Poetry,* etc.

I've been interested in your work for some time. I especially liked the pieces in *The Hound and Horn* and *New Verse.*

If you think you could venture such a meeting, let me have your address and telephone number. I am writing monographs for a Cleveland philanthropist and can't be sure of my future movements.

Yours truly,
Theodore Roethke

———

[3] Dorothy Gordon.

———

[1] Canadian-born poet, editor, and professor of English.

To Dorothy Gordon

[*Hartland, Michigan*]
July 19, 1934

Dear Dorothy: Please forgive the departmental stationery—I haven't any other.

I've been wondering why I haven't heard from you. Perhaps my last letter was whining and contemptible. I hope not. I remember that I was in a very low and desperate state of mind. When you have other people depending on you, you don't act quite normal. So forgive me for being a bore.

I'm still working on my booklets about the Hartland Area Project. One is going to be a Primer somewhat like the New Russian Primer.

This really is a most extraordinary experiment. I'd be very happy here, only I get bored with life in the country. And the damn cook here is lousy. She spends piles of money and the results are wretched. No one will direct things because this is *father's* country place.

Now you in England don't have these problems of stupid and inefficient and sloppy servants.

I have very pleasant quarters all my own—the second floor of a building by the lake. Across the lake are lovely rolling hills with trees and fields but no houses.

———————

There hasn't been very much published here of any interest. Very few books of poetry this year. The last issue of *Poetry* was some better.

I've been reading Emily Dickinson considerably.

(Dinner bell)

Here's a little piece I wrote the other day.

No Bird[1]

Now here is peace for one who knew
The secret heart of sound.

[1] Published in *Atlantic Monthly* (November, 1934), and included in *Open House. CP*, p. 17. In this letter Roethke crossed out the title "Musician" and substituted the present one.

The ear so delicate and true
Is pressed to noiseless ground.

Light swings the breeze above her head,
The grasses faintly stir;
But in the forest of the dead
No bird awakens her.

What do you think?

Did I tell you that I am doing publicity work for the college too? What rot it is! I went to a convention in Cleveland for publicity directors. The hotel had a marvelous bar with a Georgia negro who made the best mint juleps I've ever tasted. He used only twenty-year old American bourbon. Do you like juleps?

———————

I keep thinking in a curious fashion that I'll be hearing from you. Yesterday I got a bill from England and I was annoyed that there was no letter in that delicate handwriting of yours.

———————

We don't have a bodyguard against kidnappers this year, but the other night a machine-gun bandit escaped from a hospital nearby and caused some excitement. It wasn't Dillinger, though. I saw several weeks ago that a London paper said that even Indians with bows and arrows were out chasing him.

The toy manufacturers are making little submachine guns for children to play with. A crazy country—these United States.

> Please do let me hear from you.
> Ted Roethke

[Words and phrases in parentheses were crossed out by the poet.]

EVENING EYE[2]

The (sharp) long eye pins the object fast
In seeking out a shape of grace,
And all within (my being's range)
    (my narrow round) the vision's rim
Is held transfixed in its place.

The faint stars wane above the hill,
The moon a laggard course has run,

———————

[2] Unpublished.

And now this minion of the will
Has bound the sky and land as one.

The leaves are lost in change, the bough
Moves out to meet the dying light,
But soon, caught in a velvet maze,
The branches vanish on the night.

As if to fathom dusk, the gaze
Grows wider still; but lashes fall,
Undone by subtle dark, and eyes
Are sealed, their lids in summer's thrall.

TO DOROTHY GORDON

[Hartland, Michigan]
[August 18, 1934]

Dear Dorothy: All your letters came to me at Hartland on the very same day. I've read all of them several times.

What a dear person you must be! I am very touched that you should be so kind to me.

People like you always make me feel like a pot, as we say here. Do you know the expression? A "pot" in Americanese is a low, clownish, objectionable fellow; he is a worm, a louse, a "gloob."

You see, it's like this: you seem such a very fine person—almost another kind of superior human being. Honestly, you do.

And I find myself feeling very abject yet strangely tender. Do you mind my saying that? I suppose it's silly since I've never even seen you.

_____

You were correct in thinking that my father had died. I was just quoting the Crouse family at whose place I am staying.[1] Mr. Crouse was a big shot in the electrical business—made Mazda lamps. He's retired now, but is sponsoring this Hartland Area Project, which is an effort to improve in every possible way a district in Michigan. Well, I'm here writing about the whole business for Mr. Crouse. I've been very intimate with the family for a long time.[. . .]

_____

[1] See letter to Dorothy Gordon, July 19, 1934, with its reference to *"father's country place."*

I'm glad you liked "No Bird." Funny thing, I wrote it out in long hand, sent it [to] *The Atlantic Monthly.* They took it. Isn't that swell?

Look, Dorothy, would you do something for me? I take it that most of the poems are locked up in a drawer. Would you hold all of them until further notice? If any are out, hold them when they get back. If by any miracle an editor does take one, that's O.K., but let me know as soon as possible. Here is the reason: *The American Poetry Journal* wants to run about five poems of mine as a feature along with a short article. John Holmes has some connection with the magazine and is responsible for the idea. This autumn is going to be a very critical time for me, as I told you, and the more things I can get published the better.

You won't be annoyed at me for doing this? Please don't think that I'm going over your head in this matter. And if an English editor does take a piece that's out, it won't be printed in this country. The poems won't be published here until October or November. I can always have pieces taken [letter breaks off here].

Several Days Later

Last night I read A. P. Herbert's "Holy Deadlock." It was the first time I ever got through anything of his. It had come in the mail for Susie Crouse, and was the only thing I had to read.

It was pleasantly amusing. Some of these English novels with their incredibly unworldly males who let themselves be imposed upon so easily. I suppose such people do exist.

I'd read just before James Cain's "The Postman Always Rings Twice." Now there's a lovely little American idyll for you!

I was interested in what you said about the Germans. Even you show the influence of propaganda perhaps? I mean the no-matter-what-we-think-of-them attitude.

I think the Germans are a tragic people. They're so painfully honest and forthright and yet childish and naive. They get to blustering and saying stupid things.

Certainly the Germans can't be expected to lie down forever. They weren't responsible for the war. There isn't a reputable historian who will say that. And as for the poor old Kaiser, maybe he did stamp around once in a while, but was he as bad as that God damned Edward Grey?

Oh well, this is all old stuff. But it makes me sore the way the English press is always ready to line up with the French and jump all over the Germans.

You see, both my father and mother were from Prussian families.[2] In fact, my grandfather, when they lost their money, became Bismarck's forester. But he was a fanatic pacifist in later life, wouldn't allow uniforms of any kind, even for children.

I may go up to Canada next week, but probably won't.

Fashion note: The holes in the knees of my flannel pants got so big that I cut them off at the knee. The effect is picturesque.

I seem to write nothing but poems about death. And I've been using the same darn form too: But the effects are different I think. What do you think of this?

THE TRIBUTE[3]

There is no word that may be said
In this imperial peace.
The quiet wrapped about his head
Bespeaks the mind's surcease.

His shadow's dispersed, its size
Is lost in rolling shade.
Withhold the anguishment of eyes
For tongueless accolade.

[EDITOR'S NOTE: *The following six poems, though not assignable to any specific letter, were sent to Dorothy Gordon in 1933 or 1934. They are included here as the most appropriate place. All but one were later published.*]

DIFFICULT GRIEF[4]

This is no surface grief, but care
That catches at me unaware,

---

[2] An exaggeration. Only Roethke's father was Prussian; his mother came from southern Germany.
[3] Unpublished.
[4] Sent to Dorothy Gordon, probably 1934. Unpublished.

A grief too difficult for tears
That ravages my greenest years,
Destroying innocent peace to start
A swell of sorrow at the heart.
Since I am young, it does not find
Sufficient mastery in the mind.
Since I am careless, it may be
As treacherous as ecstasy,
And though it leave, it will return
To mock me with embittered scorn:
A sorrow ponderable as clay,
Old desolation, young dismay,
A fear too shameful to confess,
A terrible child-loneliness.

UNESSENTIAL TRUTH[5]

I sought a measure for your subtle being,—
A plumbline that could accurately sound you,
A figure quite sufficient to propound you.
I sought to find the angle of your seeing,
To learn your reason's reason for agreeing,
To send a shaft of vision to confound you,
To aim at you, to pierce, but not to wound you,
To trap your startled blood, forever fleeing.

When I had found the sources of your wrath,
Appraised the purest substance of your youth,
And marked the ordered pattern of your path,—
I still possessed but unessential truth.
My efforts were ambiguous and dull:
I could not learn what made you beautiful.

MORE PURE THAN FLIGHT[6]

Some day I'll step with arrowed grace
Into a brighter realm of space:

With grave felicity of motion
I'll tread an incidental ocean

[5] Sent to Dorothy Gordon, *circa* 1933–34. Published in *American Poetry Journal* (November, 1934) under the title "I Sought a Measure."
[6] Sent to Dorothy Gordon, *circa* 1933–34. Published in *American Poetry Journal* (November, 1934) under the title "Someday I'll Step."

Lightly; wander minutely where
Confederate clouds divide in air;

Place accurate feet upon the brink
Of nothingness: obliquely sink

In crystal wind; more pure than flight
Of curving bird, I'll walk the night.

Death shall not drift my limbs apart
When ancient silence storms my heart.

Before my patterned dance is done,
I'll pace on shadows to the sun.

How delicate will motion be
In this, my fleet identity!

EXHORTATION[7]

Infertile quietude
Now dominates the blood,
The barrenness of pause
From passion and its vows,
Bleak juncture of distress,
The mind's blank loneliness.

Thou gusty hope, release
Me from this sodden ease,
Rouse my quiescent will
With sudden miracle!

THE KNOWING HEART[8]

In ecstasy at being sure
Of what Time has reserved for it,
The flesh will burn a meaning pure
And make its dying exquisite.

O this mortality will break
The false dissembling brain apart—
The uninstructed soul will quake
In terror at the knowing heart.

[7] Sent to Dorothy Gordon, *circa* 1933–34. Published in *American Poetry Journal* (November, 1934).

[8] Sent to Dorothy Gordon, *circa* 1933–34. Published in *American Poetry Journal* (November, 1934).

FUGITIVE[9]

Her flesh is quick: a furious vein
Impels a subtle heart,
A fierce resilience in the brain
Makes fugitive her part.

Her foot is light: no step marks where
This innocent has stept;
She is the ambulant of air,
The fluent wind's adept.

Headlong she runs: she is the bright
Precipitant of grace,
Impetuous changeling of delight,
The sudden child of space.

To Rolfe Humphries

[November 2, 1934]

Dear Rolfe: Please forgive my delay in not replying after so memorable an evening at your house.

I was, as I said, too completely overwhelmed. A case of hero-worship I guess. I was like a country boy at his first party,—such an oaf, such a boob, such a blockhead. I don't think I was ever much worse.

And then when she[1] asked me whether I really figured out for myself that Taggard [2] was no good—that was the pay-off. Damn her, anyway. She and her Irish digs.

The thing that impressed me most (pompous word) was the way both of you have turned your full powers to poetry. It is this dedication that I have forgotten of late.

Please give me her address. I'd like to write her a note at least. Some time I hope to gain her respect.

---

[9] Sent to Dorothy Gordon, *circa* 1933–34. Published in *Trial Balances,* ed. by Ann Winslow (1935).

---

[1] Louise Bogan.
[2] Genevieve Taggard.

I re-read your MacLeish review[3] and one or two others while up in the store-room tonight.

John Holmes wrote that the *American Poetry Journal* is out today. Lord, I hope he hasn't laid it on too thick.[4] Holmes has too high an opinion of me, it seems. There are some pieces I shouldn't have published.

The piece on Time very good.[5]

Everyone around here has gone nuts.

Ted

To William Mather Lewis[1]

December 22, 1934

Dear President Lewis: I am reluctant to thrust upon you my personal problems, especially at a time when your hours and energies must be completely absorbed in directing the College through this most critical period. But contemplating the blackness (or blankness) of the outside world, and having developed a sincere attachment to the College in the few years I have been at Lafayette, it seems to me not inappropriate to submit to you a statement of why I wish to remain on the College staff and what I believe to be an honest evaluation of my services to the College.

My work in the College has been in four fields of activity. First and naturally most important is teaching. The quality of the work being done by one teacher is very difficult to estimate, since it is not simply a matter of academic preparation plus an ability to stand up and talk to undergraduates. The personality of the teacher, as you have frequently, and it seems to me very sensibly, pointed out, provides the leavening which makes a pedagogue, using the word in its popular and somewhat invidious sense, a

---

[3] According to Mr. Humphries, the review "was published in V. F. Calverton's *Modern Monthly*," probably in 1934.

[4] The November, 1934, issue of *The American Poetry Journal* contains a group of Roethke's poems and an introduction to them by John Holmes.

[5] Cannot identify.

---

[1] President of Lafayette College.

genuine teacher. Now, I do not care to present myself to you [as] a rare and glittering personality. As a teacher and a person, I am content to rest my case on the opinions of my colleagues and the many students for whom I entertain warm feelings and who, unless I am being continually deceived, reciprocate that warmth of feeling. And in the revived course in advanced composition I feel that I am dealing with a group of the finest minds in the student body, men who will someday bring credit to the College.

A second field of activity has been creative writing. This is not the place to attempt an estimate of my poetry. I do not claim to be the white hope of American literature, but it can be said that only one other poet of my age has been published as widely as I in journals of quality, journals which reach almost the entire educated class in our country. (Besides editorial recognition such discriminating critics as Louis Untermeyer, Louise Bogan, Robert Hillyer, Rolfe Humphries, Padraic Colum, Clemence Dane, Ellery Sedgwick and Stanley Kunitz have commented favorably on my work.)

Third in importance is the work in College publicity. Since, if I am to be retained after this year, at least half of my time would be devoted to publicity work, a note on what has been done and what can be done is called for. The most important feature of this year's publicity has been the systematic exploitation of the small local interest news item, a large and constant flow of such pieces having been maintained, and this in spite of a comparatively unsuccessful year of football. Furthermore, both in sporting news and general news there has been a generous amount of space devoted to Lafayette College in the metropolitan and Philadelphia papers as well as in the papers of smaller communities throughout the state.

There is an enormous amount of running around and consulting, urging, pleading, advising, and so forth, with student leaders, athletic coaches, teachers and officers of the College in the day to day routine of publicity. I state this as a fact, not as self-pity. Some reasonably literate person has to be responsible for getting the work done. There are limits, or so it seems to me, to the amount of publicity which we, a small, conservative liberal arts College can get, and I do not think that the most expensive and most expert publicity director could do much more than has been done in the past year without either changing the general policies of the College, or compromising its good name.

The main source of College news, whether we like it or not, remains athletics, and on this point I shall be very forthright: I believe that I know more of our own College athletes, and know more and care more about College athletics in general, than anyone at Lafayette except only the coaches themselves.

In one sport, tennis, I have served as coach. Working with the young men of the College in one of their vigorous competitive games, as well as in the class and conference room, has meant a good deal to me and has placed the sport of tennis on a basis of gentlemanly amateurism which, I think you will agree, is an ideal which all College sports, at least in the better class colleges, are aiming for today.

I have described my work in the College in four fields of endeavor: teaching, writing, publicity and coaching. There could be added to this a considerable amount of committee work, preparation of the annual Catalog, and the visiting of secondary schools. This last, by the way, is work which I genuinely enjoy, and hope to do more of. And I think that the method which I have already used, that of taking along a graduate of the school being visited, especially when a very presentable and outstanding undergraduate fills this requirement, promises, or logically ought to, great effectiveness in this work.

The above statements, President Lewis, constitute my case for retention on the College staff. I quite realize that you already have serious problems of personnel and especially serious problems of budgeting to cope with. Immodest as it may sound, I simply feel that I have served the College well and can and want to continue to do so. I have gone far beyond my assigned duties in order to be of use in many departments of College activity, and if in this I have failed I have not only over-rated my work but have been misled by my friends and colleagues as to its value.

It is important, at least to my own peace of mind, that I know of your decision at the earliest possible date.

I hope that you have found Mrs. Lewis in an improved state of health. Please convey to her the season's greetings and my best wishes for her recovery.

Very truly yours,

To Rolfe Humphries

[Easton, Pennsylvania]
[March 1, 1935]

Dear Rolfe: I was in town for three days a while back but didn't call up because I didn't want to wear you out.

Look, when can you come out here?[1] The boys have been pestering me about it and of course you know how I feel. I'll see that it won't be tiresome and we can have a bit of fun. You'd like Norton,[2] and these boys are O.K.

I've been in a hell of a state for weeks but seem to have come out of it.

I had dinner with Stanley Kunitz on one of the nights. He has plenty of stuff, I think. I liked him.

Here's a new poem in which I try to get away from the grunt and fart rhythm.[3] It's really a revision of an earlier one.

I had a note from Bro. Cowley. He wanted to know whether I was really a Middle Westerner or not. He said they'd get many howls from boys not included and thought it might be better to print me separately. The piece is the one about the Eye.[4]

Holmes sold *The New Yorker* a prose piece for $200 and got $60 for those light verse pieces. Also sold *Atlantic* and *Scribner's*. Maybe I'm wrong.

My regards to Helen.
Ted

To Harriet Monroe

Easton, Pennsylvania
March 3, 1935

My dear Miss Monroe: I have noticed your great interest in the public reading of poetry, and am wondering whether you could

[1] To Lafayette College.
[2] Theodore Norton, head of the library at Lafayette College.
[3] "We Sighed for a Sign."
[4] "Prayer," published in the *New Republic* (July 10, 1935). *CP*, p. 8.

give me some advice regarding a rather special kind of poetry-reading.

The students at Lafayette College are conducting a series of vesper services which are simply the reading of various poems with a musical setting. A student organist provides the music.

Although I am considered pretty much of a heathen around here, the students have been asking for advice and want me to do the reading for several programs. I am rather in the dark about just what would be effective—with music. The poetry need not be religious; in fact, the boys say they want good poetry, no matter what the subject. And they are anxious to avoid sentimental drool such as David Ross broadcasts.

So I would like to get some good musical settings for good poems, if there are such things. I remember a note in *Poetry* a long time ago saying that Israel Citkovitz (sp.?) of New York had put Joyce's lyrics to music. Do you know anything about this, or any other such attempts?

It's easy enough to get the poetry, of course. Suitable music is the real problem.

If you could give me any information, it would be greatly appreciated. And if you are interested, I will let you know how the series gets across.

And now I would like to speak my mind in another matter. I have noticed several statements to the effect that poetry—modern poetry—can't be taught effectively. That's just bunk. For two years I've been giving a very stiff course in modern literature, with the first semester devoted to poetry. Each year I've had about twelve or fifteen honor students—the ablest men in college. There isn't a poet among them, but their interest has been most enthusiastic. And this in spite of the fact that the approach has been technical. For instance, there were two lectures each on Hart Crane and Hopkins—certainly not easy poets. These were followed with the closest of attention.

Yours truly,
Theodore Roethke

To Rolfe Humphries

[Probably 1935]

Dear Rolfe: I haven't answered your letter because I've been in a strange state of jitters which were caused by a stupid weekend of drinking. The doctor has just given me some junk, but my writing isn't all that it should be.

Your vacation corresponds almost exactly with ours. Ours runs from March 7 to April 4. (School starts on the 4th.) But one of the boys suggested that April 3 on Wednesday would be fine. But that would leave out some others who would like to come but can't get back on account of arrangements with other people, etc. I wanted to have the class today for final decision, but couldn't. But you just name any date if you can't make it on April 4.

The program you outlined sounds swell. The boys are reading Spender and [Day] Lewis and Auden. They are very enthusiastic.

Oh, there's something I wanted to explain. [. . .] Ann Winslow said that she had written you about the possibility of your doing a small notice for her anthology.[1] Originally when she wrote she had suggested Archie MacLeish and asked me whether I could suggest anybody. I named you, said that I knew you, but that you were tough, wouldn't log-roll. But the damn fool didn't tell me she wasn't paying the critics. She never answered me when I asked her about the whole thing later.

I've spent more time with that twitch, sending one batch of twenty odd fresh copies, then another, *etc.* She's been saying all along that she was going to give me one of the biggest sections, if she used me. (Seems I was a bit over the age limit). Now it appears she's only going to put in six or seven poems.

Well, if I didn't need publication so badly right now for professional reasons, I'd tell her to go to hell.

But if you are too busy or would be embarrassed by the business, or have already told her to go to hell, why it's O.K. by me. I won't be offended. But let me know if possible. Lewis[2] keeps

---

[1] *Trial Balances* (1935). The introduction to Roethke was finally written by Louise Bogan (pp. 138–39).

[2] President of Lafayette College.

dangling me around and this is just the sort of thing that impresses [him].

If this is incoherent or goofy, blame the drugs the M.D. gave me.

Hastily,
Ted

To Rolfe Humphries

[*Hartland, Michigan*]
[*August 14, 1935*]

Dear Rolfe: I just found your piece "Meditation for Sext" again.[1] I liked it before, but now it seems to me one of the best pieces I've seen in a long time.

I'm still doing damn little on Crouse's work.[2] Written a few hinky-dink pieces of light verse such as the enclosed which I hope to palm off on the N. Yorker.

Bro. Cowley still has that ancestor-worship piece.[3]

The countryside is still nuts about the achievements of the Tigers.[4] Seats are all sold far in advance. They're playing to more than 100,000 for a single series.

General Motors is expanding in Michigan—especially in Saginaw.

Were you depressed that day at the farm? Norton[5] had got things pretty balled up.

I have a dandy cold coming on.

Have been reading the back issues of *New Verse* trying to see what those pots have. Some of them are pretty good, but in general they try to be too-too smart in the reviews. Grigson's taste is anything but catholic. It's a closed corporation, I think.

Write me at Waldenwoods, Hartland, Mich. if you feel the urge.

1 Included in Humphries' volume *Out of the Jewel* (1942).
2 The Hartland Area project.
3 "Feud." It was published in the *New Republic* (Sept. 11, 1935). *CP*, p. 4.
4 The Detroit Tigers won the American League pennant in 1935 and defeated the Chicago Cubs in the World Series.
5 Theodore Norton. See letter to Humphries of March 1, 1935.

Did you ever see the anthol. *Eng. Galaxy?* [6] Louise loaned me it. Really good, mostly. Good early stuff.

Ted

Regards to Helen and Johnny

HURRAY FOR WEEDS[7]

"Long live the weeds . . ." Hopkins

Long live the weeds that overwhelm
My narrow vegetable realm,
The bitter rock, the barren soil
That force the son of man to toil,
All things unholy or perverse,
The ugly of the universe.
These do I cherish, that provide
A burden for the back of pride,
The rough, the wicked, and the wild
That keep the spirit undefiled.
With these I match my little wit,
And earn the right to stand or sit,
Hope, love, create, or drink and die,—
These shape creature that is I.

Too short?

I wished to hell I'd stop writing 4-ft. couplets.

TO ROLFE HUMPHRIES

[*August, 1935*]

Dear Rolfe: I received a letter asking me whether I wanted to apply for membership in *The American Writers' League.* You had recommended me. What I've seen of their activities seems most commendable. Are you a member? I'd be glad to join if it didn't cost too much. For the first time in my life I'm about flat on my tail.

[6] Edited by Gerald Bullet.

[7] Later titled " 'Long Live the Weeds' " and published in *Poetry* (July, 1936), and *Open House*. This is an early and longer version of the poem. *CP,* p. 18.

Bro. Cowley took that piece, "Feud." [1]

Been poking around in the library at Ann Arbor looking for stuff for this text on the Hartland Area.

Tell me, is this ditty too silly, or is it worth doing?

Song for Hemingway

The season wakes within my side.
The pulse leaps to command.
The push of May, the stallion's pride
Informs my thrilling hand.

Old cunning stirs behind the brow,
The blood begins to shove,
I'm stuffed with sun; the time is now
For turning to my love.

Kick me in the ass the next time you see me.

To Rolfe Humphries

January 1, 1935 [*1936*][1]

Dear Rolfe: Thanks for a very funny letter. I showed it to the house M.D. a good guy, age 29, who will probably be at the neurological center in June. We both want to get a bet in if they ship Captain Gilbert[2] to Mexico.

---

[1] *New Republic* (Sept. 11, 1935). *CP*, p. 4.

[1] Roethke dated this letter inaccurately; it was written in answer to Humphries' letter of December 24, 1935.

[2] "Capt. Gilbert was not in the military, but was a pretty beat-up old racehorse owned by my brother and a fellow named Healy, who ran him one day at the old track just south of San Francisco. . . . Anyway, the old rogue was cunning and lazy and disliked to run, but would respond if stimulated by an illegal instrument, a handbuzzer, carried in the jock's palm, and properly applied to cause a mild shock of electricity. Trouble was, the boy felt it so risky that he demanded not only most of the purse, but in advance, so H & H [Healy and Humphries] had only a buck left to wager across the board. In spite of the handicappers' advance opinion that the Ethippian army was calling Capt. Gilbert, he won the race. All this is fact, and Tanforan (that's the track) would bear this out as far as the record of the winner goes; my brother in California has a photo of the finish." (From a letter to the editor from Rolfe Humphries, Sept. 9, 1966.)

The administrative bastards at Mich. State are trying to give me a screwing.[3] I find out December 27. (Second term opens right after New Years.) But they are going to screw themselves this time because old Theophil Klingman, top-dog neuro-psychiatrist in these parts, is doing all my dirty work for me, and I have plenty of other legal, political protection to call upon if need be. One of the rumors about me, I understand, is, or was, that I was a Red—me whom Norton always claimed was an incipient fascist.

Well, don't say anything to any of your comrade friends about this, because I don't want to be made a martyr just yet. This involves real money which I can get without being tough or causing a stink.

They're trying, you see, to give me a leave of absence, *without pay, because of ill health,* from Dec. 1 until the rest of the year. I started classes Sept. 30 and taught until November 13 without missing a class. Then I landed in the hospital for twelve days in Lansing. This cost me a neat sum, and cost me more than it should because of the young punk in charge of my case. Well, after following all instructions very explicitly from the M.D.'s in Lansing, going home for a rest, then I came back up for my interviews with the boys at Mich. State—still everything was lovely—

Interruption—mail going out.

Ted

To Rolfe Humphries

January 21 [*1936*]

Dear Rolfe: A while back you asked whether Crouse might be interested in the new magazine.[1] I doubt it, because he's in an odd frame of mind right now, but if you had any dope that I could feed him in little batches, I might get a rise out of him.

I haven't gone down to Michigan State since going to the Sani-

---

[3] This letter and the one following are concerned with what was the first of Roethke's serious "breakdowns," which occurred shortly after he began teaching at Michigan State. He did not resume his work there, but in the fall of 1936 joined the faculty at Pennsylvania State College.

[1] A proposed literary quarterly to be published by the League of American Writers.

tarium. I gather that the ad. thugs are showing wonderful toler-
ance & lovingkindness in putting me, a mere instructor, on leave
of absence. It seems that the usual custom at state institutions out
here is just to lop a guy off the pay roll, when he's sick, at Michigan if a guy wants a year's leave to complete a thesis or book, he
isn't even promised a job when he comes back. Louis Strauss, head
of the dept., told me this himself.

I have more interest in polishing up my Latin than in doing
Dante. What's a good grammar?

What do you think of the piece on the reverse side? [2] It's nothing very profound, God knows.

Ted

Assailants lurk behind the door.
This is a treacherous time. Beware
The shadow darkening the floor,
The foot that scuttles on the stair.

Escape the paralytic hand
That fumbles at your sleeve, the spies
Who mark you for a sudden end.
Be quick to pierce the fool's disguise.

You hesitate to step beyond
The narrow room; congeal with fear.
Your indecisions will confound
Your friends, while enemies draw near.

The knuckles of the spine betray
The heart: the marrow's drained away.
You need to resurrect the will
To fight when backed against the wall.

To Louise Bogan[1]

May 25, 1936

Dear Louise: It's three o'clock in the morning, and I've just finished reading, of all things, "Time Out of Mind" by Rachel Field.

---

[2] A later version of this poem accompanies a letter to Humphries on
November 20, 1937.

---

[1] Poet, critic, and translator.

Just twenty-eight years ago today little Theodore came into the world. Touching, isn't it? I've never thought much about the passage of time over my flesh, but this time it really gets me down. Twenty-eight, and what have I done? No volume out and I can't seem to write anything. You can say what you want, but *place* does have a lot to do with productivity. Hell, I don't care what happens to me,—whether I go nuts or my entrails hang out; but I can't stand being so mindless and barren as I've been [Apparently page missing here.]

I sent another letter off to that wrong address. For some reason I can't find your last letters.

Love,

Ted

To Rolfe Humphries

[*Saginaw, Michigan*]

[*1936*]

Dear Rolfe: I'm very glad you liked the piece[1] and I'm trying to revise the stanza at the end.

Here's a new one—the last one, in fact.[2]

An eminent poet and critic was up in these parts last week— Louis Untermeyer. In October he suggested that I send him something for the *Am. Mercury,* which I did, finally, about two weeks ago. He sent the poems back, as I expected, but said he liked this one "exceedingly," wished it were more "marketable," etc. But he also gave me a very detailed train schedule about his arriving in Saginaw on Tuesday at eleven, etc., so I thought he wanted to be asked to lunch or be rescued from the Women's Clubs. So I met his train, then went up to Midland with him where he talked at four o'clock. I must say that he does shovel the culture out with amazing fortitude. I enjoyed watching him and the audience. Afterwards I talked to him for some time, and he seemed to be a quite amusing guy. Some of his opinions are a bit odd, of course. I asked him whether he'd seen your article on MacLeish. He said no, which I don't believe.

[1] The poem beginning "Assailants lurk behind the door."
[2] Cannot identify.

Untermeyer laughs at himself a good bit—but not quite hard enough, I feel.

God, I can't seem to be able to put down two consecutive sentences about anything anymore. Yesterday I tried to say something intelligent about Stevens,[3] but couldn't. I gave a decent lecture on Stevens two years ago.

It's been cold as hell here for weeks.

. . . .

I guess I'm hellishly naive.

God, I'm writing a lot of inane crap, but put it down to the weather and my innate stupidity.

To Rolfe Humphries

[June, 1936]

Dear Rolfe: How are you & what have you been doing? Has *The Law*[1] come out yet? How are Helen and Johnny?

Me, I'm in fairly good spirits. I haven't a job for next year yet, but have several pretty good irons in the fire. I guess I told you all about those Mich. State bastards.

Here is a verseling I made last night. Is it too dumb? "Bestial" is a cliche, I guess.

That little piece which you got me to revise is in this week's *Nation,* I believe.[2]

I saw & liked your piece in a recent N. Yorker.

Tomorrow I'll probably go to Detroit & Cleveland.

Where is Louise? I haven't heard from her in months. Do you have her last address? I lost it.

Stanley Kunitz writes that he has been rowing with Wilson & Co.

Ted

Conscience[3]

I grew a bawdy eye,
A slack, licentious tongue.

[3] Wallace Stevens.

----

[1] This is Roethke's way of abbreviating the League of American Writers, and the reference here is to their proposed quarterly, *American Writing.*

[2] Probably "Genesis," published in the *Nation* (June 24, 1936). *CP,* p. 18.

[3] Apparently unpublished.

My sinews were unstrung
In bestial gluttony.

I had a gosling's pride,
A wit that worshipped sense.
The blood within my side
Rejoiced in violence.

Flesh thickens on the bone,
But innocence turns cold.
I shiver in the sun
To think what I have killed.

To Theodore J. Gates[1]

Saginaw, Michigan
July 20, 1936

My dear Sir: I have been advised by Mrs. Lucille Brooks of the Bureau of Appointments, University of Michigan, that there is a vacancy in your department for the coming year. I should like to be considered for this position.

I was graduated from the University of Michigan in 1929 with the highest possible degree citation, was a member of Phi Beta Kappa and other honorary organizations. I completed the work for the master's degree in 1920 [*sic.* Should be 1930]. The year 1930–31 I spent in the Harvard Graduate School.

Most of my courses at Michigan were in English literature and rhetoric. At Harvard my most important work was in practical criticism and contemporary British literature under I. A. Richards. My principal interest has always been writing and the teaching of writing.

From 1931–35 I was an instructor in English at Lafayette College, Easton, Pennsylvania, where I taught freshman English, a composition course for sophomore engineers, and a special course for honor students in advanced composition and contemporary literature. The usual tenure for English instructors at Lafayette is two years, but I was kept four—the longest anyone has been retained in twenty-five years. In addition to regular teaching, I did considerable administrative work as director of public relations

---

[1] Department of English Composition, Pennsylvania State College.

during 1934–35, and editor of the catalog. I was also varsity tennis coach for three years.

Publications of mine have appeared in such magazines as *The Atlantic Monthly, Scribner's, The New Republic, The Nation, The Adelphi, The Saturday Review of Literature, The Commonweal, The Sewanee Review, Poetry, The American Poetry Journal,* and others.

If you should wish to write directly regarding my ability, I would suggest as references:

Dr. James W. Tupper, Department of English, Lafayette College

Professor Louis A. Strauss, Department of English, University of Michigan

President Arthur A. Hauck, University of Maine, Orono, Maine

Professor Carl G. Gaum, Rutgers University, New Brunswick, New Jersey

Professor Henry C. Hutchins, Department of English, Yale University

Professor Robert Hillyer, Pomfret, Connecticut

The Appointment Bureau at the University of Michigan has a full set of recommendations and credentials regarding me.

I shall probably come East during the next month and I could very easily come to State College at your convenience if I were being seriously considered for the position.

Yours truly,
Theodore Roethke

TO ROLFE HUMPHRIES

[Saginaw, Michigan]
[1936]

Dear Rolfe: Glad you liked the piece.[1] I've changed the last stanza to

The knuckles of the spine betray
The heart; the marrow's drained away.

---

[1] See letter to Humphries, p. 36.

> To fight when backed against the wall
> Requires unremittant will.

The line is made irregular, but the word may do, or does it? The syllables are all of equal value, or approximately. I seem to be getting dumber week by week.

Did I tell you I could have had a part time job at Michigan, but didn't take? Had a bum cold at the time, with a throat & medicos thought better not. My mother has been in pretty bad shape, so it's been a dandy winter.

Read Frederick Prokosch's novel.[2] Not bad. Saw three poems of his in *New Verse* which I liked.

Did those notices of Stevens & the Deutsch book in a slight coma.[3] I could have kicked my tail for being so easy on Wallace, the finicky bastard. But Deutsch I called a compendium of common knowledge or something dumb like that.

To the movies.

Ted

God damn it, I hate Saginaw. I'm beginning to think I was born out of my time, or am just plain dumb.

To Louise Bogan

[*Probably 1937*]

Dear Louise: Last night I re-read some of your letters. (I'm saving them for posterity.) I hope you're touched.

Glad you liked the poem.[1] I'll try to fix it up as you indicated. The dear old *Atlantic* has had it for a month, sent me one letter about it, etc. *The Commonweal* bought that piece M. Cowley said sounded like a hymn, so I suppose he was right.[2] But God bless the Catholics, I say.

---

[2] *The Asiatics* (1935).

[3] Reviews of Wallace Stevens' *Ideas of Order*, *New Republic* (July 15, 1936), and Babette Deutsch's *This Modern Poetry*, *New Republic* (July 22, 1936). Both reviews are extremely brief.

---

[1] Cannot identify.

[2] Probably the poem "Statement," published in *Commonweal* (Dec. 31, 1937).

Old John is not quite such a pot as he sounds.[3] He's really a very decent guy & only sounds off—or rather drools—to a few of his intimates. He's the sort who drives Rolfe nuts, I should imagine.

Is this eppygram any good? I was quite pleased with it for a time.[4]

> Expect the staring eye,
> The insolence of hate,
> The churlish pedantry
> Of those inveterate
>
> Defilers of the good.
> They mock your deepest thought
> And jeer the fortitude
> Whereby the good was wrought.
>
> There is no need to give
> Them deference or guile:
> Their malice can't survive
> The missile of a smile.

too grotesque? too Christian?

To Rolfe Humphries

[State College, Pennsylvania]
[1937]

Dear Rolfe: I'm going to read next week, and again on the 24th. Do you have a carbon of that morning poem[1] that Wilson liked so well; in fact, do you have any other poems that you'd care to have read? I'm going to read from Kunitz, Louise, Auden, Spender, and you. I'm rather badly off in your case since I don't have a *Europa*,[2] even, right now.

---

3 Most likely John Holmes.
4 The final version published as "Reply to Censure" in *Open House*. The letter of August 5, 1937, to Morton D. Zabel contains another, later but not final, version. *CP*, p. 20.

---

1 Possibly refers to Humphries' "Bright Morning Song," later included in *Out of the Jewel* (1942).
2 Humphries' collection *Europa, and Other Poems, and Sonnets* (1928).

Don't bother if you're busy because it's my own dumbness, as usual.

I haven't done much in the way of verse recently. I pawned off a lyric with mildly revolutionary implications on the *Sewanee Review*,[3] which doesn't pay. The other week I dug a fair lyric out of that well-worked carnal vein.[4] But in this bleak area one is grateful for anything. The N. Yorker bought a light verse effort a while back,[5] etc., etc.

This semester I'm teaching nothing but freshman exposition, 110 students in four sections. It's like turning a crank after a few days.

Any news from the Guggenheim boys?

Ted

HAY-FEVER LAMENT

With all the windy hills of space,
With earth a vernal garden place,
With field and forest close at hand,
With cracks and crannies that God planned,
With air so willing to disperse
What's loose upon the universe,
With dust bowls wider than a state,—
Why must I suffer such a fate?
Oh, why in hell must all that grows
Deposit pollen in my nose?

N. Y.er

TO ROLFE HUMPHRIES

[State College, Pennsylvania]
[Probably 1937]

Dear Rolfe: Thanks very much for sending the poems. It was swell to see them in a group. I read six of yours, I believe, and they went over very well. God, that "Meditation for Sext" is a beautiful poem.

---

[3] "Sign Though No Sign," *Sewanee Review* (January–March, 1938).
[4] Cannot identify.
[5] Probably "Hay-fever Lament," *New Yorker* (Aug. 14, 1937). Reprinted above.

The second time I had a big room with a very mixed audience & much outside noise, but I pitched it out pretty well, I think. About ten had to stand, God help me. Just a Louis Untermeyer am I.

. . . .

I hope your row with the school officials turns out all right. One of the new instructors here just up & disappeared without a word. So far everything has been kept quiet.

This place isn't doing me much good.

My best to Helen & John—
Ted

To Katharine Stokes[1]

[Saginaw, Michigan]
[June 11, 1937]

Dear Kitty: It was so nice to come home and find a letter from you.

We made the trip, mostly through rain, without mishap. For two nights I stayed at Henry Hutchins' former "residence" which is filled with Italian furniture, eighteenth century originals, etc. I had a swell canopied bed.

Ann Arbor seemed pleasanter than ever before. I saw Allan Seager, a guy whom E. J. O'Brien[2] thinks is the white hope of the Am. short story. He was very funny on the old Vanity Fair people whom he knew when on the staff. He liked the Chief No Pain story. Seager's a lunger. You may have read a story of his on that theme in Scribner's about two months ago.[3] Read it.

One night I was out to Norman Nelson's house. He's a power (for a young man (37)) in the Eng. Dept. He gave me a fight talk about doing a thesis for Ph.D. on modern poetry, or at least drawing up a plan so he could get Bredvold [4] (dept. head) to accept it.

Look, would you send me the carbon or first copy of that letter

<hr>

[1] First Circulation Librarian, then Assistant Librarian for Reader's Service at Pennsylvania State College during the period Roethke was teaching there.

[2] Critic of the American short story.

[3] Miss Stokes guesses that "Chief No Pain" might have been a joke or anecdote she and Roethke shared at the time [letter to the editor]. Seager's story is "Pro Arte," *Scribner's Magazine* (February, 1937).

[4] Louis I. Bredvold, head of the English Department at the University of Michigan.

to Miss Leetch or Mrs. Brooks? It seems that Mrs. Brooks isn't with the Michigan Bureau and I need to send another copy to Dr. Purdom[5] who is in charge. When I saw this guy he was very cordial, etc. etc.

John Holmes got an offer from New Jersey State Teacher's College in Montclair at a one third jump in salary. He turned it down because Tufts is raising him this year & much more next.

The London *Sat. Rev.* turned down all the pieces.

The Headlight came & looks good. Runt isn't so hot on Steinbeck, is he?

I caught a cold, of course, in my travels.

Let me hear from you, Kitty darling.

I have Spender's Burning Cactus[6] & a couple of other things.

Ted

To Rolfe Humphries

[June 19, 1937]

Dear Rolfe: At the last minute I got a ride all the way to Ann Arbor, so I couldn't take advantage of your invitation. I would have liked to see you. (Hell, is that the right grammar?)

I found this piece, "The Bringer of Tidings," in a notebook last night. Somehow, it pleases me right now. What do you think? Is the third stanza too obscure or something? The other one is the best I've done in some time, I think.

I showed some of your poems to Leo Kirshbaum, a Yidd who has just won a major Hopwood award for poetry. He was very enthusiastic and made copies of several. Two undergraduates there liked them very much, too.

Did I tell you H. Gregory turned me down cold on a whole batch for his old annual?[1] That's what I get for sticking my neck out.

Is Louise back? I got a card from Limerick, Ireland some weeks ago, but nothing since.

---

5 Luther Purdom, head of the Bureau of Appointments and Occupational Information, University of Michigan.

6 *The Burning Cactus* (1936), a collection of Stephen Spender's short stories.

---

1 *New Letters in America*, ed. by Horace Gregory (1937).

I'll probably be up in New England in late August.

Nothing came of my sucking around old Homer Watt[2] of N. Y. U. I don't think Eda Lou fancied me.[3] Did you notice her quite favorable review of John Holmes in the Herald Trib.?

I re-read your sonnet on music[4] again. It's a swell piece.

Let me hear from you.

Give my best to Helen & John.

Ted

THE BRINGER OF TIDINGS[5]

An early bearer of the news,
You suffer neighborhood derision.
The men of property refuse
To countenance your least decision.

Your faith is counted lack of mind
By gossips at the corner store.
The wives who lift the parlor blind
Inspect you with a furtive stare.

They do not heed your warning, or
Accept you as relief from harm;
But they will seek you out before
The daybreak of the first alarm.

Custodian of common sense,
You strip our actions of pretense,
And gauge a generation's mood
And are the harbinger of good.

TO KATHARINE STOKES

July 4 [1937]
Written in post office

Dear Kitty: Here's a new kind of poem which I hope you like.[1] If

---

[2] Professor of English, New York University.
[3] Eda Lou Walton, poet and teacher at New York University.
[4] Possibly "For a Shy Partner."
[5] This is the version of the poem published in *Poetry* (December, 1938).

---

[1] Cannot identify.

you have time, type it out for me, will you? My sister has gone to Quebec.

. . . .

The *N. Y.er* bought a verse I wrote about hayfever.[2] They're still only paying me 50¢ a line.

It's very hot but fairly quiet today.

John[3] sent me the unfinished book he has made of my poems. He has 39, and I have counted up 18 which he doesn't have which I like, including the light verse. However, there are at least 7 of those he has which I wouldn't print in the volume, but that still leaves about 50,—a surprising total.

I miss you.

Love,
Ted

TO KATHARINE STOKES

[*Saginaw, Michigan*]
[*July 14, 1937*]

Dear Kitty:

. . . .

I've been enjoying myself a good bit sitting out in the garden. There has been much rain this year and the flowers are very beautiful. Last night I saw a hummingbird, several goldfinches, swallows, a song sparrow, grackles, a flicker, a mourning dove, a catbird, a wren (it nests close to the house) and just before sundown a big heron flew over. Right now a pair of goldfinches, male & female, are eating seeds from Shasta daisies only about ten feet away. They eat very voraciously—almost fall off the stem, sometimes, in their haste.

Thanks for the MacIntyre review.[1]

The Nation in recent weeks has had some reporting on Youngstown that might interest you.

[2] "Hay-fever Lament," *New Yorker* (Aug. 14, 1937). See p. 43.
[3] John Holmes.

---

[1] Probably a review of the poet C. F. MacIntyre by William Rose Benét in *Saturday Review of Literature* (July 3, 1937).

These smears are raindrops. I've been driven indoors now.
I love you, Kitty, and often I want you terribly.

. . . .

                              Ted
It's rained like hell again.

To KATHARINE STOKES

                              [*Saginaw, Michigan*]
                              [*July 23, 1937*]

Dear Kitty:

. . . .

I've been in a thoroughly bad state of late. I wish I could see
you.

The editors have been turning me down: *The Virginia Quarterly* that Prairie piece; *The Nation* that "Interlude" & the "Dixie
Highway"; the N. R. also the Dixie.[1] Well, it is the chance you
take.

Ben Belitt is taking over Léonie Adams' job at Bennington.
What I wouldn't give to have it.

My sister gets on my nerves, but I suppose I get on hers.

I've been reading some of Jesse Stuart's stories. Also read a dumb
(fairly) campus novel, "Winds Over the Campus." About Chicago.
James Weber Linn the author.

                              Hastily,
                              Ted

Your very sweet letter just came. It's swell to know that you are
thinking of me. Love, T.

To ROLFE HUMPHRIES

                              [*July 24, 1937*]

Dear Rolfe: I'm sorry that the Bennington thing fell through. I've

---

[1] The poems are "In Praise of Prairie," "Interlude," and "Highway:
Michigan," all of them later included in *Open House. CP,* pp. 6, 13, 33. The
"N. R." is the *New Republic.*

always had a kind of yen to teach there, but I daresay I never will.[1] Today, along with a rejection, Ben Belitt of *The Nation* staff said he was going "to teach verse at Bennington next year." Was that the same job or were you applying in Latin? Hell—I don't mean to be nosey—never mind, but I thought the Belitt item might interest you.

I like the new poem very much. A. J. M. Smith liked it, too. He was up here a while back. He also liked the ditties on the Congress, and copied them out.[2]

I've been in a sour state of mind of late. The editors boot me in the tail with monotonous regularity, although Bruce Bliven did buy a piece about a heron[3] a month ago or longer, I guess. Or did I tell you? And the N. Y.er one on hayfever[4]—*very* light. Light verse enfeebles the mind and other centers, I fear.

We (Art Smith and John Clarke[5] of East Lansing) were going to Olivet[6] for a meeting or two of their "conference," but I haven't heard from Smith as yet.

I expect to be diddling around New England and New York at the end of August. I hope to see you.

I enclose a piece[7] which Louise said she liked, but which *The Nation* & *N. R.* bounced. What do you think?

I must be in Norton's[8] black book, for he never answers mail any more.

Ted

---

[1] Roethke did, however. He was on the Bennington faculty from 1943 to 1946.

[2] Cannot identify these poems.

[3] "The Heron," published in the *New Republic* (Sept. 1, 1937), and New York *Herald Tribune* (Sept. 14, 1937). *CP*, p. 15.

[4] "Hay-fever Lament," published in the *New Yorker* (Aug. 14, 1937).

[5] Of the Michigan State University Department of English.

[6] Olivet, Michigan, where a writers' conference was held.

[7] Cannot identify.

[8] Theodore Norton. See letter to Rolfe Humphries of March 1, 1935.

To Morton Dauwen Zabel[1]

Saginaw, Michigan
August 5, 1937

My dear Mr. Zabel: Thank you for your letter of July 24 and for the suggestions which I have tried to follow. I believe the piece is much stronger, for I have eliminated most of the abstract words.

Sincerely,
Theodore Roethke

Old version—in case you wished to make a comparison.[2]

Expect the staring eye,
The insolence of hate,
The churlish pedantry
Of those inveterate

Defilers of the good,
They mock your deepest thought
And jeer the fortitude
Whereby the good is wrought.

Though passion is reviled
And cravens cry you down,
Delight keeps undefiled
A wisdom of its own.

Hope has a toughened skin
That keeps sufficient store
Of dignity within,
And quiet at the core.

To Katharine Stokes

[*August 14, 1937*]

Dear Kitty: I've just had that impacted wisdom tooth out along with the one next to it which had become too decayed to save. It

---

[1] Critic and professor of English at Loyola University and the University of Chicago; succeeded to the editorship of *Poetry* at the death of Harriet Monroe.

[2] Published in its final form as "Reply to Censure" in *Open House. CP*, p. 20.

wasn't too terrible, all things considered. The guy who did it refused the chair of oral surgery at Michigan and is supposed to be one of the best in the country.

I've been reading detective stories—Erle Gardner and H. C. Bailey. Also Coward's[1] *Present Indicative.* Have written nothing of late, but don't give a damn.

The University gave me a lead on a job at $2500, but I didn't bother going down to see the man. It was in a foreign country— with expenses over paid. Guess where—*China.*

Eight X-rays were taken before Goodsell operated.

I think I missed a swell job at the Edison Institute which was to pay at least $3,000. It seems the Bureau sent a picture taken eight years ago. The man practically told me that he'd have taken me if he'd seen me soon enough and had known my complete record. He had to make a decision & offered it to a guy now in Europe. He said if the man didn't take it, he'd let me know right away. (Say nothing of this, of course.) It's been quite a while now and he hasn't let me know, so it's probably fallen through, like all my projects. I'll tell you more later.

I'm getting groggy from the after-effects.

Love,

Ted

Gee, I wish I could see you. You are a darling.

To Katharine Stokes

[August 23, 1937]

Dear Kitty: My mouth has kept me out of the letter-writing mood, or any other mood except profound irritation. It seems he will have to keep dressing it, or someone will, for ten days at least. However, I'm going to New England and probably will have to get other dentists to finish. Incidentally, are you going to be in State College about then—meaning Aug. 25 or 26? If I take a bus, I might stop off to see you, if you wanted me to. (Don't be frightened—I'd *stay* at the U. Club.)

. . . .

[1] Noel Coward.

I sent Bill Werner[1] a clipping from his column the N. Yorker had sent me & he wrote a very decent letter.

The N. R. bought *Interlude* this week.[2] I sent them your typed version, for luck, even though I had to make a change in ink. You bring me luck, Kitty. *Poetry* also bought the staring eye piece, somewhat revised—by me, of course.[3] And Allen Tate wrote me a swell letter, and you know what a sour puss he is. He said Howard M. Jones' *They Say the Forties* was written in the style of Godey's Lady's book.[4] John's book he dismissed in part of a sentence.[5] All this was in the *Southern Review*.

Read a swell murder book. *The Deadly Dowager* by Edwin Greenhood or Greenwood, I've forgotten which.

Love,

Ted

To Rolfe Humphries

[State College, Pennsylvania]
[November 20, 1937]

Dear Rolfe: I'm surprised about Scribners & Random House. I was sure one of them would want to publish the book.[1] I was just beginning to think things were getting better.

Several people here have commented on your poems in *Poetry*, especially the embassy one & *Green Mountain Scene*.[2] [. . .]

Here is a poem I showed you once which I have changed somewhat. Is the conclusion all right, or would you cut the second couplet to the last? (You need to resurrect, etc.)[3]

---

[1] William L. Werner, professor of American Literature at Pennsylvania State College, had a column, "The Bookworm," in the *Centre Daily Times*.
[2] Later published in *Open House. CP*, p. 6.
[3] "Reply to Censure." *CP*, p. 20. See letter to M. D. Zabel, August 5, 1937.
[4] Refers to a popular American magazine of the nineteenth century.
[5] John Holmes's *Address to the Living* (1937).

[1] Refers to Humphries' manuscript.
[2] The poems referred to are probably those which appear in Humphries' *Out of the Jewel* under the titles "Bread-and-Butter Letter, On an Official Occasion" and "Green Mountain Seminary."
[3] An earlier version accompanies Roethke's letter to Humphries on January 21, 1936.

Is Gregory[4] poetry editor of *New Masses* now?

I thought for a while there might be some money to bring up Louise and/or you or somebody for a Liberal Arts "lecture." But now it's all fallen through.

Ted

Assailants lurk behind the door.
This is a treacherous time. Beware
The shadow darkening the floor,
The foot that scuttles on the stair.

Avoid the paralytic hand
That fumbles at your sleeve, the eyes
That mark you for a sudden end.
Be quick to pierce the fool's disguise.

You hesitate to step beyond
The narrow room; congeal with fear.
These imbecilities confound
Your friends, while enemies draw near.

The knuckles of the spine betray
The heart; the marrow's drained away.
You need to resurrect the will
To fight when backed against the wall.
The fingers limp upon the wrist
Must clench the palm in hardened fist.

To Stanley Kunitz[1]

State College, Pennsylvania
November 29, 1937

Dear Stanley: I've had a copy of *Froth,* the Pennsylvania State College "humorous" magazine, sent you. The student editorial on the library may interest you. The proposed expenditure for a new building here has been reduced more than one-half. It's a disgraceful situation. The literary magazine and college newspaper also have put up a howl.

[4] Horace Gregory.

[1] Poet and editor.

That poem I sent you[2] wasn't much good, I'm afraid. Just surface statement. A long time ago you made some suggestions about a poem beginning "Old passions haunt the brains; you mull the memory for dark despairs"—or something like that.

Anyway, here is the revision I finally made which I hope is an improvement. Ben Belitt says the lines aren't fused, but damned if I think that is valid in this case.

. . . .

Ted

The Cure[3]

The fantasies of sorrow breed
Acedia in the active brain.
The hands are useless for the deed;
You spoil the richness of the vein.

Your flesh is wasting on a frame
Designed for swift, explicit wrath.
Denials of the spirit tame
The conscience into stupid faith.

So bleed yourself of love, the blood
That melancholy feeds upon,
And learn the marrow's fortitude,
The hatred burning in the bone.

I've progressed beyond this viewpoint, I think.

The Summons[4]

Now all who love the best,—
Old and rebellious young,—
Must contemplate the waste
Of countenancing wrong:
The human mired, the brute
Raised up to eminence,
The mimic following suit
Until devoid of sense,

[2] Cannot identify.
[3] Apparently unpublished.
[4] Published as one of a group of "Seven Poems" in *Poetry* (December, 1938).

The good becoming gross,—
All this we may discern;
By slow degrees we learn
The full extent of loss.

Though the small wit we have
May nullify belief,
The simple act can save
The heritage of life.
With secrecy put by,
The heart grows less obtuse,
And fervency of eye
Is put to better use.
The impulse long denied,
The lips that never move,
The hatred and the pride,—
These can be turned to love.
Now we must summon all
Our force, from breadth to length,
And walk, more vertical,
Secure in human strength.

RIVER INCIDENT[5]

A shell arched under my toes,
Stirred up a whirl of silt
That riffled around my knees.
I waded further from shore.
Whatever I owed to time
Slowed in my human form;
Seawater stood in my veins,
For a moment I turned to lime;
The elements I kept warm
Crumbled and flowed away;
And I knew I had been there before:
In that cold granitic slime,
In the dark, in the rolling water.

Here's the swamp one finally ended. Do you like it? Rolfe doesn't like the ending but I do.

[5] Published in *New Yorker* (Sept. 11, 1943), and subsequently in *The Lost Son and Other Poems* (1948). Lines 4 and 8 were later dropped. *CP*, p. 49.

"Dark" is to be a noun. Do you take it as a noun? Or must I use semi-colons?

ELEGY[6]

Her leaf-like hands on the long branches of willow
Move in my eyes as they move on the face of the river.
The long willow arms bend with the wind but do not beckon.
Whatever shines or reflects returns me that image.
But her voice, light as a brook over stones, I cannot remember,
Though I listen at the wind's heart, at the center of whirling water,
Or wait by cold rocks in the stillness of low country.
My ears stay on the stretch for that unearthly timbre.

I saved this because you liked part of it. Now I like it, of its kind. Last line was a bastard,[7] but I think O.K. now. D'you?

TO STANLEY KUNITZ

[December, 1937]

Dear Stanley: Did the copies of *Froth* and *The Bell* finally reach you? The *Froth* editor is my best student in verse-writing, Robert Wistrand.

Curse me if you will, Stanley, but here is one more poem.[1] I won't send or show you another until I see you, I promise. I've been making a desperate effort to turn away from negation and "hatred" and this is the result. The shadow of Yeats is on the page, but is it too heavy? In other words, is it my poem or a series of echoes? I believe it mine for I had to fight through much to get even this on the page. God knows what I say isn't new, but is it worth saying in this way? I mean with this many abstractions?

Oh hell, never mind *all* the questions. What's troubling me is the "influence" business. It's so easy to say: "Yeats: (1) three foot alternate rhymes (2) enumerations."

---

[6] Published in *Poetry Quarterly* (England) (Summer, 1943).

[7] Line 5 originally read, "But the light voice I never remember,"—it was scratched out. Line 8 originally read, "Only the dry air of silence closes upon me." It is also scratched out.

---

[1] Possibly "The Summons." See letter to Stanley Kunitz, November 29, 1937.

Please be patient with my frantic questioning. I get in a terrible stew every so often for fear that I'm writing like Lionel Wiggam or Frances Frost. It's theme correcting that addles the brain perhaps.

When I was in Chicago for the M.L.A. meetings your name came up several times: (1) In the *Poetry* office (where I was taken by some friends—it wasn't my idea.) G. Udell is a great fan of yours. Dillon wasn't there.[2] (2) At Elder Olson's. He, incidentally, is a much more mature guy than you'd imagine from his *Thing of Sorrow*. Really an impressive intellect. (Stupid phrase) An "Aristotelean" who is taking his Ph.D. at Chicago this year. But I must say Olson's teacher, R. S. Crane, was damned dull to my mind. Have you read any of Crane's books? I haven't. But Olson is O.K. I hope the damned academics don't turn him into another snivelling carper (paradox) with a "system" that has all the answers.

Another fellow & I drove 700 miles in one trip last night & today. We had much trouble with batteries, lights, etc. I'm a little groggy still.

Ted

I do hope you like that piece.

[EDITOR'S NOTE: *This poem, while not assignable to a specific letter or correspondent, belongs to this period of Roethke's career. It is placed at the end of this section because it was published in* Commonweal *on December 31, 1937.*]

STATEMENT

My former self goes out;
The flesh is purified.
The past will be my foil
Against ridiculous doubt.
Discord shall not prevail
While blood beats in my side.

The body learned its length
And breadth; my darkest mood
Was written with my name.
Now I declare my strength

-----

[2] George Dillon was then editor of *Poetry;* Geraldine Udell was on the staff.

And find a proper theme:
My vigor is renewed.

I drop my foolish ways
For wisdom dearly bought,
And salvage what I can
Out of my wasted days.
The present is my span:
I move to richer thought.

1938-39

To George Dillon[1]

State College, Pennsylvania
January 4, 1938

My dear Mr. Dillon: I was sorry that I missed you last week when I visited your office.

I have enclosed five poems for your consideration. Three, "The Cure," "Against Disaster," and the one beginning "All those who by design would clean," were written in a period of terror before a "breakdown." The other two were written more recently. I set most store by "The Summons," which I hope you will like. I mention all this because the two sets of poems are contradictory.

Because of reasons I need not enumerate, it would be a kindness if you could give me a decision on these as soon as possible.

Please thank Miss Udell for a most pleasant half hour.

Yours sincerely,
Theodore Roethke

At the last minute, I have decided to include two more.[2]

[1] Poet and translator; then editor of *Poetry* magazine.
[2] Not able to identify these, or the fifth, unnamed poem mentioned in paragraph 2, above.

To Rolfe Humphries

[State College, Pennsylvania]
[January 29, 1938]

Dear Rolfe: By a curious circumstance, I'm supposed to be reviewing *And Spain Sings* for *Poetry*.[1] I feel like a horse's ass about it, for I know practically no Spanish.

It happened in a curious way. When I was in Chicago, I ran into a guy I know, Dan Sparks, who was on his way to the *Poetry* office with a dame named Marguerite Young.[2] He wanted me to come along, so I did, since it was only about five blocks from the Drake. While we were there, the business manager[3] asked me if I did any reviewing. I said occasional snippets for Cowley. Then she asked me whether I'd be interested in *And Spain Sings*. I said yes, but, . . . etc. etc.

Later the book came along.

Well, all this has no interest for you. But I didn't want you to think me the complete jackass for even attempting the job. At the time, my chief idea was that this was a chance to plug the book.

All this leads up to the main idea: Have you several of the originals around in carbons that you could send or lend me? I don't mean to try to evaluate any pieces as translations,—I just thought I could learn a little Spanish and perhaps ease my conscience a bit.

Don't bother if they're not close at hand. The most I could handle would be, say, half a dozen.

———————

If this sounds dumber than usual put it down to my being slugnutty from reading papers and having conferences. The teaching load here is terrific. A lot of the boys don't bother with conferences, but I try to have three or four with each kid.

For two weeks I've had pharyngitis with complications.

[1] Roethke's review of *And Spain Sings: Fifty Loyalist Ballads,* ed. by M. J. Bernardete and Rolfe Humphries, appeared in *Poetry* (April, 1938). Reprinted in *On the Poet and His Craft.*
[2] Later author of *Moderate Fable, Angel in the Forest,* and *Miss MacIntosh, My Darling.*
[3] Geraldine Udell.

Zabel was at the Modern Language meeting. He seemed a fairly decent guy, especially when placed against a background of academic great men.

I see where you're having another poetry class.

Hastily,
Ted

To Katharine Stokes

[*Saginaw, Michigan*]
[*June 22, 1938*]

Dear Kitty:

. . . .

Today I helped my mother with the washing. She likes to use rainwater, which must be moved by tub from a big cistern. Some of it must be heated on a special stove downstairs. So I got all that ready, helped run some things through, put out the lines, carried baskets in and out, etc. She has a terrific routine: washer then wringer to rinsing tub, then through wringer again. But when it's all over, the clothes smell sweet and fresh, without a trace of soap.

I've written one poem[1] which I will send you shortly. It's fair, perhaps, but may be pedestrian.

I think you are too generous in comparing MacNeice[2] & me. But it's nice.

Love,
Ted

I've busted my good pen. I'm just sick about it. But maybe the pen people can fix it.

Bud Roethke, my big operator cousin from Beverly Hills is in town, but I haven't talked to him. My Aunt Elise, one of the more fancy relatives, sold her house & is moving to Detroit to live with her lawyer son & wife & child.

Yes, it is not interesting.

T.

[1] Cannot identify.
[2] The poet Louis MacNeice.

To Rolfe Humphries

[Saginaw, Michigan]
[June 29, 1938]

Dear Rolfe: I got the manuscript off in time, with a good many of the revisions you, Louise & Kunitz suggested.[1] I threw out some of those dumb pieces you didn't like ("To measure love by love's machine," "Be proud to live alone," for instance). Found one or two others, revised about eight or ten; changed the order—made no divisions.

But hell, it will be too sour puss for I-Love-Life Benét.[2]

I've been home nearly two weeks and have scratched out a few lyrics. Here's a dubious effort which I wrote this afternoon. I'd just read that slop in the back of the edition of Rupert Brooke and "Perfidious Albion" in an old N. R. and was really mad for once. Is it too bald and blunt? I don't suppose old Malcolm[3] would touch it.

Things are lousy in Saginaw. My mother is in pretty bad shape, physically and financially.

Three or four kids were working on that League contest, but some were overwhelmed by the subject.[4] I'm positive Robert Wistrand will hand in a fairly good entry in poetry.

Give my best to Helen & John.

Ted

COWARD'S SONG[5]
(For Lady ———, endorser of cold cream)

> Though gas and roaring guns
> May reap your blue-eyed sons,
>
> I'll not put up a stake,
> Or fight for your sweet sake.

[1] Roethke submitted a manuscript for the Yale Series of Younger Poets competition, but it was rejected, as he guesses here.
[2] Stephen Vincent Benét was the judge for the Yale Series.
[3] Malcolm Cowley.
[4] A contest sponsored by the League of American Writers for undergraduate writers in American colleges.
[5] Unpublished.

Why should I give a limb
To keep *your* figure trim,

Or bear with roach and louse
To save that country house?

I think of Sikhs and Boers.
Humanity like yours

Has come to a dead end.
There's nothing to defend.

I'll not pick up the torch,
But leave you in the lurch.

I'll keep what I have got,
Though Albion be not.

To Stanley Kunitz

[*Saginaw, Michigan*]
[*1938*]

Dear Stanley: Here are two verses which I wrote last week.[1] Neither is much, I suppose, but maybe they were worth doing.

I've played a little tennis and caught the usual Saginaw Valley cold.

Very dumb and silly I feel.

Did I tell you that I gave the manuscript the title you suggested —*Open House*? Another addition to my debt. But I don't think anything will come of the Yale competition. I never won first in anything. Always place or show. But one can always hope, anyway.

Let me hear from you, even though my infantile scribbles don't deserve an answer.

Ted

[1] Cannot identify.

To Katharine Stokes

[Saginaw, Michigan]
[July 5, 1938]
Monday night

Dear Kitty: After my confident scribble of Friday or so, I've lapsed into complete creative inactivity, as you might expect. In addition, I have more cold, blisters on toes of both feet, and one hand from playing tennis. It took me 4–6, 6–4, 6–4 to beat a guy I licked 6–0, 6–2 the first day I was out here.

Today I read a lot of John Peale Bishop in Louise's copy. He's very good in his way although sometimes it's the wrong way.

Today, since June[1] went on a picnic, my mother & I were home alone. She (my mother) made some ice cream that was most successful.

Well, pray I start writing some more. I made a good start, I think.

Love,
Ted

Haven't heard from Stanley. Had a nutty card from Louise—a pictorial representation of Dante's *Inferno*. John Holmes wrote asking me to come in July—which I won't, of course.

Could you send me John Crowe Ransom's book of criticism? [2]

. . . .

To Katharine Stokes

[Saginaw, Michigan]
[July 26, 1938]

Dear Kitty:

. . . .

Funny thing: George Dillon reacted just as you did to "Like Walkers in an unfamiliar place"—he said he liked the first two stanzas

---

[1] Roethke's sister.
[2] *The World's Body* (1938).

very much, but thought the last too flatly didactic. So I've revised it & made it a much stronger poem. Dillon added "The Signals" [1] —or did I tell you that? He keeps asking to see more, although he says he's overstocked.

I'm still pretty sore about the Yale thing,[2] but I'll forget about it in due time.

The ad for *Poetry* in the July *Poetry* has my name along with some twenty others.

Well, I licked what I think will be my toughest opponent in the News Novice tournament, 6–2, 7–5. It was Jack Wallace who plays no. 1 for Bay City Junior College. But there's still a kid named Ike Garber who is the Valley Junior Champion and one of the best juniors in the Middlewest. (He was seeded no. 8 in the western junior.)

I'll probably get licked eventually, but I've been playing pretty fair tennis, all things considered. I'll probably get a sore toe or sore arm, or something silly.

I'd rather write poems, but my mother & sister seem to think a diet of tennis & sunshine is better right now.

You're a sweet child, Kitty, and I love you.

. . . .

Ted

To Katharine Stokes

[Saginaw, Michigan]
[July 29, 1938]

Dear Kitty: Well, I play the finals of the Novice Tournament to-morrow. I'll probably get licked.

It has rained hard each night for three nights. Today there is a high west wind and sun—just the sort of day I like.

My mother sold some stock for $1400 for which she paid $4,000. Nice going, eh. I *hate* business.

---

[1] Later included in *Open House. CP,* p. 8.
[2] Roethke's manuscript was rejected in the competition for the Yale Younger Poets' prize.

Gee, it's just a marvelous day. I wish you were here, Kitty.

Tonight I'll probably see my first movie in Saginaw for this summer—Jezebel.

Love,

Ted

Here is a poem I wrote after scratching out the note to you:

WINDY WEATHER[1]

Last night a rain broke up the summer's drouth.
The branches of the elm bend north and south.

The countryside has turned to softer green
As leaves and grass lift up their under sheen.

The fattest clouds have split apart or thinned.
Goldfinches pitch through pockets of the wind.

The young colt snorts and paws from fence to fence.
He likes commotion of the elements.

All living things are straining at the tether
To claim their freedom in this windy weather.

To Rolfe Humphries

[*August 2, 1938*]

Dear Rolfe: Thanks for the letter & comments.

Last week-end I saw Art Smith (A. J. M. Smith) & John Clark in Lansing. They are pretty sharp guys, I think, & among your true admirers. They're going to be in New York Christmas & were disappointed to learn you'd probably be in Mexico. I recited your Yeats parody with great success. They copied it down.

Clark gave Edmund some boots in *The Commonweal* about a month or so ago,[1] but whether for the right reasons I don't know. I looked at it just hastily.

Well, I got a printed rejection slip from Horse's A. Benét. I guess I'll have to learn to write like Paul Engle.[2] Sometimes I think I haven't far to go.

---

[1] Later published in the *New Yorker as* "Summer Wind" (July 22, 1939).

---

[1] John Abbot Clark, "The Sad Case of Edmund Wilson," *Commonweal* (July 8, 1938).

[2] Engle's volume *Worn Earth* won the Yale Prize in 1932.

Art Smith, especially, is a very bright & amusing guy. But sometimes I think his verse is a bit too unhuman & nutty. But some very good.

Did you quit your job? What's this about finding a new one?

It's hot & I feel stupid & gloomy.

If you have time, let me know whether any of these verses have any merit.[3]

My best to Helen & Johnny.

Ted

THE VICTIMS[4]

Muddled their dreams of love and rich disguises.
Their furtive gestures bid for fellowship.
Mother alone such beauty recognizes;
They loll about with sullen underlip.

[This stanza scratched out]

Who squirmed by the wall at the earliest childhood dances,
Uneasy at play, the victims of classroom jest,
Walked with averted faces past scribbled fences,
In competition always came second best.

Infection's bloom expands in secret places.
They strip themselves of strangeness to survive,
But death puts on a set of falser faces
To lure them down the highway to the grave.

For the horrible figures that haunted the farthest corner,
The bogie men who rapped on the nursery sill,
Return in their sleep,—but the horse-like features are sterner.
Only the unloved know what it means to be ill.

TO BEN BELITT[1]

Saginaw, Michigan
August 8, 1938

Dear Ben: Since I haven't heard from you since last winter, I have been wondering whether you were offended by my silly dictated

---

[3] "The Victims" and "Summer Wind."

[4] Published in *Twentieth Century Verse* (London) (September–October, 1938).

---

[1] Poet and translator on the faculty of Bennington College.

letter about the verse writing course. I hope not, for I sent it with the best of intentions. I can't type: hence the dictation.

I liked your last poem in *The Nation*;[2] so much, in fact, that I copied it out. Indirectly I heard from the book store at State College that you were bringing out a volume.[3] Who is publishing it? I hope Cowley or Dillon gives it to me to review.[4]

My own fortunes in publishing have been unlucky: a printed slip from the Yale Series of Younger Poets. Louise Bogan & Stanley Kunitz thought the mss. would win by a wide margin. But that's the chance you take, I suppose. I'm both mad & discouraged because it did seem like a pretty good book once it was put together. Kunitz arranged it.

For me, the summer has been fairly dull but pleasant. Wrote about half a dozen verses, then quit. Brain fog or something.

Did I ever send you a copy of a piece called "The Summons"?[5] I practically wrote it under your direction—after your warning to escape from negativism. Maybe it's too easy a solution. But most people liked it.

Did you see Rodman's anthology?[6] My God, what a sophomore! What do they teach them at Yale, anyway?

I've enclosed what verses I can dig up. Do let me know what you think, Ben. I'm reacting against poems of straight observation: too easy for me to do 'em.

> Cordially,
> Ted Roethke

Don't forget to tell me about the volume. I'll try to plug for it in the course of my travels: Ann Arbor, Connecticut & New Jersey & other points.

---

[2] "A poem then called 'Tarry, Delight,' but now called 'The Enemy Joy'" —Ben Belitt.

[3] *The Five-Fold Mesh* (1938).

[4] "Ted *did* review it for *Poetry* (January, 1939)—severely, as it deserved" —Ben Belitt.

[5] Published in a group of seven poems in *Poetry* (December, 1938). See letter to Stanley Kunitz, November 29, 1937.

[6] Selden Rodman, *A New Anthology of Modern Poetry* (1938).

To Katharine Stokes

[August 17, 1938]

Dear Kitty:

. . . .

A letter from Ben Belitt. He said he didn't think the poems I enclosed were as interesting as those he'd seen in print recently I can't recall what I sent him. The Auction, Feud,[1] & one or two others.[2] He thinks I need to break up my line & stanza units. I do, but not quite to the extent he suggests.

It's been raining a lot—several times a day.

Tomorrow the tooth comes out, I guess.

Love,
Ted

To Katharine Stokes

[Saginaw, Michigan]
[August 22, 1938]

Dear Kitty:

. . . .

Nothing new except that I'm doing B. Belitt's & W. Maas' books for *Poetry* when they come out.[1] *Harper's* turned down three with a note. I'm to have a poem in John's book, *The Poet's Work*, Oxford Press, out in October.[2] "This Light" is the piece.

My mother & I are going to an old movie "Dr. Rhythm," with B. Lillie & Bing Crosby.

Love,
Ted

---

[1] Both poems were included in *Open House. CP*, pp. 4, 21.
[2] Including "The Summons."

---

[1] Reviews of Ben Belitt's *The Five-Fold Mesh, Poetry* (January, 1939), and Willard Maas's *Concerning the Young* (March, 1939); both are reprinted in *On the Poet and His Craft.*
[2] John Holmes.

To Louis Untermeyer[1]

State College, Pennsylvania
September 18, 1938

Dear Mr. Untermeyer: Now that I am one of the several hundred instructors who use your anthology in the classroom, I reserve the right to dispatch letters to you on any pretext.

My chief reason in the present instance is to tell you of a mild dissatisfaction among the more alert young with your failure to include Stanley Kunitz, Kenneth Fearing, and Rolfe Humphries in the last edition. Surely these poets have more stuff than, say, David McCord? I know the anthologist can't please everybody, but I thought I'd put in a plug for these three.

I remember your telling me blandly in Midland that your long piece about the rapture and response of food was a great poem.[2] At the time, I thought you were pulling my leg, but now I believe you. Quite in the same spirit, I am enclosing, for your private perusal, one of the greater pieces of light verse of our time, "For an Amorous Lady," [3] along with one or two more serious efforts.

Last spring I got together, finally, a collection which Stephen V. Benét of the Yale Series did not accept but which was praised by Louise Bogan and others of my betters. If you know of any publishers who are anxious to lose some money, let me know.

Yours sincerely,

To George Dillon

State College, Pennsylvania
October 16, 1938

Dear Mr. Dillon: Thank you for the suggestion about the last poem. I hope you think that the change I have made is an improvement. I have also made a minor change in the last couplet of "The Signals."

Here is the order I should prefer:

[1] Poet, anthologist, and critic.
[2] "Food and Drink," in Untermeyer's 1932 collection of the same title.
[3] *CP,* p. 23. Cannot identify others.

Prognosis
The Reckoning
The Signals
Against Disaster
The Pause
The Bringer of Tidings
The Summons

If you don't like "Prognosis" for a title of the #1, call it "The Crisis." If you think that particular piece should not open the group, put "The Reckoning" first and "Prognosis," second.

For a group title I have no good ideas. Perhaps "Seven Poems" or "The Summons and Other Poems"? [1]

I had one other piece that I really wanted in this group, but it got out of my hands. However, perhaps I have enough space—too much, perhaps.

One other minor point: My job up here has been inaccurately reported in the past because there are two departments. I'm an instructor in the department of English composition (not English department). And it's *The* Pennsylvania State College. Not, of course, that this matters to me, but there are always local boys who brood about such matters.

I teach courses in verse writing and argumentation, incidentally.

My longwindedness is no doubt due to the fact that your acceptance of this group constitutes the most important recognition I've ever had.

Sincerely yours,
Theodore Roethke

To Louise Bogan

January 4, 1939

Dear Louise: That was a rather inane sonnet[1] I sent you, I guess.
Home was as usual: my mother half-sick [. . . .] I ate too much,

[1] The group was published in the order Roethke gives here under the collective title "Seven Poems" in *Poetry* (December, 1938). A different group of seven—but with some of the same poems—was submitted to George Dillon with Roethke's letter of January 4, 1938.

[1] Cannot identify.

drank nothing, read some, and wrote a light verse and made a new tail for an old piece.

The other night I almost called you up, in a burst of sentiment.

The academic life over the country looks pretty gruesome. The lazy guys—some of them anyway—are all right, but those in power or coming to power make the worst writing heels look like princes among men. Honest.

Do write me, Louise. I'm sort of veering about, inside.

Love,
Ted

Berryman[2] said of four poems I sent him that he liked "Highway: Michigan" [3] best, but then gave about four reasons why he was returning it. Oh well.

To John Ciardi[1]

State College, Pennsylvania
April 5, 1939

Dear Ciardi:

. . . .

I was grateful to you for your detailed comments on my verses in Poetry,[2] and they make me ashamed to ask that you let me reserve final remarks on your pieces until a later time when my ideas are completely resolved. Only one thing: be careful of the "big theme," the I-have-the-sense-of-infinity sort of thing out of Aiken via MacLeish[3] or vice versa.

And one further remark: I liked "Continent's Edge" the best I think, because the imagery is more concrete, for the most part, although the syntax at times leaves something to be desired. Try some poems based on a single figure sometime.

"I Warn You Father" seems in part subtle and fresh, in part too

2 John Berryman was poetry editor of *The Nation* in 1939.
3 *CP*, p. 33.

---

1 Poet, editor, and critic.
2 Refers to Roethke's "Seven Poems" in *Poetry* (December, 1938).
3 The poets Conrad Aiken and Archibald MacLeish.

obvious. I think you should try more pieces in this vein. Work on this one a bit more.

Well, I seem to be pontificating.

I hope that you make out with the Hopwood.[4] And the job.

Sometime I'd like to sit down and talk about your writing: that method is much better.

We had MacNeice[5] here for his first American appearance. About five hundred people turned out to hear him, lured by Theodore's artful & intensive publicity.

This letter has turned into a succession of afterthoughts.

> Cordially,
> Ted Roethke

To Rolfe Humphries

> [*Saginaw, Michigan*]
> [*1939*]

Dear Rolfe: Please accept my apologies for not having thanked you for taking me to the farm. It was a swell evening.

I have been occupied with final exams and conferences, packing books and notes, and getting out here. Now, when everything is done, I catch rose fever or something like it. But I've started to write some stuff again. Here are examples, some of which I hope you'll like.[1] Let me know if you have time.

Do you by any chance have Taggard's[2] summer address? I told her I'd send her some of Kunitz's latest poems. I suppose I could reach her c/o The League.

Things out here (with the family) are no worse than I expected. My mother was sued by the bank for double indemnity on some bank stock she held. (Bank crashed.) Etc. etc.

Have been reading some of the English snot noses in back numbers of *New Verse*. Those guys have been overrated if you

[4] Ciardi did win the University of Michigan's Hopwood award for his poetry in 1939.

[5] Louis MacNeice, English poet.

---

[1] Cannot identify.

[2] The poet Genevieve Taggard.

ask me. It makes me sore the way Random House and others will push those blue-eyed bastards. Very American. Hip, hip.

I expect to start Caudwell's[3] book, "Illusion and Reality," pretty soon. Have you read it? I've re-read parts of MacNeice's book,[4] and there is good stuff in it, but he's so goddamned smug: "There are a few good poets I have not mentioned . . ."

. . . .

I hope you like some of these pieces. Best to Helen & John

Ted

THREE POEMS ON F. PROKOSCH[5]

I

The poet of the caterwaul,
I find I like him not at all.

II

I don't like the fake demonic
Even when architectonic.

III

[. . . . .]
[. . . . .]

TO ROLFE HUMPHRIES

[Summer, 1939]

Dear Rolfe:

. . . .

Here's my problem: could I have your permission to quote from a letter you wrote me back in 1934 about that piece that was eventually published in *The Nation* called "Genesis." The excerpt is pretty long and makes you look very good (dumb, but you know what I mean). The "article" is just for a new student-faculty magazine that some kids are trying to start at Pa. State.[1] I had

[3] Christopher Caudwell, British Marxist critic and poet.
[4] *Modern Poetry: A Personal Essay* (1938).
[5] Frederic Prokosch, poet and novelist.

[1] Published as "Verse in Rehearsal" in *Portfolio* (September, 1939); reprinted in *On the Poet and His Craft*.

used some examples of revisions in the verse course and also for the guy who teaches esthetics, and they wanted me to repeat on paper. I want to use your remarks first, because they're good and second, because it makes the thing a bit more effective & less exhibitionistic.

I hope it's O.K. with you because these kids have been howling for the mss. Let me know, will you?

I never did get that letter to the League[2] written. My sister went away and I had no one to type for me.

I'll send a carbon of the thing shortly, but I need it for reference right now.

Ted

To Louise Bogan

[Saginaw, Michigan]
[1939]

Dear Louise: I was pleased that you liked the new pieces. You're probably over-generous about the spring poem[1] because of private associations, but I hope not. Pretty-boy Maxwell[2] returned it.

Monday I learned that I'm allergic to many of the things with which I've been stuffing myself for years: coffee, cocoa, oranges, grapefruit, peas, asparagus, onions, etc. Also Timothy Hay, Red Top, and the like, which I've eaten only on occasion. My damned eyes seemed to have collapsed, also. The Disintegration of Roethke, 1928—

J. Holmes is [at] a place called New Fane or New Fangle, Vermont. Know it? His wife has begun selling verses to the *N. Y.er.* I suppose they'll incorporate. My sister is in Boston, or was,—and thinks it an obscene and frightening city. Now she's in New York, I believe.

Today my activities were as follows: (1) picked up papers (2) got my own breakfast (3) repaired my mother's shoe (4) put up screen (5) dried dishes. Mamma's helper.

---

2 The League of American Writers.

---

1 "Vernal Sentiment," later included in *Open House. CP*, p. 24.
2 William Maxwell, *New Yorker* editor.

Did you see Rolfe's Columbia Ode in *Poetry*?[3] God, I think that's wonderful.

Here is a new poem[4] with some quaint sound effects. Hope you like it.

Love,

T.

I miss the polished brass, the powerful black horses,
The drivers creaking the seats of the baroque horses,
The high piled floral offerings with sentimental verses
—As the carriages passed you smelled sweat and the flowers'
    perfume

Now, as if performing a task that disgraces,
The black-flagged cars, filled with anonymous faces,
Hurry to where a man's last resting place is.
—As if in the cemetery there was not sufficient room.

To Katharine Stokes

[Saginaw, Michigan]
[1939]

Dear Kitty: It was very nice to get your two letters, especially since my cold is worse & my mother has been ill.

I'm sorry about the *N. Y.er*: but I think that magazine stinks. That last Irwin Shaw sketch has made me mad as hell: just a piece of sly hun-baiting. Incidentally, they sent back "Vernal Sentiment" suggesting that I re-submit in February. Hell with them. L. Bogan liked that piece "very much indeed." Said it had just the right feeling, tone, emphasis. I think it must have struck a chord of private association. C. Widow[1] she said was good too, but she wished the W. didn't go Simplified Left at end. (She doesn't—only I couldn't think of any other common & human symbols other than hands & faces.) Elsewhere she said I was writing

---

[3] "Draft Ode for a Phi Beta Kappa Occasion," *Poetry* (June, 1939).

[4] Later titled "On the Road to Woodlawn." This is an earlier version than the one included in *Open House. CP,* p. 22.

---

[1] "The Ballad of the Clairvoyant Widow." This poem and "Vernal Sentiment" (which the *New Yorker* finally did publish on March 3, 1940) were both later included in *Open House;* however, Roethke here appears to be talking of an earlier version of the "Ballad." *CP,* pp. 24, 27–28.

"real well, as we say in New England." Later she repeated something to the same effect.

Me, I'm not so impressed.

I guess I sent you the epigram Cowley took?

Hero of phantasies, etc.[2]

Well, if you want to do tasks so badly, here is a tough one. Sometime, several years [ago], the collected or Haverford Edition of Christopher Morley's works was reviewed in the *New Republic* by—I think—T. S. Matthews. Now at the end of that review there is a remark about Morley's being carried off by an attack of whimsey with puns as a complication. Copy that sentence down exactly. Reason: I made up an epigram which uses a somewhat similar idea. I've just recalled where I think I got it.

Don't work hard at it, because the epigram isn't very good anyway. I'm hoping the reviewer's idea isn't close to mine.

It's been raining pretty hard here of late and now it's turned pretty cool.

The movies have been simply unspeakable. Even the second & third showings are terrible. Haven't been once.

Last night I read a bunch of sea stories: one swell one called "Professional Aid" by Alfred Loomis.

Just heard that the administration was defeated on neutrality by *4* votes: it was only one of those committee [as] a whole things or something.

I still feel bum.

Love,

Ted

To Katharine Stokes

[*Saginaw, Michigan*]
[*1939*]
Sunday night
(*really Monday morning*)

Dear Kitty: Last night I made my second trip "down town": just

---

[2] "Poetaster," first published in *New Republic* (Nov. 29, 1939), and later republished in *Open House. CP*, p. 24.

to the west side library, very briefly. On returning, I found my mother very ill with a combination of gall stones & upset stomach. Spent much of the night making her hot water bottles & various medicines and reading Ruth McKenney's *Industrial Valley* in the interims.

Today she's been some better, although confined to bed, of course. She really needs rest because when up she's always washing or cleaning or baking something.

My eyes still trouble me a good bit. Think I'll have them checked next week. Washing them with boric acid seems to help.

I've revised the ending of the ballad [1] somewhat, but I'm not sure it's right yet. Sent it with others to *Poetry*. Pray. But it's Oxford that really concerns me. Boy, I wish they'd take that book! —Yet often I think I'd rather wait a couple more years.[2]

The weather is nice & cool now.

. . . .

Haven't heard from Stanley for a long time.

The local librarian, a Miss Prall, won't order Steinbeck's *Grapes of Wrath,* although her staff wants her to. The world is the same, alas, wherever we go.

Love,

Ted

I drew my mother a picture of my room[3] the other day to amuse her. She was appalled—by the smallness & proximity to other people & the toilets.

To KATHARINE STOKES

[*1939*]

Dear Kitty:

. . . .

Here's an epigram I revised & improved, I think.

[1] Probably "Ballad of the Clairvoyant Widow." *Poetry* did not publish it, however; it appeared in *Partisan Review* (Fall, 1939). *CP,* pp. 27–28.

[2] The book is *Open House;* and it was two more years before the manuscript saw publication.

[3] The room referred to was undoubtedly Roethke's at Pennsylvania State.

AGRARIAN

The graceful gesture and the cadenced drawl,—
These do not serve your purposes at all.
It's grand you look in great-great grandpa's britches,
But the fit's too tight: you're straining at the stitches.

If you want to type it up some time, do.

Love & cheer up,
Ted

To Katharine Stokes

[*Saginaw, Michigan*]
[*August, 1939*]

Dear Kitty: I haven't written because I've been busy on this trip[1] and helping take care of mamma, who had a gallstone attack the morning after we got back. She's a bit better but still is on the couch. She just had one of these last month.

The trip was really good fun. My cousin did all the driving. I have marked in brown ink the trip up and in a black wiggly line the trip back. We stayed in Newberry the first night, then went to Soo Junction where we took a narrow gauge railway through an absolute wilderness to the Tahquamenon River where we took a boat 22 miles up the river to the Falls. On the way I talked to owner of the boat and found that he took my father & Joe Fordney to hunting camp for years. He showed us the road that led to the camp.

That country, as I said, is really gorgeous. The falls can't be reached or even approached by automobile. It's really unspoiled wilderness. We saw a deer swimming and mother and some other people saw a little bear. There are plenty of beaver and even otter around, but we saw none.

The trip across the straits was also fun. In fact the whole thing was jolly, and I was especially glad that all three of us could go.

---

[1] A trip to upper Michigan, described here, which Roethke made with his mother, sister, and cousin.

Tuesday

. . . .

The Oxford mss. was here on Monday along with a rejection of the ballad [2] (second time) from Poetry. Also cemetery poem[3] & one other.[4]

. . . .

Love,
Ted

I'm getting a Writer's Yearbook for you—a market guide.

To Louise Bogan

[*circa 1939*]

Dearest L.: Nothing new here: the same themes, the same wait-resses, the same jokes, the same silly sunshine.

Been reading A. Tate's novel, "The Fathers." I rather liked parts of it. Also Ransom Tansom T.'s[1] "The World's Body." This a bit pretentious, but sometimes shrewd. Shrewd, or even crafty, is the word for some of those agrarian guys.

I have a new pair of shoes and a new coat and a new air of respectability, in consequence. A bit like Babar the Elephant. Do you know Babar? He is wonderful. Ferdinand the Bull is pretty good, too.

. . . .

Say, did you ever see Auden's poem, "Song for the New Year," —the one beginning

> It's farewell to the drawing-room's civilized cry
> The professor's sensible whereto and why
> The frock-coated diplomat's social aplomb
> Now matters are settled with gas and with bomb.

[2] "Ballad of the Clairvoyant Widow." *CP,* pp. 27–28.
[3] Probably "On the Road to Woodlawn," later included in *Open House. CP,* p. 22.

[4] Cannot identify.
[1] John Crowe Ransom.

There's a wonderful stanza along toward the end:

> I shall come, I shall punish, the Devil be dead
> I shall have caviar thick on my bread,
> I shall build myself a cathedral for home
> With a vacuum cleaner in every room.

Oh, why am I not smart like Auden?

What have you been up to, dear Louise? I drank some Guinness recently & thought of you. But it still made me feel lousy.

Ted

To Louise Bogan

[circa 1939]

Dear Louise: Funny thing: I had just popped a letter into the box when I got yours, which was welcome indeed in spite of the P. R.[1] boys' being alienated news.

Well, I hope you told them that I was conscious of what I was doing, at least to the extent of bringing up the matter when I showed you the piece.[2] I may be self-deceived, but I still think that piece is good enough to have an independent existence. And what is an ancestor for anyway? (Ans. To assimilate, not to imitate . . . Thought I had assimilated, etc.)

Fact is I had sent the piece to Grigson[3] with the title "Hopkinsesque" (a Godawful word—should have been Hopkinese, I suppose), and I was intending to write Cowley when the N. R. up and printed it.

From the practical point of view, certainly a blunder, I suppose. But I really did think, and still do, that the piece is something more than imitation. The rhythm seems "righter" for instance. But I won't reprint it.

If you're not too bored, who were the people and how caustic were they? Hell, that's a tiresome request, but I always seem to

---

[1] *Partisan Review.*
[2] Probably the poem "Praise," *New Republic* (Dec. 20, 1939).
[3] Geoffrey Grigson, editor of *New Verse.*

learn faster from my enemies & detractors. And I don't hold grudges—just am more careful.

It has been sweet of you to bother thus far, since it's always so much easier to say nothing and let people blunder on.

You know, I asked two academic guys who were supposed to know Hopkins well whether they thought this was imitation Hopkins. Nothing like him, said they. This probably proves two things: (1) how dumb I am (2) how dumb and/or knavish they were.

————————

Well, I hope you think that *Sale* thing is really a good one now.[4]

Jesus, knowing me is very trying a good bit of the time, I begin to realize. But do bear with me just once more.

The weather is wonderful today: alternate snow and sunshine. I got out my old raccoon and felt nostalgic for 1925.

Love to you both. Do write some more.

Theodore Flopkins-Hopkins Roethke

[4] "Sale," later included in *Open House. CP*, p. 32.

1940-47

To Stanley Kunitz

Saginaw, Michigan
June 30, 1940

Dear Stanley: I'm sorry to hear about your hand and hope it's all cleared up by now. Your decision to quit the publishing business I think very good news. Funny thing: the day before your letter came, in reading and talking about some of your pieces, I had said that I wished you could have more time for writing and not be tied to such a terrific routine. (Jesus, it's two o'clock and my syntax is worse than usual.) Anyhow, my kids were pleased—really,—when I said the next day that you were going to be a poet and nothing else.

Did I ever tell you the story about the kid who came to me & said there was a swell copy of *Intellectual Things*[1] in the State Library at Harrisburg that he could swipe very easily and then we could have a copy for the College Library or at least for the poetry class? He is now working on a newspaper in Harrisburg and I daresay he *has* swiped it by now.

Did I tell you that the University of Michigan Press is publish-

---

[1] Kunitz' first book of poems, published in 1930.

ing an anthology of contemporary Michigan poets? [2] May God be my witness, they're putting in 10 pieces of mine! However, this is not astonishing in view of the fact that there are few bards in these parts. But I think it's a good sign when the academies do something like this. Actually, one book at the U. of M. Press recently was devoted, I understand, to an analysis of commodity prices in ancient Abyssinia—jack-ass skins and the like.

Here are some recent pieces. That doggerel thing[3] I have put on ice for a time. Don't think I'll print it. I hope you see something in this Lament thing. The rhythm is a bit odd but I hope it is in keeping with the theme.

Please write.

My best to Eleanor.

Ted

Added two stanzas. Maybe some should be cut—#3? Or is it all too dumb and involved?

SUBURBAN LAMENT[4]

Even the simple and insentient are unhappy:
Horn-honkers find their neighbors unresponsive;
Mechanical sheep stop bleating at the curbstone:
Hands yank the shade before an unlighted window;
A child bursts into tears before the hard-kneed stranger,
The pure in heart cherish obscene ambition.

Research returns to the file; lyric ardor
Chills in the cool of the academy shadow;
On the vague eye of the suburban husband
The sexual image wavers like water.
An era of waiting: household traitors
Make the usual capitulation to appearance.

Some are mild-eyed people, forlorn in freedom,
Their loves a mimic of grandiose passion,
Familiars to contempt, the cough, the studied laughter,

2 *New Michigan Poets,* ed. by Carl E. Burklund (1940).
3 Cannot identify.
4 Unpublished. A second version, omitting stanzas 2 and 8, is also included under the title "Mid-Western Reverie" or (this title scratched out) "Lament for the Torpid."

Mumblers and fumblers, true to a hazy vision,
Believe compromise the necessary method of wisdom,
Give up at the tree's base: a rabbit surrender.

Not enough feet have passed in this country,
Stones are still stones, and the eye keeps nothing,
The usurious pay in full with the coin of the gentle,
Follies return on the heads of innocent children,
The evil and silly remain too long in tenure,
And the young, mimetic, fall into the old confusion.

Some travel by train to the fourth largest city,
Holy of holies for all who live by objects.
Those with the wire-like antennae of purpose
Are the magnificent and sterile makers.
With them it is useless to put the question,
"What else do you do with your time? Are you ever lonely?"

Worst are the aging rich, the red-eyed complainers
For whom a change in menu is cause for excitement;
But money is not enough, and power is empty:
The pot-bellied banker deserts the dining table,
A great-grand uncle drops his Christmas package,
And the habit of gossip becomes an illness.

Insistent as cicadas the noise of their sorrow,
Yet most spend their lives in pretense of contentment;
The blood loops lazily on its alarming mission
And the quaint town sleeps in the arm of an ominous shadow.
O what can rouse them from the coma of indifference,
What frenzy relax the muscles of pride and smugness?

Though the geography of despair had no limits,
To each was allotted some corner of comfort
Where, secure as a seed, he could sit out confusions.
But this is another regime: the preposterous bailiff
Beats on the door with his impossible summons
And the mad mayor holds nightly sessions of error.

Mid-Country Blow[5]

All night and all day the wind roared in the trees,
Until I could think there were waves rolling high as my study floor;

---

[5] Later included in *Open House*, but with a very different second stanza.
CP, p. 12.

When I stood at the window, an elm bough swept to my knees;
The blue spruce lashed like a surf at the door.

That night the wind fell; the moon rose, all of a piece;
The elm branch swung back as before.
But I could still hear, as if in the tops of trees,
The sound of waves breaking on some inland shore.

[EDITOR'S NOTE: *The following three poems, all unpublished, were sent to Katharine Stokes in the summer of 1940; the letters accompanying them are not reprinted here.*]

THE CURIOUS PEOPLE[1]

Even beyond the suburb with automatic oil burners,
And miles from the super market and illuminated church steeple,
It might easily have been one of the world's frightful corners—
A place in which to be careful with people.

Poverty was there in those streets without name or number,
Yet windows were clean or boards kept out the weather.
Though I forget the streets and faces of these people, I remember
How intense was their desire to live decently together.

FOR THE SAKE OF THESE . . .[2]

For all the wit of the future, for the unpursed kisses,
For tumultuous children racing around tomorrow's corners,
For animal grace, the dignity of hounds and horses,
For all that is holy or human,
We ask guidance.

For the mist rolling like tumbleweed out of valleys,
For the broad lakes, the mountains of stone, the nodding clover,
For ripening fields where even the wind is peaceful,
For this our land and these our people,
We require wisdom.

SIDE-LINE COMMENT[3]

If I had a brain like Ambassador Bullitt,
I'd take each little idea and carefully mull it.

[1] Unpublished. Sent to Katharine Stokes, July 3, 1940.
[2] Unpublished. Sent to Katharine Stokes, August 27, 1940.
[3] Unpublished. Sent to Katharine Stokes, August 27, 1940.

If I were Senators Burke, Wadsworth, or Barkley,
I'd try not to see everything through a brass hat, darkly.

To Katherine Anne Porter

Saginaw, Michigan
July 24, 1940

Dear Katherine Anne Porter: When I wrote Bob Wetteran[1] asking whether he thought you'd care to glance briefly at the verse mss. for arrangement and general effect, I had no notion how the "Conference" was run.[2] Consequently I was embarrassed about the whole business. I was not trying to presume on a slight acquaintance—that I wish you to understand.

It's a very small matter, I daresay.

Sincerely yours,
Ted Roethke

To Katherine Anne Porter

Saginaw, Michigan
August 22, 1940

Dear Katherine Anne Porter: Your letter was very sweet and made me feel a complete ass. But, unabashed, I send along the verses anyway, with the hope that some of them will give you pleasure. If they bore you, just stuff them in the other envelope. Some of them, written between intervals of groaning and roaring, may seem hardly relevant to the present day. But I have tried to be honest and unpretentious and make plain words do the trick. I hope you will like some pieces and the general effect; will think there is enough substance or body. I remember your casual remark about B. Belitt's *The Five-Fold Mesh* and hope that this book does not affect you similarly.[1]

[1] A mutual friend who worked in a bookstore near Pennsylvania State College.

[2] Miss Katharine Stokes told the editor that Roethke attended the writers' conference at Olivet, Michigan, in July, 1940.

[1] References to Roethke's "book" are doubtless to the manuscript of *Open House,* not published till the following year.

Oh God, how boring one can be about one's first book! I feel like a mother about to have her first child—at the age of, say, 42.

I hope Herbert Nipson did not cause you any inconvenience. He was my student, but he did not come to Olivet at my suggestion, much less to Saginaw, where he arrived when my mother was quite ill.

Now, dear lady, please do not fret over these in any fashion. There are times when poems of any kind can be insufferably dreary. People who send manuscripts are a bore, I know, but, somehow, I seem impelled to send these to you. Believe me.

Sincerely,
Ted Roethke

To George Dillon

Saginaw, Michigan
August 27, 1940

Dear Mr. Dillon: This is a small matter and a long time back, but it has been upon my mind for some time. It concerns some inaccuracies of statement in my review of Ben Belitt's *The Five-Fold Mesh* in January, 1939.[1]

(1) In the last paragraph, the sentence occurs, "Except for half a dozen poems—and that is enough—he creates no more than remarkable language." This is ambiguous, to say the least, and harsh if it is taken to mean that there are only six poems in the book. I was thinking, there, of a "poem" as something that has a chance to stay in the language for a time. It was unfair not to indicate this definition of the term.

(2) In the previous sentence, "Too much of his work seems to spring from an act of the will rather than from an inner compulsion," the last phrase should have been "from some deeper compulsion." The will is something "inner," of course.

(3) I am afraid that sometimes in the review there is a tendency to create Belitt in my own image—to insist, in other words, that he do the kind of thing that I do. This is a common failing among reviewers, I believe.

[1] Included in *On the Poet and His Craft*.

Perhaps all this is silly, but it has disturbed me a bit. However, this does not mean that I am shifting my general position on Belitt, though I do believe that I went after him pretty hard, primarily because he does have a piece of the real thing which he is in danger of spoiling by becoming pretentious.

Curiously enough, at least two able, sourpuss professional critics praised these remarks.

Yours truly,
Theodore Roethke

To Katherine Anne Porter

State College, Pennsylvania
October 19, 1940

Dear Katherine Anne: I am immensely in your debt for your kindness in troubling about my verse.[1] I'm afraid you were much too generous, but I shall always cherish the remarks none the less. The point you made about the arrangement is absolutely right, of course; as a matter of fact, I had already moved these pieces, which might have been written by almost anyone, to the center of the book.

I do hope my sending the poems didn't interrupt your own writing. There are times, I know, when the necessity to read a particular thing at a particular time can be most irritating, to say the least.

Your good wishes for a publisher have come to pass: Knopf is doing the thing next spring. I have thrown out a few more, tightened up a few, written one or two. Pray for me.

I hope some time we can have lunch or something in the city and laugh and talk. Somehow I'm always a sourpuss with more than three or four people.

You *were* very sweet to wade through the mss.

Sincerely,
Ted R.

I hope the tooth has subsided!

[1] Roethke had sent Miss Porter the manuscript of his book, *Open House*. See letter to Katherine Anne Porter, August 22, 1940.

TO KATHERINE ANNE PORTER

State College, Pennsylvania
March 7, 1941

Dear K. A. P.: If you have occasion to write to John Bishop, please tell him this: Auden referred to him as one of the two really good critics of poetry in America. There's so much malice and back-biting going on that I like, sometimes, to pass on praise if it doesn't have to be directly. I'd tell him myself except that he might think it boot-licking. Matter of fact I never thanked him for being so decent last summer.

Item: there is an American white wine at Macy's which I think you would approve of. It's called Santa Cruz Folle Blanche and costs $1.44. When I drank some with Italian cutlets, I thought of you the other night. (Even with the "when," the coherence isn't too good.)

Well, my damned book[1] is out Monday. Say a little prayer if that isn't too blasphemous.

Sincerely,
T. Roethke

[EDITOR'S NOTE: *This unpublished poem was sent to Dorothy Gordon, probably in 1941; the accompanying letter is not included here.*]

SUBURBIA: MICHIGAN

When superior steel made craftsmen archaic,
The moon-faced moron became boss's darling;
The immediate past remote as Carthage;
Bulldozers levelled the curving hillside,
Up sprang the cities of lathe and plaster:
Who said, "Yes, but," was never a hero.

Not enough feet have passed in this country:
Stones are still stones and the eye keeps nothing.
The passenger pigeon is gone; half-breed trappers
Set tarpaper shacks on battered oil drums.
Tourists stare at an absolute marvel:
A monarch pine, saved by quixotic fancy.

[1] *Open House.*

Eggs are tremendous and the local churches
Blaze with thirty miles of electrical wiring:
A land of lubritoriums, super milk-shakes,
Wrinkled peas, pie, veal without savor.
Fun disappears from the list of choices;
There is always something else we wanted.

Beyond the super market and illuminated church steeple
Live men for whom no factory whistles.
Some, driven from the land, seek the comfort of water,
Crawl back to the eternal womb, the beneficent mother.
Like dazed turtles in spring, they creep to the river
To dangle bent pins at the mouth of a roaring sewer.

Others travel by air to the fourth largest city,
Holy of holies for all who live by objects.
Those with the wire-like antennae of purpose
Are magnificent and sterile makers,
With them it is useless to put the question,
"What else do you do with your time? Are you ever lonely?"

Though the geography of despair had no limits,
To each was allotted some corner of comfort
Where, secure as a seed, he could sit out confusion.
But this is another regime: the preposterous bailiff
Beats on the door with his impossible summons
And the mad mayor holds nightly sessions of error.

To Rolfe Humphries

Saginaw, Michigan
July 16, 1941

Dear Rolfe: Glad to get your note and the poems. Am I being dumb or too smart—is the end of "I" supposed to be an allusion to

> O Western wind when wilt thou blow,
> And the small rain down can rain,
> Christ, if my love were in my arms
> And I in my bed again

or something like that? [1]

[1] Mr. Humphries writes the editor that he cannot recall the poem referred to here. Possibly it is an early draft of a poem later revised and given a title; but there seems to be no piece in Mr. Humphries' *Collected Poems* which would suggest this allusion.

I'm not sure the two parts are effective together this way because of the pronounced difference in rhythm. I like II a lot, but maybe, as you say, it needs something further to give it completeness. Maybe you could get rid of one of these "is's" in the last lines.

However, I'm not very bright tonight: hay fever has given me a headache.

When I got back from Smiths,[2] my sister went out West. On Thursday my mother was taken very ill with gallstones—had two doctors, etc. Now she's some better but still is in bed. I've been cook & nurse. It doesn't leave much time for writing, I must say.

However, here are two pieces which are better, I hope, than that swing rope thing. Is the idea in "City Limits" clear enough? Should I not use an analogy and just say "Metallic rubbish" or something like that? The hand-written one is an old theme, but maybe there is an inch of progression. At any rate it has nouns & verbs mostly. Hope you see something in it. Did I send this versicle?

SPECIALIST

If the compass of his mind
Matched his Renaissance behind
He could range like Paracelsus
Through his field and someone else's

I have a longer funny one which you will like, I think—about a guy in a sanitorium being cured by good feeling.

I finally saw the review in *N.R.*[3] It looked nice, I thought. And many thanks for belaboring them to bring it out. Now if the *Times* & *Nation* would only do a little something. But maybe I'm naive.

As far as I know I'm going to Breadloaf. Haven't heard from Morrison[4] since I saw you, though.

Ted

Afterthought: I like II a good bit just by itself. "Veins of stones" is a beautiful phrase.

2 Probably A. J. M. Smith.
3 Humphries reviewed *Open House* in *New Republic* (July 14, 1941).
4 The novelist, Theodore Morrison, long associated with Breadloaf School.

CITY LIMITS[5]

Frayed rugs, rags, grease, harsh cinders everywhere;
A beggar's face cracks like a rusty sieve;
The soot of evil sifts through falling air
Streaking a baby's bib, a drunkard's sleeve,—
These are the images by which I live.

Unclean! Unclean! That carrion crow, the eye,
Flaps through a haze of hate in vicious weathers,
A starving portent in a grimy sky.
The spirit's rubbish that no bird beak gathers
Repels the pungent death of flesh or feathers.

Our phantasies, like flies[6]
That buzz from ear to shoulder,
Keep just beyond our gaze,
Too quick for hands to smother.
We double in our tracks
Pursuing tails of shadow,
The atavistic Other
That jumps on careless backs.

But throb and heave of breasts,
Self-conscious in their sighing,
Dispel the dread of beasts;
We look and there is nothing
Where phantoms stiffly moved,
Because our glance is human;
The lips curled back for loathing
Relax with the beloved.

Too short? A middle stanza? No, I hope.

[EDITOR'S NOTE: *The following two poems were sent to Rolfe Humphries on July 25, 1941; the accompanying letter is not reprinted.*]

PASTORAL[1]

The elder bush is loud
With catbird rasp and nicker;
The mower's axle-rod

---

[5] Published in *Partisan Review* (November–December, 1941).
[6] Unpublished.

---

[1] Sent to Rolfe Humphries, July 25, 1941. Unpublished.

Outshrieks the noisy flicker.
The wheels grate over ground
And the long knife cuts the clover
Until a quail flies up,
Flushed from well-hidden cover.
Wheel-sound and bird-song stop;
Before the blade creaks over,
Across the meadow comes
The hum of early summer.

DOUBLE FEATURE[2]

Before Buck even gets to the ranch, the operator switches the light.
Lovers disengage, move sheepishly toward the aisle
With mothers, sleep-heavy children, stale perfume, past the manager's
    smile
Out through the velvety chains to the cool air of night.

We dally in groups near the rickety pop-corn stand;
Dawdle at shop windows, still reluctant to go;
Teeter, heels hooked over the battered curb; drag a toe
To gear shifts, "Good-night, all," vague lifts of the hand.

A wave of Time hangs motionless on this particular shore.
We notice a tree, arsenical grey in the light, or the slow
Wheel of the stars, the Great Bear glittering colder than snow,
And remember, dimly, there was something else we were hoping for.

[EDITOR'S NOTE: *The following four poems were sent to Stanley Kunitz in 1941 but are not assignable to specific letters.*]

"Cast on the field from their full height . . ."[1]

Cast on the field from their full height,
The oak leaves turn upon our sight.
Sun doubles them upon the land,
Their shade is wider than a hand,
The shadows move from left to right.

A hundred years, to this same sound,
The tree repeats its daily round,
The drama of revolving shade.

[2] Sent to Rolfe Humphries July 25, 1941. An early version of the poem later included in *The Lost Son and Other Poems* (1948). *CP*, p. 47.

[1] Sent to Stanley Kunitz, 1941. Published in *Poetry* (February, 1941), under the title "Second Shadow."

A hundred years its leaves are laid
In rich profusion on the ground.

But man a second shadow throws
Beyond the visible he knows;
The mind, untrammeled, can outfly
The nets of mutability
And shake the shade that hugs us close.

Slow Season[2]

The light is less; noon skies are wide and deep;
The ravages of wind and rain are healed.
Late afternoons a scent drifts from the field
Until clear eyes put on the look of sleep.

The garden spider weaves a silken pear
To keep inclement weather from its young.
Straight from the oak, the gossamer is hung.
At dusk our slow breath thickens on the air.

The hue birds lost, the trees take as their own.
Wide waves of wheat are gathered into sheaves.
The walker trudges ankle-deep in leaves,
The feather of the milkweed flutters down.

The shoots of spring have mellowed with the year.
Buds, long unsealed, are litter in the lane.
The blood moves trance-like through the altered vein.
Our vernal wisdom has grown ripe and sere.

A sequel to "The Light Comes Brighter." Some clichés but I needed them for pattern. Do you like this? I've tried to push the observation a bit beyond mere observation.

"Like walkers in an unfamiliar place . . ."[3]

Like walkers in an unfamiliar place,
We lift our hands for twigs that are not there,
While phantom cobwebs trail across the hair
And brambles sting an unprotected face.

[2] Later version of this poem included in *Open House*. Sent to Stanley Kunitz, 1941. *CP*, p. 12.
[3] Apparently unpublished. Sent to Stanley Kunitz, 1941.

> We cannot gauge a switch's swinging back,
> Or keep in step with someone just ahead.
> While looking left, we bear to right instead,
> And stumble on a weatherbeaten track.
>
> Let us take care in picking up our clues.
> Of all the forces that can pelt our form,
> The things we see, least often do us harm.
> The mind can teach the heart what to refuse.

I hate to fall back on the mind-heart business, but I had to get something simple & pretty explicit. How did you like that last stanza of that oak tree thing?[4]

POEM[5]

> The loutish and the mad
> Our destinies appoint,
> The good is fouled with bad,
> The times are out of joint.
> The gun prods in the back,
> The club finds out a skull;
> When bellies hang too slack,
> The sensitive grow dull.
> O when will hate be gone,
> The blood begin to buck,
> The foolish all atone,
> And love renew its luck?

A kind of sequel to "The Summons." I'm going to desert this form. I like it too well.

To Earl Robinson[1]

State College, Pennsylvania
March 7, 1942

Dear Mr. Robinson: Thank you for your thoughtful letter of January 21, 1941, regarding my "Ballad of the Clairvoyant

---

[4] Seems to refer to " 'Cast on the field from their full height.' "
[5] Apparently unpublished. Sent to Stanley Kunitz, 1941.

---

[1] American composer.

Widow."² I am delighted to learn that you "will be interested in doing something to it" after you finish the music for Sandburg's "The People, Yes."

There is one point in your letter which I do not quite understand: "I wish that the finish could be a little stronger, make it possibly in terms of hope for the country coming through the people rather than nature exclusively." Of the things that the Widow sees—the signs of hope—five are entirely human (the harbor, alive with men and ships; the surgeon; grandpa; the unemployed; and the men on rail and roadway). It is true that the last couplet has non-human symbols, but I thought that the above-mentioned images had driven home the point that the hope lay in the energy, the good humor and the pride of the people; by the last couplet I mean to imply that there is a deep and abiding energy in all living things which can aid our human strength and contribute to our destiny. I don't think this is just mystical bunk; even the anthropologists seem to believe this. At any rate, I cannot see how I can make this piece much more explicit without going too simplified left.

[. . .] I have a real faith in the "Ballad" because it is my one piece that seems to have a considerable underground circulation; it has even been read at labor meetings and I hear about it from people of various types from time to time.

If you have any ideas or themes you think I could handle, please let me know. I sometimes work better on direct assignment. Anyhow, I'd be deeply grateful if you will let me know whether you have had time to do anything with "Ballad."

Yours sincerely,

TO STANLEY KUNITZ

State College, Pennsylvania
July 5, 1942

Dear Stanley: How are you? Good, I hope and Eleanor too.

Kitty said you didn't go to the meeting at Milwaukee. She did and now is going to summer school at Michigan.

² *CP*, pp. 27–28.

By me nothing is unusual. We kept right on this summer with the accelerated program: maybe a week off in September. In April I went to Harvard on the Morris Gray.[1] Everyone was very nice. I really had a hell of a good time—and don't think I made an ass of myself. Frost came, and Matthiessen; also Philip Horton, to whom I talked about you.[2]

For a time I was below 200 lbs & playing quite good tennis. Now my No. 1 kid beats me usually. I win when the courts aren't too dry.

I hope you like some of these poems—especially *The Return,*[3] which no editor wants, apparently. Let me know, some time, about *The Return* & the mud & slime one.

I thought you were very good on Louise B. & Moore.[4] Haven't heard from B. in a long time.

Best to you both,
Ted

RUNE[5]

In scum and terror
Of noisome fen
Grow fronds of error,
Deceptive fern.

Who, careless, slips
In coiling ooze
Is trapped to the lips,
Leaves more than shoes.

Who, chilled to the marrow,
Would still keep warm,

[1] Harvard's Morris Gray Fund is used from time to time to finance readings there by contemporary poets.

[2] Robert Frost, F. O. Matthiessen. Philip Horton is the author of the well-known *Hart Crane: The Life of an American Poet* (1937).

[3] *CP*, p. 47. Other poems sent with this letter were "The Minimal," *CP*, p. 50; and "Rune" and "Germinal" (printed here).

[4] Kunitz reviewed Louise Bogan's *Poems and New Poems* in *Poetry* (April, 1942), and Marianne Moore's *What Are Years?* in *Poetry* (November, 1941).

[5] The title "Gnomic" is scratched out on the typescript, and "Rune" is written in. The poem is apparently unpublished, but the last stanza with "Must" replacing "Or" in the first line appears in section 2 of "The Shape of the Fire." *CP,* p. 65.

Must writhe a furrow
Like pristine worm,

Or pull off clothes
To jerk like a frog
On belly and nose
From the sucking bog.

GERMINAL[6]

Slowly, slowly, without cracking the thinnest varnish,
A building settles.
There are many changes without drama, days without sunset,
Merging of mist and mist, boredom upon boredom;
Cities of fog and ambiguous pigeons;
Lacklustre eyes that see only grey like the lion.

Drop by drop the last grey day leaks through a rain pipe;
A potato sprout pokes through rotting burlap;
Cold seed, long buried in a crush of mud and sticks,
Begins to stir;
In the vein, in the long vine,
Time matures.

TO STANLEY KUNITZ

[*July, 1942*]

Dear Stanley: I'm glad you liked the letter and hope something comes of it.[1]

Thanks for taking all the trouble with that sludge thing.[2] It seems too written, somehow. I'll put it away.

Yes, *Germinal* is a bit abstract at the end, but I'd hoped the lines "In the vein, in the long vine" would carry it off sufficiently . . . God I never thought of *Gnomic* as being literary, except for "fen," maybe. Words, they is slippery.

. . . .

If you think your *Mercury* friend would be interested in any

---

[6] The title "Mutation" is scratched out in the typescript, and "Germinal" is written in. Poem was published in *New Yorker* (April 3, 1943).

---

[1] A letter recommending Kunitz' manuscript to Alfred A. Knopf.
[2] Possibly "Rune," sent to Kunitz with letter of July 5, 1942.

of the enclosed, show them to her.[3] *Minimal* & *Germinal* are sold. Some of these are slight.[4]

T.

[EDITOR'S NOTE: *The following unpublished poem was sent to Stanley Kunitz, probably on July 16, 1942, but cannot be assigned definitely to a specific letter.*]

"Love curled in many laps . . ." [1]

Love curled in many laps;
My own, my secret lips
Babbled in urinals;
Wrenched from its spine, my head
Bounced through deserted halls.
Not all of me was dead.

Vague transitory wish
Rattled my bones like a bush;
Nerveless, a mangled hand
Kept jerking at my side;
I sucked the sores of pride,
The blackened staunchless wound.

I saw my several selves
Dismembered in neat halves,
Each on a spot in space
Grimacing like a fiend;
Dervish of horror, spun
Faster upon my spine,
Writhing until the last
Forms of my secret life
Lay with the dross of death
Out of myself I rose,
Fervent and whole of skin.

---

[3] Kunitz had suggested that one of the *American Mercury* editors would be interested in seeing Roethke's poems.

[4] Cannot identify.

---

[1] The last stanza of this poem clearly becomes part of the later piece "The Exorcism." *CP*, p. 147.

To William Carlos Williams

State College, Pennsylvania
November 11, 1942

Dear Bill: I've just nearly croaked from pneumonia, but I'm fairly well out of it now, I guess. The saw-bones didn't diagnose it as pneumonia at first, didn't give me sulfa though I kept asking for it, etc. etc. The nurses said I was a 1–2 shot. I'm glad you liked "The Minimal." It's in the current *Harper's Bazaar*,[1] along with your praise as to my steak-cooking—hope you don't mind.

Look: answer me truly: Has this one about death got the true indignation?[2] It seemed to write itself and by God I mean it. I hope very much you'll like it, but if you don't say so. You're my toughest mentor.

The factory one will amuse you, I hope.[3] I worked for those Heinz bastards four summers.

Well, all this is written in the dither and wobble of convalescence. I'm pooped and a bit nutty, I suppose.

I know you're busy, but write if you can.

Ted

To Stanley Kunitz

[State College, Pennsylvania]
[Late 1942]

Dear Stanley: I am convinced that Hoffman[1] is on the level. I'm sorry as hell and I really thought something was going to come of this. You ought to be a cinch at Macmillan for G. Taggard[2] is a reader, or used to be, at any rate. Hell, someone has *got* to take it. Want me to write Holmes for ideas? He's a dope in some ways, but very honest & thinks no end of your work. Didn't I mention

[1] Later included in *The Lost Son. CP,* p. 50.
[2] Probably "Judge Not." See letter to John Crowe Ransom, p. 123.
[3] "Pickle Belt," included in *The Lost Son. CP,* p. 46.

[1] Paul Hoffman of Knopf, to whom Kunitz had sent his manuscript.
[2] Genevieve Taggard.

Holt's once? The guy there cares about poetry. What ever happened to W. W. Norton? Or didn't you try him?

Oh God, it's the Age of Ass-holes, or something.

About the army, I can't be anything but futile. Everyone says don't go in just as an ordinary draftee: try for a commission in Navy (administrative job) or intelligence. But that would be too loathsome for you to do, I know. I should think they'd be ready to put you in the medical corps anyway.

Me, I'm in fairish shape and back at work. I burn up far too much energy, emotional & intellectual, in teaching, damn it. Been giving regular harangues against the hate propaganda; on being aware of self & mastering own world, etc. Kids seem to love it. They do react when you give them the truth. But it's all blood in the sand and makes you a dangerous man in the profession. Someone has sowed a very dirty canard in re me a while ago. It probably cost me that Hunter job, I understand. Hell, like Veblen, I'm doomed to the provinces, I guess.

Flight of ideas: Does your office (Wilson & Co.) still want that biographical crap? [3] I remember your mentioning it in New Hope, but I always felt rather silly about it & figured you'd write again or something. I saved about 150–200 words from the Harvard appearance, etc. But if someone else is doing that now or this is not the time, to hell with it. It just crossed my elephantine memory.

It's Sunday night and I've just had dinner with La & Ma Stokes.

Yesterday I got out Winters' review of *Intellectual Things*.[4] (I had saved it.) He's a funny guy, but better than those damned agrarians by a good deal. Narrow but sharp and really honest. (Boy, is that becoming a rare quality!) Oh hell, I labor the obvious.

I daresay you're in no mood for looking at other people's things. Scratch something on the margin of these[5] if you feel inclined, or throw 'em away. I thought the death one[6] had the sacred indignation, but maybe not. It's an open vulnerable poem, but not defeatist, I insist.

This is getting long-winded and idiotic, Stanley, but I write it

[3] Refers to the autobiographical material Roethke prepared for *Twentieth Century Authors*, of which Kunitz was the editor.

[4] Yvor Winters' review in the *New Republic* (June 4, 1930).

[5] Cannot identify.

[6] Probably "Judge Not." See letter to John Crowe Ransom, p. 123.

with the best will in the world. Disregard the gaucheness and accept the impulse, if possible.

One practical thing: if you say the word, I'll wire or write Sloan[7] (sp.?). He was very nice to me and I've seen him since at Bread Loaf.

Best to Eleanor & yrself—

Ted

To Léonie Adams[1]

State College, Pennsylvania
March 5, 1943

Dear Miss Adams: In talking to Mr. Jones[2] over the telephone recently, I asked him whether a memorandum to you on our conversation about course possibilities might be of any use. For the moment I had forgotten you were writing, and now I curse myself for having such an idea. But he seemed to think this a good scheme; and since he has mentioned it in a subsequent letter, I am sending along these remarks, some of which are repetitious, for you to glance at or throw away, as you like. Please do not think this a presumption or an effort to scrounge courses. I am simply trying to clarify by answers to your questions and to indicate what I can do best.

Creative Writing

I have included an old syllabus—which tells, I suspect, very little about what actually went on in my course at Penn State. This was never followed slavishly and all the ground has not been covered in a single semester. The course attracted various types of students, some of whom never wrote well but at least learned what goes into a piece of verse. Every effort has been made to adjust work to the student: to get him reading writers with whom he has an affinity. The "syllabus" was supposed to be suggestive, not arbitrary.

---

[7] William Sloane, editor at Henry Holt.

[1] Poet and the wife of the critic William Troy.

[2] Lewis Webster Jones, president of Bennington College.

Since leaving Lafayette I have not taught the writing of short fiction, except a bit in "A" freshman sections. I used to have students read Chekhov, Maupassant, Hemingway, Anderson, Turgenev, some of Maugham, D. H. Lawrence, Kipling, Mansfield, A. E. Coppard, H. E. Bates, K. A. Porter, Arthur Calder-Marshall. The only new writers I have noticed of late are Eudora Welty, Dylan Thomas, and some of the young English in *Horizon*. There are always Saroyan enthusiasts, I find, among the young.

I am not sure I have a "story sense," whatever that is. I suspect people who think of the short story as a sacred form. My students were encouraged to observe closely, write sharply, catch speech rhythms. Keeping a journal was a useful exercise, as I mentioned to you.

Possible Course in the Analysis of Poetry

If the sole consideration were teaching efficiency, this would be the best possibility for me. Such a course would be a chance to range around in time and yet concentrate on individual poems; to deal with minor or special writers for whom I have a real enthusiasm (Skelton, Henry Vaughan, Marvell, Herbert, John Clare, Beddoes, Lawrence, Hardy, and the like) and introduce little known people (I have rather good files on Kunitz, John Betjeman, and some of the Canadians like A. J. M. Smith). Actually, such a course could provide a real complement to existing courses, it seems to me.

Perhaps I labor the obvious. I daresay all this has been considered and said better in department meetings. But I really think I could contribute something; could hold up my end. And it might prod me into doing a small book.

Blake

I was quite overwhelmed by the Blake possibility: an almost unbelievable chance, as it were. It would be better, if I were asked, to have some time to work up the longer symbolical poems.

American Literature

My reading in this field is less sketchy than I indicated, probably. I did some fairly intensive work on the stuffier writers under two good men at Ann Arbor. The early writers, including Cooper, bore me. Dickinson I know pretty well; and Thoreau. I am weak on James: have only read about five of his novels. Melville I think I have read in entirety, though some years ago.

General Background

From one point of view, my formal education was an example of what can happen under the elective system. In college I took no Latin, no Greek, no philosophy (except esthetics under DeWitt Parker) no mathematics. On the other hand, I did intensive work in 17th, 18th and 19th century literature under such men as Henry Hutchins, Defoe scholar now research professor at Yale; Earl Griggs, Coleridge man now at Pennsylvania; Louis Bredvold, authority on Pope, and Babbitt and Murray at Harvard. The point is this: except for linguistics I have had a fairly severe academic training in the methods of literary scholarship. But I remained rebellious against graduate schools. Actually, my best work was done for close interpreters of the text like Gingerich (Wordsworth), Strauss (Browning), Campbell (Shakespeare),[3] and I. A. Richards.

But your patience has been tried long enough. Just one specific request: could you, on the enclosed post card, indicate which basic course will be taught the coming semester? I want to do a little reading before I come up.

Yours sincerely,
Theodore Roethke

I hope I don't sound like an opinionated ass!

Note: This is a rough outline of a course in verse writing which was developed to meet the needs of intelligent students who are not particularly well read. One cannot teach a young writer to use the past as a tool if he does not know what that past is; consequently, students are expected to read widely and deeply in the whole field of English and American poetry and to get considerable practice in a variety of verse forms. One cannot be too grandiose about results: after all, there are only from five to

---

[3] S. F. Gingerich, Louis A. Strauss, and Oscar J. Campbell were professors of English at the University of Michigan.

fifteen people with real talent for writing poetry in any one generation. But a bright student can be taught to write cleanly; he can learn—and this is most important—much about himself and his own time.

"Form" is regarded not as a neat mould to be filled, but rather as a sieve to catch certain kinds of material. Students, whatever their other defects, rarely become stanza-paralyzed.

First week.	Purpose of the course. Some definitions: Dickinson, Housman, Frost, Jeffers. Some differences: Poetry-prose, poetry-verse. Class analysis of poems written before course.
Second week.	Rhythm: Time and accent in English poetry. Lines with their musical equivalents. Metrical feet: Iambic, trochaic, etc. Rhyme: Full; half, slant or tangential; suspended; assonance, consonance, "dissonance." Examples: Anglo-Saxon, Hopkins, Owen, Ransom, Wylie, Auden. Alliteration: Effective (Hopkins and Yeats); excessive (Swinburne).
Third week.	Imagery: Metaphorical thinking as opposed to analytical. Sensuous image: early lyrics, Keats, Yeats, Cummings, Auden. Intuitive image: Blake, Dylan Thomas. Cerebral image: Donne, Crashaw, Marvell, Dickinson. Complex "fused" image: Dante, Milton, Baudelaire, Lorca. Students write poems based on images they associate with a particular mood or subject.
Fourth week.	Tetrameter couplet. Seventeenth century: Jonson, Milton, Marvell, Vaughan, Butler's "Hudibrastic couplet." Eighteenth century: Swift, Prior, Parnell. Nineteenth century: Coleridge, Scott, Byron and Morris.
Fifth week.	Tetrameter couplet (continued). Present day examples: Housman, Yeats, Warren, Betjeman, Auden. Bad couplet poems: Auslander, Coffin, Kilmer.

Sixth week.	Revising a poem. Bad first draft of a Roethke piece; revisions and final version. Revisions of Blake, Yeats, A. J. M. Smith, Humphries. Class criticism of couplet pieces.
Seventh week.	Pentameter couplet. Differences in rhythm from tetrameter; differences in types of material which can be treated in this form. Closed couplet: Pope, Dryden, Dobson. Open couplet: Keats and Swinburne (over-embellished). Modern examples: Kunitz, Brooke.
Eighth week.	Diction. Poems with excessive adjectives: Zaturenska, early Yeats. Poems with few or no adjectives: Bogan, Humphries, Blake, later Yeats.
Ninth week.	Poems of objective description: Shakespeare, Clare, Frost, E. Thomas, Marie de L. Welch. Static description: Georgian poets. Description with analogy or symbolic meaning: Léonie Adams, Bogan.
Tenth week.	Melody and tone color: Shakespeare, Pound, Stevens, Léonie Adams, Crane, Joyce, Hopkins, D. Thomas. Poems based on two or three combinations of vowels: Campion, Bogan, Joyce. Further revisions: Auden, Tate, Bridges.
Eleventh week.	Quatrains. "Common meter" of hymnal; folk ballads, Auden, Mallalieu. "Long meter." Heroic quatrains. Variations.
Twelfth week.	Sonnet: Spenser, Shakespeare, Drayton, Donne, Milton, Wordsworth, D. G. Rossetti, Wylie, Millay, Madge.
Thirteenth week.	Epigrams and light poems: Blake, Landor, Praed, Locker-Lampson, Belloc, Gogarty, Winters, Allott. Poems based on a single image: Frost, Yeats, Humphries, Bridges, Bogan.

Fourteenth week.   Free verse poems: Eliot, Marianne Moore, early Pound.

Fifteenth week.   Poems of more intricate stanza patterns: Hardy is studied in detail.

Sixteenth week.   Poems with a three-foot line: Bridges, Yeats, Bogan.
                   Songs: Shakespeare, Campion, Donne, Auden.

*   *   *

Regular assignments: (1) Poem in tetrameter couplets.
                       (2) Poem: objective description of nature.
                       (3) Poem without adjectives.
                       (4) Poem based on a single image.
                       (5) Poem in pentameter couplets or optional.
                       (6) Poem in heroic quatrain or sonnet.
                       (7) Ballad or poem in "common meter."
                       (8) Optional.
                       (9) Poem with fairly intricate stanza form.
                      (10) Optional.

Special assignments: (1) Translating poems. If student knows German, translations from Heine, Hölderlin, Rilke; Spanish, translations of Lorca; French, translations of Valéry, Rimbaud, Baudelaire, Goll.
                       (2) Rewriting bad poems. Student is given a bad poem from Braithwaite or some such anthology and asked to rewrite.
                       (3) Notebook or workbook. These are kept not only for revisions but also to record isolated phrases or images; anything that might be the material of poetry.
                       (4) A little "anthology." Student's favorite but little-known poems found in course of reading.

To Allan Seager[1]

Bennington, Vermont
May 8, 1943

Dear Allan: You haven't had an answer to your letter of April 19 for several reasons: there was a delay in forwarding my mail; I've been down with a misplaced sacro-iliac and busy as hell the rest of the time on a different job.

I'm very glad about the daughter and *Equinox,* and anxious to see both. [. . .]

. . . .

This place so far has astonished me. I teach three courses "Literature and Humanities" (a freshman course which emphasizes close reading of the text (various versions of *Antony & Cleopatra* and a damn good poetry selection made here). This meets 11–12:30 on Mon. & Thurs. "Lyric Form" (to be changed to "Verse Form" next term) which meets 11–1:00 on Tues. In this I have 8 bright witches and 1 goon. Then another writing course which meets 2–3:30 on Thursday. But in addition to this, I have ten "counselees" and "tutees" whom I see individually an hour each week. I gather I have an exceptionally good batch.

This didn't open up because of losses to the Army: one guy, Wm. Troy, just resigned because he was tired of teaching and especially of teaching women. (His wife, Léonie Adams the poet, is still here. A very able dame and a good writer in my book.) It seems I was hired because, according to the president, Lewis Jones, I'm "a grass roots American with classic tastes." So, simple fellow that I am, I'm to teach a course in American literature (just people that interest me) next year. Also a new course in Mod. English Poetry and Verse Fawm, which will be a perpetual course, I gather.

All this is a bit nutty to me because officially I'm on leave of absence from Penn State. The president seems a hell of an able guy and a decent guy. He's been so enthusiastic that I worry that I will veer the other way with equal vigor.

To sum up: nobody seems to think of the place as something permanent, though some have been here since it started. Contracts

1 Novelist and professor of English at the University of Michigan.

are always for one year to begin with, then 3, then 5 years. Some people are nuts about the place—turn down headships (there are no ranks or dept. heads here) and deanships at places like Minnesota and Columbia. Others like it two or three years, then lose their enthusiasm. Others get fired. These last, I understand, have been Ph.D. types, punk teachers or dull dogs in some way.

It's anything but stuffy. The president is a very competent whisky drinker, so are most of staff; the kids invite you in for drinks before dinner, on occasion. Yet all this has produced no untoward results. Most of the kids and all of the faculty work hard.

Well, by now you're probably bored stiff by all this prattle. Somehow I thought you'd be interested. Whether I'll like the place later is difficult to say. If I find I do no writing, I'll quit, of course.

Well, best to Barbara & Pa & the kid. Let me hear from you.

Ted

TO ALLAN SEAGER

[*Bennington, Vermont*]
[*September 13, 1943*]

Dear Allan: On August 17 I tried to wire but Western Union wouldn't accept because it was congratulation.[1] I didn't call because of some dumb feeling that you might think I was fishing to come down.

It's a swell book, it really is. Certainly the best to come out of the Middle West in some time or indeed out of the U. S. A. But to hell with my idiotic superlatives. It's done, it's there on the pages. I hope it makes a real hunk of dough, too.

By now you may be in the army, but I hope not. Let me know what's up, anyway, if you have time. And let me know how Barbara & the kid and pa are.

Bennington is still hysterical in some ways,—a trying place to teach in, though my efforts have been overpraised, if anything. I have been conducting a feud with some of the senior intellectuals

---

[1] On the publication of Seager's novel, *Equinox*.

in an effort to get them to be a little less arty. Some of them need a goose in their most sacred place, but I am not their man.

Mr. Kenneth Burke is here this semester to reduce them, by other means, I have no doubt. He's a good guy of the verbose Irish type.

Sincerely,
Ted

All this is stupid. But believe me: I am terribly pleased about *Equinox*.

To William Carlos Williams

[circa 1944]

Dear Bill: The only reason I haven't written sooner is that I was afraid I would over-whelm you with gratitude, like a St. Bernard. In fact, I carried the letter around for a time: something to hold against the world.

Which sounds like self-pity, but ain't.

All those greenhouse ones and the nutty suburban ones came back from Ransom, from *Poetry*, etc. What the hell. But as an old pro, I suppose I should realize that the better you get, the more you'll get kicked in the ass. I do think the conceptual boys are too much in the saddle: anything observed or simple or sensuous or personal is suspect right now. Anything with images equals Imagism equals Old Hat. Oh well, you know all that better than I; have seen it, have been fighting it.

I thought I'd mislaid the letter, but found it and read for the 15th time.

Notes:

1) I'm particularly pleased you like *The Return*,[1] which I thought one of the best I've ever done: exact psychologically and no slop. It's been turned down by everybody.

[1] *CP*, p. 47.

2) I know I understate too much, and I'm trying to work out of this.

3) I'm glad you liked the cuttings pieces.²

4) As to the general problem,³ you're very coonie, as the kids say here.

———————

Another matter: I put your name down on a Guggenheim application and you may be getting a letter. One item in my Plans for Work may seem dubious—the Paul Bunyan idea. The more I think about it, the less I like it. But I've got to get some device to organize some of my ideas & feelings about Michigan, etc.—not too solemn or God bless America or Steve Benétish. Maybe it's worth trying, anyway.

I think I can say there's a real need for me to get out of teaching for a time. I'm getting too caught up in it: too obsessed with making real dents in these little bitches. The best ones keep urging me to quit: not worth it, etc. etc.

God, I get sick of all these "I's" "I's." Another time, it'll be different: when I get the Cummington Press book, which I've ordered.⁴

Here's a few new ones; one good one, I think.⁵

Best,
Ted

To Kenneth Burke¹

State College, Pennsylvania
February 27, 1945

Dear Kenneth: I hate like hell to do this, but I have put you down once more as a sponsor: this time for the Houghton Mifflin Literary Fellowship Award in poetry.² This is positively the last time

———————

² "Cuttings" and "Cuttings (*later*)," both included in *The Lost Son. CP,* p. 37.
³ Would seem to refer to "the general problem" of verse writing.
⁴ Williams' *The Wedge* (1944).
⁵ Cannot identify.

———————

¹ Critic and essayist on the faculty of Bennington College.
² Roethke did not win the award.

I will pester you. It's a thousand bucks. I enclose a statement of the general nature of the project. My deciding to apply for the damn thing occurred just last night. Some friends of mine here were looking at some of the new pieces. One of them, a Houghton Mifflin author, E. J. Nichols,[3] suggested this thing. I found out by wire that I could still make the deadline if I get my manuscript off today. That is why I couldn't ask you ahead of time. If for any reasons you have misgivings about this, just shoot me the statement of the project and I'll dig up somebody else.

I've been travelling around, and for all I know you may have sent me a letter about that longer piece.[4] I'm going to expand the central section of that, I think.

. . . .

I am leaving for Saginaw tomorrow. My address there is 1805 Gratiot Avenue.

I really hate to be bothering you, but one G is a lot of hay. I hope you're happy and otherwise undisturbed.

Sincerely,
Ted

Statement of General Nature of Project

My plan is simple. I wish to complete the various groups of poems on several levels of experience in the enclosed manuscript and also write a longer meditative or speculative piece. The poems in manuscript include the following categories:

(1) An uncompleted sequence about my father's greenhouse called *News of the Root*. In this I am trying to avoid the sentimental and literary diction of the Georgians or the earlier *Floral Offerings* of the nineteenth century and write a natural sensuous poetry with some symbolical reference in the more complex pieces. The poems done so far are not sufficiently related and do not show the full erotic and even religious significance that I sense in a big greenhouse: a kind of man-made Avalon, Eden, or paradise.

(2) A sequence of satirical poems, more violent in rhythm, mostly

---

[3] A friend and colleague of Roethke's at Pennsylvania State College.
[4] "The Lost Son." *CP*, pp. 53–58.

about the suburbs. These will be bitter or even brutal in tone, but not without humor, I hope. The examples like "How needles and corners perplex me" or "Last Words" approximate what I am trying to do in this vein.

(3) A series of three longish poems about a mental and spiritual crisis. The first of these, *The Lost Son,* is included. The central section of this poem will be revised and expanded.

(4) A group of pieces about rivers and watery places. In these I try to suggest the relation between the visible and invisible reality by a merging of sound and imagery. ("The Minimal," "River Incident").

(5) A series of dramatic lyrics. "My Papa's Waltz" or "Pickle Belt" are examples of this kind of thing.

My whole effort of late has been to write a lively understandable poetry that a good many people can read with enjoyment without having their intelligence or sensibility insulted. My first book was much too wary, much too gingerly in its approach to experience; rather dry in tone and constricted in rhythm. I am trying to loosen up, to write poems of greater intensity and symbolical depth.

To Kenneth Burke

[Bennington]
December 21, 1945

Dear Kenneth: I make a very poor return for your swell letter by taking you up on that offer to run interference for the long piece.[1] Here it is, with I think all the changes you suggested, plus some more. I think it's tightened up; is done. And I hope you do. But if for any reason you feel dubious about it, give up the project and return.

Tate is probably the best bet, wouldn't you say; and Ransom next.[2] Anyway they're the only ones I care much about. The hell with *Chimera* or *Accent*: rather bury the piece in the garden.

I wouldn't be doing this, I suppose, if I didn't feel so much hung on this damn thing. For some reason I have ended the year

[1] "The Lost Son." *CP*, pp. 53–58.
[2] That is, *Sewanee Review* and *Kenyon Review*, respectively.

with a feeling of absolute psychic and physical exhaustion. Without wallowing in self-pity, I keep thinking that this is the end of my 15th year of teaching. I really thought for a time this semester that I was slipping: not enough bounce, no real hot flashes or improvisational rides. But at the end, a lot of them trooped in with the usual palaver and some of the freshmen even cried, as God is my witness, as they walked out of the last class.

By such things do we live I daresay. But it does seem a hell of a life, on occasion. No property, no security, no nothin'.

So, pa, if you can revive my drooping spirits as a writer, it would be just dandy at this point.

Forgive the caterwauling. But you would be ready to permit it if you had suffered all the fools and low-grade bitches I have in the last month.

. . . .

Part IV

Hope you and Mrs. and the kids are all in good health.
Forgive the burbling.

Ted

Postscript

Auden was here for a day and night. He's coming on for one semester, anyway. He spoke of you with great respect. In fact, he indicated you were the only person he would want to see, apart from the administration. He didn't want to stay in the guest room either. So we drank and roared down in Shingle until 3:30 or 4:00, at which time I retired virtuously to one of the upstairs rooms. (Sounds sinister; it wasn't.)

I like him very much, and always have. He's cockier than he used to be, but still a very fine man underneath the British exterior. And damned smart.

He wants me to go to Greece, for some reason. Seems I should learn what suffering really is. Then go to Germany and work in UNRA.

Best again. Wish I could see you.

T. R.

To Kenneth Burke

[circa March 1946]

. . . .

Postscript

Dear Kenneth: Forgive the pencil—but I'd clam up writing with a pen.

Your letter meant a great deal to me, particularly since it came when I was lower than a snake's ass about what I am and what I do. Not that *I* had any doubts about the poem;[1] but I know that poems that run back into the unconscious and depend upon associational rightness have a hard time breaking in on readers who are conditioned by the purely literary kind of thing. Maybe, eventually, I'll ask you to run interference for the piece somewhere.

I was struck by the fact that some of your points I have down in notebooks as observations of my own. One belief: "One must go back to go forward." And by back I mean down into the consciousness of the race itself not just the quandries of adolescence, damn it. (Though I don't resent the phrase, really. Rimbaud was an adolescent, too.) I suppose at this point you will say that any regression does go back or repeat what has happened before and not merely in the individual man.

It's always seemed to me that many of these blood-thinkers or intuitives aren't or weren't tough enough. They just fart around with the setting sun like William Wordsworth or if they do get down in the subliminal depths they get punchy or scared and bring nothing back from the snake-pit (or hen-house).

But my real point is: Your belief and interest in the piece has set me up very much, and I'm overwhelmed that you should consider writing about it in your next book. Hope you do. I've been flowering in obscurity so long that it would be startling to wake up in a book.

If all this sounds nutty, put it down to the fact that Bennington has me as tired already as I usually am in December.

[1] Apparently "The Lost Son." *CP,* pp. 53–58.

Sorry you had to spend so much time on permissions and, I suddenly think guiltily, damn fools who write letters and send verses.

Say hello to Mrs. B.

Ted

To Kenneth Burke

[circa March, 1946]
Londonville, New York[1]

Dear Pa: Thanks for the kind words about the poems.

I don't know what to say about what to do with Tate. All I know is that I want very much that he print the poem[2]—and God knows it's a better piece than most of those he prints. So use your own judgment; but don't make him sore, if you can avoid it.

I've been crawling in and out of hospitals the last three weeks. For two weeks I was in the Albany Hospital taking some electric treatments. Mary Garrett and J. Jackson[3] have been keeping track of me. Now I'm out in the country at some nursing home with a lot of old ladies. Am leaving tomorrow or the next day, I think.

Somewhere I have some other chrysanthemum poems; but not here. Will send when I find.

I wish I could sit down with you and throw it over the fence, pa. The list of people I can abide is very small, I assure you. I haven't seen Lewis Webster[4] in a long time, though I still like him; but am not sure how he feels.

_____

If this scribble is nuttier than usual, put it down to the electric shock treatments and the prime stupidity I have been subjected to of late.

Say hello to mamma and the kids. If you can, get Tate to print the poem. It would improve my spirits.

Best,

Ted

1 Written from Leonard Nursing Home.

2 The poem is apparently "The Lost Son." It was printed in the *Sewanee Review* (Spring, 1947). *CP*, pp. 53–58.

3 Mary Garrett was Director of Admissions at Bennington; James Jackson, one-time student of Roethke's, later taught at the University of Washington.

4 Lewis Webster Jones, president of Bennington College.

To Kenneth Burke

[Saginaw, Michigan]
May 2, 1946

Could I spiral like this, like these strung
-up young chrysanthemums tethered on strings,
My face always pushed toward the sun, all impulses in
Place, a fir flower shaping itself out?

The directionless learn only by moving.
Here in this carnation-house, in the man-made
Mountainy air, it becomes more clear:
Faith moves me, less than a mountain, much more.

Will I stretch out of wretchedness? Yes.
Even these clumps wrapped in burlap stir
Up hope; the last least parts of me strain
When I see maimed roots grappling granitic stones.

Theodore Roethke
Written in the Sag. Pub. Library

Dear Pa: Your letter of Feb. 15, 1945[1] *ast* me to refer you to other
lines of mine which had chrysanthemums in them. Here's one piece
[above]—which I liked a lot once; but don't know now. Will you
be insulted by any explanations? As you'll see (he says politely),
each stanza implies a shift in place: the first stanza in the warm
chrysanthemum house (oriental flower, etc.); then, as the aphorism
opening stan. 2, implies a movement (not of the bowels but to the
cooler carnation house); then, in the last to the coolest part of the
greenhouse—the nursery—at least 600–700 feet from the second
boiler.

Maybe these are ideas and symbols here that deserve a better
settling: say part III of the longer things I'm grunting over and
will inflict on you eventually, never fear, O Critical Parent.

Actually, in *this* piece I was just practicing or showing off: Having read all the encomiums heaped on M. Moore winter before
last, I said to myself, Shit, I can break up syntax too and do it with
less mannerism [. . . .] (Or is that too cocky or only a half-truth

[1] Roethke had misdated Burke's letter; it was written February 15, 1946.

—probably; and a disloyalty to a pretty good poem, even though nobody will buy it.)

Also you asked me, specifically, why no chrysanthemums present in "Flower-Dump." Well, in part this is explained by the factual aspect: this was an enormous greenhouse (250,000 feet of glass) and there were *two* dumps and the one I was most cognizant of as a child was only about a block from the house and could be seen out of the back window; while the chrysanthemum houses (about 500 feet long they were and connected with the second boiler-house) were almost three blocks away (still on our property, y'unnerstand): Besides the height of the chrysanthemum season occurs in late November—by which time the spoiled or too-old stuff when thrown out would soon be covered with snow. (Still not the whole answer, of course.)

As to why chrysanthemums are the accusers. Notice the "half-grown," i.e. adolescents. I meant (among other things) this act of being up on top of this greenhouse was something that even the most foolhardy older kids condemned because if you slipped you pitched through the glass to if not certain death, a broken back or neck and bad cuts. . . . Again there's the factual part: there were five or six of these 300-foot houses all together, side by side, with nothing but chrysanthemums.

Do I betray myself as too literal? But I try to be true to the actual (be exact) and also to get the widest yet most honest symbolical richness too. Me and Proust: we got to put it all down.

Another place where the chrysanthemum turns up is in the end of the fourth section of *The Lost Son*, where the lines occur

The rose, the chrysanthemum turned toward the light, etc.

(D'you have a final copy of this long one or do you want to wait till it comes out in *Sewanee* in Oct. they have just written.)

Now the predominant color associations here are red (of the rose): a deep red and tall stems (the old man cross-bred some of the roses and developed some used all over the country) and the yellow of the chrysanthemum (*you* take the ball from here, Pa, old Man, on what was meant by the buried color symbolism here.)

Time out for a long interruption by the head librarian of the

Hoyt-Public who also, for some reason, brought up that piece, "Child on Top of a Greenhouse."

And, Pa, I found *Salute* for May, p. 19. At first I thought you had some broad hint about for-Christ-sake-quit-bothering-*you*-about-what's-over-the-dam-and-do-what-you (meaning me)-should-be-doing; and also, a hint that I might read *your* works on occasion. But damn it, I'm always afraid to: it's a whole world of its own and furthermore I don't want people to say I'm hanging on to your coat-tails—(even if I do on occasion). I do read 'em sometimes, even so.

. . . .

My plan of English publication will probably come to naught, since those bastards monkey around for months and then make only political moves: no chance for A meddicans or merit, I always say. But I'll try, anyway. *Horizon* asked twice to see work.

Had long, scarcely decipherable letter from Judy Bailey.[2] Apparently she hasn't sold out to the suburbs as yet. They (Sarah[3] and she) may come west, it seems. I said, sure. Stop off, only I *can't* put you up. (My mother's entrails are practically out half the time, if I can believe my sister. Can't operate—she's a cardiac, etc., etc.) But my reply was probably too blunt or crass for those delicate ears again. I'm fond of them both and hope I didn't offend them.

. . . .

Now look, Kenneth, please don't feel obliged to answer these long-winded communications: I'm just trying to answer the questions you asked. I have a tendency to be over-grateful to the point of exhausting the patience of other people, wearing out my welcome, as it were. And I've actually thrown away several letters to you simply because I didn't want to bother you. It's been about ten years since any literary person (apart from E. L. Walton speaking to the Troys about me[4]) has ever bestirred himself in my behalf in a matter of real importance. I mean like sending that piece[5]

----

[2] A Bennington student, later an editor with New York publishing firms.
[3] Sarah Moore, daughter of the composer Douglas Moore, one of Roethke's students at Bennington.
[4] Eda Lou Walton, poet at New York University; William Troy and his wife, Léonie Adams, at Bennington College. Miss Walton must have helped Roethke get the job at Bennington.
[5] "The Lost Son."

in to Tate,—offering to do it and *doing* it, as you did. I'm cynical about the human race, I guess; only actions count.

Best,

Ted

(Earlier letter—threw rest away.)

Dear Pop: I spent about five hours of my priceless time—and thereby set back the course of American poetry five years by so doing—in running down this reference on salt. (You asked me or mentioned once that you were interested in ideas about the symbol. signif. of salt.)

Will answer later other points you brought up in letters re: chrysanthemums, etc. But often your questions come so close to the heart of what I'm after that it just bitches me up if I try to explain in prose what I'm trying to get at.

Will hold off on
this until I get
another long one done.

I'm going, sometime soon, to send a long typed letter asking for advice in reading in one or two very particular areas in philosophical thought. (Sounds pompous but hope it isn't.)

Christ, Kenneth, sometimes when I go over some of these notebooks of stuff, I get a little scared: I mean I (threw rest away)

"Salt, says the learned Moresin, is the symbol of eternity and immortality. It is not liable to putrefaction itself, and it preserves things that are seasoned with it from decay."

—Brand's *Popular Antiquities,* II, 234, as quoted
in Judson's *Seventeenth Century Lyrics,* p. 297.

To William Carlos Williams

Saginaw, Michigan
May 8, 1946

Dear Dr. Bill: I have been reading over your letter written to me in July 1944 and the later one about the set of short pieces I sent you, in which you made the comparison with James Stephens. It goes without saying that these letters have meant a good deal to me and have helped me, I believe, in the laborious process of getting really loosened up.

But here's a long one[1] which I think is the best I've done so far. It's written, as you'll see right away, for the ear and not the eye. It's written to be heard. And if you don't think it's got the accent of native American speech, your name ain't W. C. Williams, I say belligerently. In a sense, it's your poem—yours and K. Burke's. He's been enthusiastic about it even in its early version. My real point, I suppose, is that I'm doing not one of these but several: with the mood or the action on the page, not talked-about, not the meditative, T. S. Eliot kind of thing. (By the way, if you have an extra copy of your last blast against T. S. E., do send it to me. I can't seem to get a hold of it anywhere.)

I've begun the Guggenheim, as you probably know; but so far I haven't traveled any place and it may be some time before I do, the way things look right now. I'll probably have to come East on business before the end of June. Maybe our paths will cross then. Hope so, anyway.

Do let me know what you think of this long one when you have time. You've had more to do with it than you think.

My best to Mrs. Williams.

Sincerely,
Ted
Theodore Roethke

This is a hell of a letter, but may the poem suffice!

To John Crowe Ransom[1]

[circa 1946]

Dear Mr. Ransom: I wrote this poem after a bout of pneumonia.[2]

---

[1] Probably "The Lost Son." CP, pp. 53–58.

---

[1] Poet and critic, founding editor of Kenyon Review, and professor of English at Kenyon College.

[2] See letters to W. C. Williams, November 11, 1942, and Stanley Kunitz [late 1942].

I have no misgivings about it, and hope you don't. It can serve as an antidote for some of the caterwauling done of late.

Yours truly,

Judge Not[3]

Faces graying faster than loam-crumbs on a harrow;
Children, their bellies swollen like blown-up paper bags,
Their eyes, rich as plums, staring from newsprint,—
These images haunted me noon and midnight.
I imagined the unborn, starving in wombs, curling;
I asked: May the blessings of life, O Lord, descend on the living.

Yet when I heard the drunkards howling,
Smelled the carrion at entrances,
Saw women, their eyelids like little rags,
I said: On all these, Death, with gentleness, come down.

To Kenneth Burke

New York, New York
October 5, 1946

Dear Kenneth: It was a high spot of the summer, being at your house, and I hope we didn't bitch up any rhythm of work, either your own or the household's. I envy you that nest, and the Mrs. and Michael, in particular, among other things.

I've been doing not much except poking through notes and writing down lines for another excursion into the underworld of nature. Bogan thinks I ought to get even more violent and go into hexantanz or whatever you call it. (This a 4th piece) Today as a finger-exercise I wrote a ballad (complete with tune) about a fifteen-year old being wooed by a fairy. I thought it quite funny at first, but now I'm having me doubts. It's too dirty, I guess. It's the sort of thing that can be sung at 3:00 A.M. at a very rowdy party, perhaps.

———————

I've tried to follow out your ideas for titles for the sections of #2 and given the whole a name, too. Let me know whether you

[3] Published in *Sewanee Review* (Spring, 1947).

like when you have time. Also, do give me the word if you see Tate and the chance comes up for that triple-play, Burke to Tate to Ransom. As long as this remains a possibility I don't want to get manic and start peddling it myself. But I realize (I hope) that you have other things to brood about than my concerns.

Went to a party at Anais Nin's[1] the other night. I liked her but not many of the others present that I hadn't known before.

Well, hello to mamma and the kids and the country side.

Best,

Ted

Send back "The Long Alley"[2] if you have no further use for it. On the other hand, keep if you like. (It's my "best" copy.)

I had a low scheme involving the academic world that might make us both more dough and be more convenient. It would not be for this year, but next; and still only a possibility. Will talk about when I see you. Idea: to teach as a team, more or less,— I feed to you, etc.

To William Carlos Williams

New York, New York
November 30, 1946

Dear Bill: Kenneth said you were wondering why I hadn't sent any more long pieces. I was going to call up and maybe drop by; but each week-end that it seemed possible, something happened.

Anyway, here's the second one[1] and I hope you like it. I'm rather glum about getting it printed in a good place, but fundamentally that doesn't matter.

These pieces seem to make quite a dent, often, in people who usually don't read much poetry. Maybe that's for the wrong reasons; but I hope not.

---

[1] Novelist and author of important literary diaries.

[2] Roethke appears to have sent the poem to Burke in early August, 1946. *CP*, pp. 59–61.

---

[1] Most likely "The Long Alley," which Roethke placed second in the sequence. *CP*, pp. 59–61.

Well, let me know what you think. I myself figure it's a vein of experience nobody else has tapped in quite this way.

While up in Bennington, re-read *The Wedge* and have copied out (several pieces). *Paterson* I haven't read in its entirety, but was glad to see Jarrell gave it a resounding acclaim in the *P. R.*[2]

Hope by now the effects of the operation are all gone and you and Mrs. W. are in fine fettle.

Me, I'm in good spirits and thinking about going South for a while. If you know about any quiet places in Fla., let me know.

This is a hell of a letter,—as usual,—but carries with it the best wishes possible.

Ted

To Elizabeth Ames[1]

State College, Pennsylvania
March 5, 1947

Dear Madam: I should like to make an official application to be granted the privilege of coming to Yaddo during this summer, preferably in July and August. Last year I talked over the possibility with Mr. Simon Moselsio, who encouraged me to make application at the proper time.

During 1946, while on a Guggenheim fellowship, I worked on a sequence of short poems and three longer poems called *The Lost Son, The Long Alley, The Shape of the Fire.* I now wish to write an even longer poem about a spiritual crisis, probably dramatic in form. The theme and much of the imagery are in my mind: I need the time and quiet which Yaddo would afford.

I have enclosed a bibliography and some excerpts of reviews of my first book, *Open House.* I can also send a copy of the book if you wish. Doubleday and Company wants to do the second volume, but it will not be out for some time.

In addition to Mr. Moselsio, may I also refer you to Mr. Ken-

[2] Randall Jarrell's review was reprinted in *Poetry and the Age* (1955).

[1] Director of the Yaddo Foundation.

neth Burke, Andover, New Jersey and Mr. William Carlos Williams, 9 Ridge Road, Rutherford, New Jersey.

If there is any other information you desire, please let me know.

Yours truly,
Theodore Roethke[2]

To Kenneth Burke

[*State College, Pennsylvania*]
[*March 16, 1947*]

Dear Kenneth: Hell, here's another request—and I make it with hesitation.

I'm trying to get into Yaddo for this summer (July, August) and I've put you down as a reference, since you and Bill Wms. are about the only biggies who have seen the longer pieces,—all of them.

I'm supposed to ask you to send a "detailed and informative statement" to Mrs. Elizabeth Ames, Yaddo, Saratoga Springs, N. Y. My project is an even longer piece, possibly dramatic in structure; or I may do that sequence about students you suggested.

Frankly, I don't think I'll be violently attached to Yaddo; but it's a way of saving money.

Another time I'll write about a project nearer and dearer to my heart: namely, getting the hell out of here & possibly going somewhere with you as a team to function as we did at Bennington, only more intensively. For—don't tell those Bennington lugs this —my coming back here was a blunder. I *do* have two very good classes in verse form and analyzing poetry; but the place as a whole has become a trade school for louts. Really it has, Kenneth. And

---

[2] Roethke wrote on application for his 1947 visit in answer to question about plans for work: "Recently while on a Guggenheim fellowship, I wrote a sequence of three longer poems called *The Lost Son, The Long Alley, The Shape of the Fire,* which dealt with a spiritual crisis. But I have not exhausted the theme: I wish to go beyond these poems. This means going into myself more deeply and objectifying more fully what I find, probably in a dramatic poem that could be staged. Much of the imagery and several rhythms are in my mind, but have not been resolved. I need time and quiet. I know that whatever comes out will not be merely meditative."

the administration is composed of hill-billies who have learned to count (mostly subtract).

I'm teaching well—if I can judge by the response—but haven't done one damned thing on my own. It's no way to live—to go from exhaustion to exhaustion.

Well, more anon on this theme.

Would you mind, then, banging off a few choice words to [her]. I really felt I was all set for a move toward something else. I need quiet & time. (I live in a 2 x 4 room, radios on all sides.)

Did you ever play those records? [1] I guess I'll have to make some sort of rationale or explanation for that second piece *The Long Alley*. If you ever get brooding on it again, and think of a way of giving some leads to the reader, let me see them. Somehow, I seem psychologically unable to "explain" something that is so close to me. Hell, these kids sense the unity all right: I don't see why trained readers can't.

> Best to mamma, Michael & Butch.
> Affectionately,
> Ted

To KENNETH BURKE

> *State College, Pennsylvania*
> [*circa May, 1947*]

Dear Kenneth: Well, your strategy worked apparently. My art belongs to Yaddo, for the month of July, at least.

Poetry bought "The Long Alley," to my amazement.

No other triumphs except what occurred when the kids effected a rating chart for courses here. In a criticism-of-verse pitch,—the only one taken so far—the results were almost too gratifying. A unanimous "superior" and "extremely stimulating." That's the kiss of death in a State School—to have the kids like the course.

How's mamma and Mike and Butch? How do you find M. Garrett's[1] husband? Or haven't you met him yet?

---

[1] Perhaps refers to recordings Roethke made of "The Shape of the Fire" and "The Long Alley" for Harvard College Library, Poetry Room, although John W. Matheson's bibliography of Roethke lists these as issued in 1948.

---

[1] Mary Garrett. See letter to Burke written *circa* March, 1946.

You talk about going to the wars. Pal, you should be in a sweat shop like this to see what's tough: people crawling over you all day long, and mostly louts at that. The best kids are fine,—but the "community,"—Jesus. I'll be glad to see those phonies at Yaddo.

I'm serious. I really feel that there are a lot of things bouncing around in me that will get killed off if I don't break away.

But that's my problem, and I don't mean to be always howling.

Wrote a poem, 1½ pages,—still in the "underworld" but much clearer.[2] Will send.

Read (re-read) your essay on Keats' *Ode to a Grecian Urn* a while back. Not to butter you up: I found it a very exciting interpretation. Promptly swiped some of your ideas for a class; did give you a credit-line, however.

Two days ago it snowed for about ¾ of an hour.

Am too sleepy for me.

Yours,

Ted

To JOHN SARGENT[1]

June 13, 1947

Dear John: Here's the third long piece[2] and some shorter ones which have not been published in magazines and which you might want to send to Mary Louise Aswell of *Harper's Bazaar* or the *Vogue* people in connection with your scheme of a possible article with poems or just poems with maybe a note. As I understand the contract, Doubleday would take 25% for any magazine publication of the poems, with 75% for me. Here are some items you may or may not want to work into a sales talk:

As you say, these people are very name-conscious. If Aswell got the idea that Auden, Bogan, Burke, Martha Graham, W. C. Williams, Shapiro, etc. think these are fresh and exciting, she would jump at the scheme, I think. Auden, for instance, liked this last

---

2 Possibly "A Field of Light," or some version of it. *CP*, pp. 62–63.

1 Sargent was Roethke's editor at Doubleday.

2 Apparently "The Shape of the Fire," though "A Field of Light" was actually the third poem printed in the sequence when *The Lost Son* was published the following year. *CP*, pp. 64–67.

one best; read it over four or five times, kept saying "This is extremely good," etc. The last part,—the euphoric section,—made him think of Traherne, as I remember: no "influence" but the same kind of heightened tone, I think he meant. I mention this because Aswell is currently on a Dylan Thomas jag: sees that Welshman in everything. If she trots out his name, give her the admirable Bogan's dictum. Said that eminent poet and critic: "You do what Thomas thinks he does."

Maybe a possible angle is that "The Shape of the Fire" represents, with its quick shifts in rhythm and association, a poem that creates a genuine imaginative order out of what comes from the unconscious, as opposed to the merely automatic responses of the surrealists. (I didn't dream this up myself: it's a point made by Bogan and others.)

Well, enough of this perhaps vomitmaking, I-love-me kind of thing. But if it's true, as Evalyn Shapiro says, that these longer pieces are acquiring a kind of underground reputation, then some scheme like this article is in order, it seems to me.

Well, let me know your reaction.

One further point: As I wrote Ken,[3] I have one or two ideas about binding, type, and jacket that I would like to talk over with whoever is in charge of that work. Perhaps the next time I'm in town—which should be the end of the month—you could steer me to the right person.

Sincerely,
Theodore Roethke

P.S. Maybe a point to make is that the poem is not difficult to anyone who is willing to think in images. Certainly after the deliberate conflicts of the first section, it's all clear enough.

To Selden Rodman[1]

Saginaw, Michigan
June 23, 1947

Dear Selden Rodman: I'm delighted that you want to use one of the long poems for the Penguin "100 American Poems." "The

---

[3] Ken McCormick of Doubleday.

---

[1] Poet, editor, and critic.

Lost Son" is available for publication anytime; *Poetry* has taken "The Long Alley," and if you would let me know when your volume is coming out, I'll see that they print the piece before any possible anthology appearance,—in case you want that one. The case of "The Shape of the Fire" is more complicated: Doubleday & Co. is cooking up some scheme for a magazine appearance, with a possible article. I won't know what the result of their activity will be for a few weeks, I daresay. But there will be no complications about the first two, I assure you. But if you do like the third the best, I'll give them a prod to find out any date-line.

As to a permission fee: whatever you think is fair for the length of the piece would be all right with me. Incidentally, it might be better to determine the fee before I send back my contract to Doubleday. After that, they control the rights and have to be given a cut.

It was indeed a pleasant meeting. On the strength of your remarks, I re-read Lowell [2] and now believe I was being uncharitable. There's a rough power in his best things, certainly. I'll do the same with Muriel R.'s[3] early work soon.

The dinner,—with tennis before and talk afterward,—is a very pleasant prospect. I'm afraid I won't be back in town before early August, however. I'll let you know as far in advance as I can when I'm coming.

Let me say once more how pleased I am that you like those pieces. I thought I went far beyond the early work, and that's what W. H. A.[4] & L. Bogan, Wms.,[5] etc. tell me, too. It's odd: I can feel very impersonal about them, for they seem to come from a tapping of an older memory—something that dribbled out of the unconscious, as it were, the racial memory or whatever it's called. Hence, my unabashedness about them,—which may be tiresome and naive.

Don't let this frou-frou ink scare you. It's my sister's—all I can find at the moment.

Sincerely,
Ted Roethke

[2] Robert Lowell.
[3] Muriel Rukeyser.
[4] W. H. Auden.
[5] William Carlos Williams.

To John Crowe Ransom

Saratoga Springs, New York
July 28, 1947

Dear Mr. Ransom: Regarding your *becoming* a convert to my work: I console myself that those slow to faith are, in the end, the firmest.

But I am nobody's Dylan: I never went to school to him. If there's an ancestor, it's Traherne (the prose).

I enclose a new piece,[1] typed by Master Robert Lowell, who says you will recognize what a labor of love his typing is. He thinks you might break down on this one, but I remain cynical and

Yours truly,
T. Roethke

Pardon the whimsey or cuteness,—the result of a hot afternoon.

To Allan Seager

Saratoga Springs, New York
July 29, 1947

Dear Allan: Via my sister, who got it from a friend of hers in summer school, came a *Daily* clipping about the jump in rank.

Congratulations—and I'm not being cynical. Any such event, apart from its personal aspects, is a kind of victory over mediocrity.

But, dear God, some of those other advances were enough to make you weep.

———————

This month has been pretty good fun. A good deal of time spent with R. Lowell: fishing, drinking, playing croquet, tennis, etc. At night we wamble into town often, with Buck Moon & Jim Powers, the short storyist.[1] My feeding habits seem a source of perpetual astonishment to these characters. This bores me.

———————

[1] "A Field of Light." Ransom did not break down; the poem first appeared in *The Tiger's Eye* (March, 1948). *CP*, pp. 62–63.

[1] Bucklin Moon, editor and author, and J. F. Powers, short story writer and novelist.

Other day caught 16 bass (only 4 legal) and the biggest perch I ever saw. One bass broke my line, and twice they have torn off hooks.

Have finished one 52 line piece,[2] which Lowell thinks one of the best I've done. But it drives me nuts that I go so slowly.

I may depart to the Northwest in the fall.[3] The deal is good, but I haven't agreed about courses. And I'm having misgivings about going even further into the provinces.

Hello to all,
Ted

Lowell says Peter Taylor[4] is an admirer of yours.

Postscript

Let me know date of book's[5] appearance.

For some reason I am restive about this one of mine:[6] want it to make a real dent. It should, I'm told, if it's handled right and some of these long-hairs take the time to read it. But it's such a damned puke-making racket, in some ways. I feel like burying pieces out in the yard, often. That "Long Alley" is in the July *Poetry* and "The Shape of the Fire" will come out in *Partisan Review*.

I still say we could function more efficiently as a Michigan mob (Seager, Roethke, Jackson, Dick Humphreys) on occasion—as those southerners do. Boy, do they stick together,—as you no doubt have noticed.

I'll be here for a while yet. I'm supposed to go to N. H. Conf.; but I'm trying to wiggle out.

---

2 "A Field of Light." *CP*, pp. 62–63.
3 To the University of Washington, Seattle.
4 Short story writer and novelist.
5 Probably Seager's novel, *The Inheritance* (1948).
6 *The Lost Son,* published in 1948.

To Elizabeth Ames

Chicago, Illinois
September 14, 1947

Dear Elizabeth: I'm very sorry that I left so suddenly that there was not time to say good-bye.[1]

What happened was this: I had a chance for a ride with John Brinnin[2]—which I didn't know about until late the night before. Since then I've been rambling about, collecting and packing books and other items. I had just one day with my family in Michigan.

But do let these hasty words say, very lamely, how much your graciousness meant to me. I was very happy, and the one longer piece I did is, I'm told, a very good one.[3] (*Very* seems to be the word in this epistle.)

With every good wish,

Ted Roethke

To Kenneth Burke

Seattle, Washington
September 18, 1947

Dear Pa: While unpacking a box, I came across some old letters from you, and overcome by sentiment, I take pen in hand.

I had hoped to see you before I left for Seattle, and at the last minute Judy and Sarah[1] wanted to wire you to come in for a fancy champagne binge on the night before I was going to leave but I realized that I'd never get done packing in State College (where I had to go next); so they were dissuaded only after considerable argument. I left N. Y. on Monday—the day they wanted to give the party.

Was glad to get your letter. One chickie told me the next day

[1] Roethke here refers to his departure from Yaddo. He is on his way to Seattle.
[2] Poet, biographer, and anthologist.
[3] The poem alluded to is again "A Field of Light." *CP*, pp. 62–63.

[1] Judy Bailey and Sarah Moore, Bennington students.

(after that session in Mary's[2] kitchen) that three students almost fell out the window trying to hear everything we said. I guess we made things pretty clear. I was a little saddened, at the time, but you seemed so over-aware of my supposed thug side: it's a mask I made to keep away fools, but you're not supposed to be taken in by it.

Yaddo was quite a lot of fun, on the whole. La Ames seemed a little wary at first but then became very gracious and asked me to stay on, etc. . . . Robt. Lowell I liked very much: we did a lot of fishing and reading and beer-drinking; went up together to Breadloaf and read to the School of English; went to see some fancy friends of his at Ipswich, Mass. etc. I don't think his ear (Lowell's) is especially subtle, and some areas of experience he doesn't seem to understand;* but the best of his stuff has a rough power, I think. It's not all that R. Jarrell says it is, but so what.

This town is pleasant enough but I'm afraid I'm going to be overwhelmed by nice people: it's a kind of vast Scarsdale, it would seem. Bright, active women, with blue hair, and well-barbered males.

The arts and the "East" seem to cow them. . . . I found, to my horror, that you have to go a mile from the campus even to get beer, and there are no bars for anything except beer and light wines in the whole of Seattle, except in private clubs. And there are no decent restaurants, either, as far as I can find out.

But I digress. (Time out for hunting a copy of a 52-line piece[3] I did this summer: a kind of interlude between "The Long Alley" and "The Shape of the Fire." But can't find; will send later.) Incidentally, "The S. of the Fire" (That's a hell of a title, I've decided) is appearing in your favorite magazine, *Partisan Review.* Current number, I'm told. The book[4] will be out in March, according to Doubleday. I think it's touch and go whether it will disappear under the waves or make quite a splash. I get some very fancy talk from characters as diverse as the Shapiro's (Evalyn and

[2] Probably Mary Garrett.

* Not very much intuitive perception; too much influence of A. Tate and too much concern and respect for formal (stanza-form) order [Roethke's note].

[3] "A Field of Light."

[4] *The Lost Son and Other Poems.*

Karl) and S. Rodman, etc. about what a pisser of a poet I am; how "The Lost Son" already has an underground reputation, etc. etc. Well, at the ripe age of 39 I could stand a few hosannahs, particularly if they lead to a larger pay-check and/or time off from teaching. Auden says he is going to write Eliot to see whether Faber would want to publish the book or a selection from both books. I doubt that he (T. S. E.) will do anything at present, on acc't of paper shortage,—even if he did like it.

Enough of this personal gabble. What's with you? Well, I hope, and mamma and the kids. . . . Your name came up the other night at a dinner; a new guy named Perrin[5] (from Colgate) admires you a good deal.

Let me hear from you. (I'm lonesome already: it would be a humane gesture.)

Best,

Ted

I still think that scheme of working as a team is a good one: but nearer New York.

[5] Porter Perrin.

1948-49

To Evalyn Shapiro[1]

Enroute on the New Empire Builder
[1948]

Dear Evalyn: In Detroit, Geraldine Udell gave me the *Poetry* with Karl's lecture in;[2] then when I passed through Chicago two weeks later, she asked whether I'd read it. Hell, I'd read *nothing* in the interim. But I did read it out of Chicago, and prompted by a Scotch or two, nearly sent a fervent wire saying it was the first mighty blow against the dreary text-creepers, the constipated agrarians, and the other enemies of life. I don't quite agree with what he says about the *song;* but otherwise I'm with him nearly all the way; and there were sections I could amplify from my own teaching experience, particularly, and at great length. In fact, I think a swell book might be done by essays from four or five poets: *Critics on Trial; The Case Against the Critics*—or some such title. Karl, me, Bill Williams (we'd *make* him be coherent), Dylan Thomas, maybe Stevens, etc. It's an idea, anyway. I've fought out some of

---

1 Then wife of the poet Karl Shapiro, who was at the time editor of *Poetry* magazine.

2 "A Farewell to Criticism," *Poetry* (January, 1948), was first delivered as a William Vaughan Moody lecture at the University of Chicago.

these things with Burke in detail: hence this especial vehemence.

The only sad thing, for me, was the possible implication that Pa was never going to raise his pen for any particular book again. I'd hoped sometime, . . . etc. *That* was no more than human, wouldn't you say? Particularly since so few people "get" the long pieces as he does.

Well, anyway,—and taking the flight of ideas to another hope: I'd *hoped* and expected to call up from Washington and see you both & the amazing child. But that proved impossible; *may* fly East in March; but that's chancey.

In the meantime, if you've survived this matchless prose this far, let me say happy New Year, and blame the travelling salesmen for the goofy prose.

Do write: one or both. And tell me about the job. Mine is wonderful as job; but Seattle's a bore.

Love,

Ted R.

P.S.

a) Oh, I almost forgot: how did those photographs turn out? Do you have any extras? Doubleday and *Mademoiselle* want something, and I have nothing except resemblances of Winston Churchill.

b) Called Babette[3] once, but never did see her, alas.

To Kenneth Burke

Seattle, Washington
January 19, 1948

Dear Kenneth: Pardon my usual electric courtesy in replying: but it's not for want of thinking about you and yours; and talking, too, in New York and even here.

I envy you the old growler, and the sunshine.

Your idea about the record may or may not come to pass. I sent a two-page letter on the subject to Ken McCormick[1] and even in-

---

[3] Babette Deutsch.

---

[1] Of Doubleday and Company. Burke had suggested that Roethke should try to persuade Doubleday to issue a recording of Roethke reading his new poems along with the book containing them.

cluded your letter. Hope you don't mind. There hasn't been time to hear as yet. One of the tough salesmen thought it a swell idea. So did the *Poetry* people.

At the moment I'm cursing my editor, an amiable Park Avenue oaf, aetat 23, who had the temerity to dump proof-sheets on Marianne Moore and, *I think,* even asked her for a blurb. Good God, for fifteen years I have hesitated even writing her on any pretext, and now she may think I put him up to this. I can't give him hell, for he has laboured mightily getting a handsome jacket, etc., and acts and talks as if I am the bard-of-the-year, to say nothing of my generation. All very pleasant,—but the Moore incident has distressed me. I do think she'd like the greenhouse poems, anyway.

There does seem to be some fancy talk, in the underground, about those long ones. For instance, a guy named John Theobald, in reviewing Brinnin's poem in *Poetry,* said something that might interest you:

"It is Hopkins, we remember, who distinguishes two sorts of illumination of obscurity: first that which yields step by step with the construing of the sentences (e.g. Browning's *Sordello*), and second, that which shines from every sentence, withholds itself from the poem as a whole on repeated readings, but when it does yield, 'explodes.' Brinnin's poem exposes itself to the first, Theodore Roethke's *The Long Alley* (*Poetry,* July '47) . . . does to the second."

In my childish way, I was pleased.

New York was fun, and your name, as I said, was bandied about; and we toasted you in wine, once, as I remember.

I did not call up Tate, since I thought he'd be suspicious, what with the book coming out so soon. I was always sorry Cummings wasn't rung in on that evening last winter. He's one guy, I think, who would hear those rhythms in that longer stuff.

I tell you, Kenneth, this far in the provinces you get a little nutty and hysterical: there's the feeling that all life is going on but you're really not there. . . . So forgive all this mother-hen anxiety. And do take (typewriter—pen) in hand again in another letter. Do you like the enclosed, for instance?[2] It was originally

2 This may refer to "A Field of Light," which Roethke says he will send to Burke in his letter of September 18, 1947; or it may be a piece which appeared in the continuation of the sequence poems in *Praise to the End!*

Theodore Roethke *ca.* 1943
Photo from *LaVie,* Pennsylvania State University student yearbook, 1943)

Theodore Roethke as Pennsylvania State University tennis coach, 1942–43
Photo from *LaVie,* Pennsylvania State University student yearbook, 1943)

Fishing at Jameson Lake, Douglas County, Washington; September, 1954
(Photo by Walter Walkinshaw)

planned as an epilogue for "The Shape of the Fire." But it seems something else, now.

It's nice to think of someone being where it's warm *and* functioning on something that matters. Have you taken any steps about an English edition?

Hello to mamma and the kids.

Best,

Ted

There's a thing here in the summer that pays pretty good dough. I've proposed your name, but there is a big committee, etc. If not this time, another time . . . etc. But I am keeping after them. Only qualm they have: you'd be too esoteric, above the heads of the customers. . . . Do you have any copies of those evening meetings lectures?

To Babette Deutsch[1]

Seattle, Washington
January 22, 1948

Dear Babette: I'll try to say one or two things; and not be too fancy, I hope.[2] I'll keep in mind these two statements from Jung which turned up in a student's notebook:

1. "Being essentially the instrument for his work he (the artist) is subordinate to it, and we have no reason to expect him to interpret it for us."

2. "The truth is that poets are human beings, and that what a poet has to say about his work is often far from being the most illuminating word on the subject."

Both these things are truisms, of course; but, as I say, I put them in front of the letter to keep me from being silly. You realize that poems like those long ones are particularly hard to comment on; and it is only a personal regard, I assure you, that forces me, at long last, into saying *something*. And now, I'm already sounding pompous. I valued very much that warm gesture of the phone

---

[1] Poet, translator, and critic.

[2] Roethke derived the form and much of the content for his later essay "Open Letter," published in John Ciardi's *Mid-Century American Poets* (1950; reprinted in *On the Poet and His Craft*) from this letter.

call last winter; and I hope your regard for these poems will continue to grow. In fact, I've hoped the process would be something of the sort John Theobald (whoever he is) indicated in an incidental remark in *Poetry* when reviewing a book by Brinnin. (Can you stand one more quotation?):

"It is Hopkins, we remember, who distinguishes two sorts of illumination of obscurity: first, that which yields step by step with the construing of the sentences (e.g. Browning's *Sordello*) and the second, that which shines from every sentence, withholds itself from the poem as a whole on repeated readings, but when it does yield, 'explodes.' Brinnin's poem exposes itself to the first, as, for instance, Theodore Roethke's *The Long Alley* (Poetry, July '47) . . . does to the second."

Is it childish to cherish this remark, and hope that this will often, eventually, be the case with those whose opinions I value? Maybe I like it, too, because a former student sent it to me.

But to more specific inquiries: 1. You are right in thinking of "The Lost Son" as an experience complete in itself. But it is only the first of four experiences, each in a sense stages in a kind of struggle out of the slime; part of a slow spiritual progress, if you will; part of an effort to be born.

"The Lost Son" is the "easiest" of the longer ones, I think, because it follows a narrative line indicated by the titles of the first four sections: "The Flight," "The Pit," "The Gibber," "The Return." "The Flight" is just what it says it is: a terrified running away,—with alternate periods of hallucinatory waiting (the voices, etc.); the protagonist so geared-up, so over-alive that he is hunting, like a primitive, for some animistic suggestion, some clue to existence from the sub-human. These he sees and yet does not see: they are almost tail-flicks, from another world, seen out of the tail of the eye. In a sense he goes in and out of rationality; he hangs in the balance between the human and the animal.

"The Pit" is a slowed-down section: a period of physical and psychic exhaustion. And other obsessions begin to appear (symbolized by mole, nest, fish).

In "The Gibber" these obsessions begin to take hold; again there is a frenetic activity, then a lapsing back into almost crooning serenity (What a small song, etc.). The line, "Hath the raine a father," is from the bible, of course—the only quotation in the piece. The next rising agitation is rendered in terms of balked sexual experience, with an accompanying "rant," almost in the manner of the Elizabethans, and a subsequent near-blackout.

Section IV is a return, a return to a memory of childhood that comes back almost as in a dream, after the agitation and exhaustion of the earlier actions. The experience, again, is at once literal and symbolical. The "roses" are still breathing in the dark; and the fireman can pull them out, even from the fire. After the dark night, the morning brings with it the suggestion of a renewing light: a coming of "Papa." Buried in the text are many little ambiguities that are not always necessary to know. For instance, the "pipe-knock." With the coming of steam, the pipes begin knocking violently, in a greenhouse. But "Papa," or the florist, often would knock his own pipe (a pipe for smoking) on the sides of the benches, or the pipes. (Now I certainly don't expect readers to get that second meaning, necessarily.)

Then with the coming of steam (and "Papa"—the papa on earth and heaven are blended, of course) there is the sense of motion in the greenhouse—my symbol for the whole of life, a womb, a heaven-on-earth.

The final untitled section, the illumination, the coming of light suggested at the end of the last passage occurs again, this time to the nearly-grown man. But the illumination is still only partly apprehended; he is still "waiting."

In "The Long Alley" a serenity, a "light," was achieved, at a cost; but it was only partial and only for a time. The beginning of "The Long Alley" is a relapse into the sinuous river-imagery: an ambivalent brooding by the edge of the city. The dead seem close. But there is a sense of unworthiness; a vague sexual guilt.

Dear Babette: I simply can't go on trying to "explain" this. It really is very closely written. Doesn't the whole clue lie here in the effort to reach, to apprehend the unnamed "Luminous one," "a milk-nose." Most of Part III is a nutty sexual dance, with wry comments on the "love," herself locked in the silo (the tower). All those last symbols are inevitable and easy, head of a match; cat (woman); goat (animal in man), etc.

Part IV the experience is sublimated—even more so—in the merging of flower, girl and fish, and in the subsequent evocation there is a kind of minor ecstasy; there is an exhortation to the self: a demand for release and acceptance of "The Fire." (I'm gliding over a lot of things, of course.)

"A Field of Light" (the piece you had without a title) is so short that it is almost an interlude. There is a stagnation period (1); then a conflicting action: an invoking of the "angel," while "hunting" tender things for the "hidden" again. A mild dance at the end. The final section is another "light" passage, with much more activity than at the end of V.

And now, dear lady, lest you feel I am insulting your intelligence with these crude outlines, I shall leave "The Shape of the Fire" to you. Again you will notice there is a regression, this time pretty violent; again a "return," at the end. But notice that the *last* section (5)—and the best—the things seen, the symbols, are apprehended by the mature man.

In doing these, I have worked intuitively all the time. I've read almost no psychology. Several people have made the point that they are at once a personal history and a history of the race itself. (That sounds high falutin'; but that's what they said.) I can make no claim, of course, one way or another. They *are* written to be heard; and they were written out of suffering, and are mine, by God. What gives me a kick is the dent they seem to make in people who don't care for poetry often, these and the young, who approach work naively. An eminent lady poet said, "You do what Thomas thinks he does." The remark seems unnecessary: I do what I do; Thomas does what he does. My real ancestors, such as they are, are the bible, Mother Goose, and Traherne.

Love,

Ted R.

In writing these, I have believed:

1. To go forward (as spiritual man) it is necessary first to go back.

2. In this kind of poem, to be most true to himself and to that which is universal in him, the poet should not rely on allusion.

3. In this kind of poem, the poet should not "comment," or use many judgment-words; instead he should render the experience, however condensed or elliptical that experience may be. (That's what has happened to Eliot in the *Quartets*. His rhythms are weakened; there's too much talk. It's a reflective, not a dramatic poetry.)

You watch: What I say is true.

To Katherine Anne Porter

Seattle, Washington
February 6, 1948

Dear Katherine Anne: I was unpacking some stuff lethargically the other day and came across some of your generous letters from several years back. I was so touched, somehow, a fat tear rolled down my fat cheek. Really I was.

Then the next day I was hauled in to a meeting about a writer's conference. "We need a short storyist," they said. "Why not try for the best," I said, "Katherine Anne." "She was first on our list, but we were told she was sick," said they.

So—I wired Elizabeth Ames and Bob Wetteran. Elizabeth thought you were fine; Bob had doubts. But I do hope you are completely well and would consider coming up here. The advantages: 1) It's only a week; 2) There are no manuscripts to read—only public lectures or lecture-readings; 3) The climate is supposed to be superb in summer; 4) Everyone wants you very, very much.

A Mr. Harold Alford has already written you, I believe. Do consider it seriously, dear lady.

And it would be nice to hear about your life in the glitter-glitter circuit.

By me, it is much the same. Last summer was at Yaddo: wrote a little, fished a lot. Also there were R. Lowell, J. F. Powers, and Buck Moon. We played croquet and made noise on occasion. All three I like fine.

Elizabeth lent Doubleday a drawing belonging to her by Charles Seide, which has made up into a handsome cover. These new longer poems, by the way, I think you might find exciting. They're a good deal different from those neat-and-tidy or grunt-and-groan effects of the first book. Allen T., prompted by Burke, printed one (enclosed)[1] with enthusiasm. People seem either enthusiastic or horrified. That's better than polite praise, it would seem. I'll see that you get a copy, if you like.

Do write; do consider, dear Katherine Anne.

Affectionately,
Ted Roethke

[1] "The Lost Son." *CP,* pp. 53–58.

To Edward Nichols[1]

[*March 13, 1948*]

Enroute on the New Empire Builder

Dear Eddie: Would this be too much?—

Could you get me a copy of the student-faculty directory[2] and send it to me care John T. Sargent, Doubleday & Co., 14 West 49th, New York City? I'll send you the dough whenever I know how much it costs. And if it happens to be a particularly sunshiney day and you are therefore amiable, and you want to check a name or so that you think would be interested in *The Lost Son and Other Poems* by Theodore Roethke,—well that would be fine. I myself will try to remember some of my ex-kids. And then forward to Bob Wetteran's bookshop in Hollywood (Pickwick Bookshop, the one he works for, I mean, 6743 Hollywood Blvd.) that is doing a special promotion job. I have lost both my address books and all old lists: I thought that such things were beneath me; but I guess they ain't. It really *is* Bob I'm thinking of, since Doubleday will never get its advance back. (It's true there is a genuine underground about this book, if I can believe the New York talk. Even the austere Mr. Eliot wrote to Auden about my "queer and individual effects," etc. But so what.)

I open up with a pitch at Wayne in Detroit, then go to New York, then New Haven, then Boston, then Ann Arbor (two appearances), then maybe Indiana and *possibly* Iowa and Minnesota. Then back to Seattle. I was touched to find on leaving that some kids had come down to the station (3 miles on the bus) to see me off. As the only serious poet within 1,000 miles of Seattle, I find I have something of the status of a bank robber in Oklahoma or a congressman in the deep south.

Story: Peg Knoll[3] heard I was coming East, asked how much I would want to come to Pa. State. I said $40 or $50, since some

1 Former colleague of Roethke's at Pennsylvania State College.
2 For Pennsylvania State College.
3 A member of the Pennsylvania State College library staff, colleague and friend of Katharine Stokes.

academies are happy to plunk down $100, plus,—and since last spring there was $60 for Shapiro, who couldn't come,—at Pa. State. Well, I thought it a pleasant notion & was going to turn back half of the fee for an anonymous poetry prize. However, later a letter came: embarrassment; no $40 or $50 forthcoming. Willie Lewis was afraid to ask, since his book budget was overdrawn already (Originally he'd thought it a fine idea, according to Peg.) and he had no special fund. The English Dept., which had been counted on, said it had no money (which would have been about 10 bucks or 5, in its case).

Well, hell, the whole thing made me feel like a horse's ass, a fallen angel, a shit merchant all at once. I reflect somewhat bitterly on the energy I spent & the dough of my own I've spent getting people to come there. You'd think that the damned place would be glad when one of its own boys breaks out with a book that, according to many smart characters, is the best book of verse of this year or last by a country mile; a book, much of which was written there etc. etc. Well, O.K., that's that. I'm getting old, but still remain naive, I guess.

Forgive this grumbling. It's just me pride that was hurt. Denied by my own people, I felt.

What's with you? You owe me a letter, you know.

. . . .

Ted

On long poems in "Lost Son"—"the most phallic poems in English."

To Selden Rodman

Seattle, Washington
April 14, 1948

Dear Selden: Delighted to get your letter and to know that you got the book[1] and are pleased with it.

I'm touched that you asked to review it, and hope that you do

---

[1] *The Lost Son and Other Poems.*

hold forth,—and at some length. What about *Sat. Rev. of Lit.,* or *The New Republic,* or that new rag, *Hudson Review.* The H. Trib. has been assigned, I'm told. Well, somewhere, anyway, I hope you speak out; for at the present rate it would seem that people profess in private to admire the book, but no one says anything publicly.

Did have a v. generous letter from Karl Shapiro . . . "I can only say this is one of the best books of poetry that has swum into my ken . . . the long thing stands easily with our best long poems." Etc.

Was pleased to be in *100 Poems.*[2] It's certainly a nice selection. Only thing that saddened me was that derived-from-Wms. business.[3] I do owe him a debt for jibing me in conversation and by letter to get out of small forms; but his own work I don't know as well as I should. (Some kid stole my copy of the *Collected Poems.*) Rhythmically, if there are ancestors, it's Mother Goose & Skelton (maybe Blake in his epigrams). His (Wms.) rhythms are more staccato, more broken, seems to me.

Well, in any event it's no great matter. But do look again, old chum.

About English permissions: It would seem to me that for *both* American and English permissions, a total payment of $25 for "The Shape of the Fire" would be reasonable—this being the sum we had agreed on if the piece weren't published elsewhere. Hope this is O.K. with you. So far they've sent no payment for Am. permission (the original $15).

Won't get to New York until summer—just was there last month, as part of a lecture-reading junket. Did about nine appearances at six colleges.

Best to your wife.

Ted

I am touched, let me repeat, to have your words about the book.

---

[2] *100 American Poems,* ed. by Selden Rodman (1948).

[3] The sentence in Rodman's introduction which Roethke mentions reads as follows: "Roethke, like Kenneth Rexroth and Byron Vazakas, and to a lesser extent Elizabeth Bishop, derived his undressed and deceptively simple style from the cross-grained imagist, William Carlos Williams."

To Kenneth Burke

[*1948*]

Dear Pa:

· ·

Did you ever get that letter [. . .]?[1] And are you keeping your card active in the Roethke Appreciation Society? Lemme know if the mood seizes you.

I've just finished a long (97 lines) poem,[2] the last probably from the dark world. The tone of some of the passages is somewhat the same; but what is said (dramatically) is different. The thing is much "clearer," I think, than the other: can really be worked at as equations: There's a more complicated "ecstasy" passage, which resolves into death-wish. I've been astonished to find that in the last 24 lines of affirmation there is not one reference to anything human except the line:

"I've crawled from the mire, alert as a saint or a dog."

And a saint is hardly human. All the other images are fish, birds, animals, etc. . . . Onan's folly.

But it's a real piece, Jack; it's got power.

But God, I need a larger structure; something dramatic: an old story,—something. Most of the myths are a bore, to me. Wish I could talk to you about it.

Well, I do hope you come. If there are any questions, let me know.

I'll be in N. Y., I think, by the end of this month.

Did you notice Bogan's review in *The New Yorker*?[3] I was astonished because I hadn't gone near her during my last trip. It's the only thing, apart from provincial bladders, that's appeared. Don't tell me [. . .] etc. aren't racketeers. That old brush-off-to-

[1] Probably letter to Babette Deutsche, January 22, 1948.
[2] "Praise to the End!" *CP*, pp. 85–88.
[3] May 15, 1948.

the provincial technique. Or avoid-what-I-can't-understand [. . . .]
Those limp-pricks: I can write rings around any of them. [. . .]
  It's late and I'm beginning to snarl.

  Best to mamma and Mike and all.

                                              Ted

Ask Jim Jackson[4] if he's sore at me. Hell, I wrote asking for dope
on how his books are coming because I wanted these guys to make
him an offer. No answer.

                   To Kenneth Burke

                                       Seattle, Washington
                                       [*February 8, 1949*]

Dear Kenneth: I) I enclose one more new piece[1] of which Palmer[2]
says—"I suggest that you send a copy of it as soon as you can to
Burke to extend the range of his examples." [3] He's going to print
it in the group.[4]
  Point a) The title is a line from Christopher Smart
  Point b) This piece is conceived as the first of a sequence of
dramatic pieces beginning with a small child and working up. A
kind of tensed-up *Prelude,* maybe: no comment; everything in the
mind of the kid.
  II) I'm to enquire whether you'd have any interest at all in coming out here from approximately June 20 to August 20 to teach
two courses *Advanced Study of Verse, Advanced Writing of Verse,*
meeting at 1 and 2 in the afternoon, either 5 days a week or 4
days,—as you elect. 50 minute classes. The enrollment is about 12
in one and around 15 in the other. You could do anything you

---

  [4] Former student of Roethke's who taught for a year at the University of
Washington.

  [1] "Where Knock Is Open Wide." *CP,* pp. 71–74.
  [2] J. E. Palmer, editor of *Sewanee Review.*
  [3] Burke was working on his essay, "The Vegetal Radicalism of Theodore
Roethke," which appeared in the Winter, 1950, issue of *Sewanee Review.*
  [4] Three poems by Roethke, "The Visitant," "Where Knock Is Open Wide,"
and "Praise to the End!" were published in the same issue. *CP,* pp. 71–74,
85–88, 100–101.

like. The pay is around $589 a month, and perhaps another $100 —at least—for a public lecture.

All this is not my idea—though the original Burke impetus is and was—and would not conflict with the fancier Walker Ames lectureship later; or a regular appointment later. I told Heilman[5] that you had the place in New Jersey and probably wanted to get the best weather here. But even after one round trip of al- most $300 rr. fare, there's still about a G clear for rather pleasant work in V-mild weather.

. . . .

Hope you like the kid's piece. Off-hand, I don't know anyone who's tried this before, with any success. Joyce is something else. (Yeah, yeah, and a slackened tension, often.) Also Faulkner in *As I Lay Dying* isn't the same, and doesn't hold up so well on re-reading.

Best to all,
Ted

Your idea: to do something with the teaching theme in poetry is beginning to take shape, and it will be good, I think. In fact, a whole lot of new things seem to be beating around inside. I just wish I didn't have to teach at all. Wish I could go through the whole of mystical and philosophical literature for about 3 or 4 years, and then write a long poem and a dramatic poem. Or just the *time*.

T.

Do write something.
Love to ma and the kids.

To Kenneth Burke

[circa April, 1949]

Dear Pa: No, I'm not mad and don't regard you as a farthandle. It's those guys like Bill Wms. that tell you by post, by telephone, in

[5] Robert B. Heilman, critic and chairman of the Department of English, University of Washington.

conversation that they're going to hold forth in print,—and then don't—who piss me off.

I've had a profound belly-ache the last two days: the world of letters seems far away.

Items:

1. No what was meant was "God, give me a near." [1] I realized the auditory pun, howl's.

2. Line 8 of "The Visitant" should be "I waited, awake as a frog," not "alert as a dog."

I think I've got hold of a really big theme: it's got everything, involves just about every neurosis, obsession, fundamental itch or what have you. I wish I could sit down and talk to you a little about it. It may take me five years or longer; but when I get done, Eliot will be nothing: a mere *litterateur*. He ain't much more, anyway.

I'm awfully weak from the shits. Will write more later.

Here's an elegy which should reduce you to tears.[2]

. . . .

Best to mamma and Mike, etc.
Ted

To John Ciardi

Seattle, Washington
May 2, 1949

Dear John: Excuse the paper: I can't find anything else right now.

It was pleasant to hear from you and to learn you want to put some work in the anthology.[1]

After brooding, here's what I think would be best: The whole of "The Lost Son" and "The Shape of the Fire." This makes me a pig by 30 lines (about 270 in all), but my "statement" will be pretty short. On that, I should like to make it in the form of a

[1] This phrase is from "Where Knock Is Open Wide."
[2] Probably "Elegy for Jane." *CP,* p. 102.

---

[1] *Mid-Century American Poets,* ed. by John Ciardi (1950).

letter (to an imaginary person) "Dear ———" saying something about what I'm up to in the longer pieces.[2] (I wrote just such a letter to a lady critic[3] who wrote enquiring, and two or three people who saw it liked the tone, contents, etc.) I could avoid being pompous or self-conscious or otherwise fancy.

Let me know your thought on this.

All the best,
Ted

P.S.

By the way, there were some mistakes in the text of the first edition; corrected in the second:

In "The Lost Son": p. 45 "Toads brooding *in* wells" ("in" is omitted, wrongly)[4]

In "The Shape of the Fire": page 63 "When the *herons* floated" etc. *not* "waterbirds"

Also page 63: "When the sun for me glinted the sides of *a* sand-grain" ("*a*" is omitted wrongly.)

Also page 60: "A dish for *fat* lips," *not* flat.[5] And stir from *your* cave of sorrow."

To Kenneth Burke

[*circa 1949*]

Dear Pa: J. Palmer said send you a copy of "Praise to the End!"[1] Here it is, a lovely virgin typescript.

Minor info:

1) Title is from a line from Wordsworth, *Prelude,* Book I, along about line 350 or so. (Ambiguities, ironical and otherwise, are intended.)

[2] Roethke's "statement" does take that form and is called "Open Letter." Reprinted in *On the Poet and His Craft.*

[3] See letter to Babette Deutsch, January 22, 1948.

[4] In the *Collected Poems* (1966), "in" is still omitted (p. 53).

[5] I have altered Roethke's letter here: he wrote "fat" twice but obviously meant "flat" the second time, since that is the printing error in the edition referred to.

---

[1] *CP,* pp. 85–88.

2) "Bumpkin, he can dance alone" is that line from an old nursery rhyme.[2]

I had some remarks about the structure: the fact you can work it out in equations, almost. But then I thought, fock him, the old critic. Let him find his own,—as if he wouldn't.

In last passage, almost total absence of human symbols isn't accidental. Ecstasy-death wish, etc. (Sublimation carried to its ultimate end.) In this respect—and some others—this piece says something different from any piece in the book, I think.

———————

Last summer I tried to promote a car to come out to Andover. No luck. One Sunday almost came out in a Rolls Royce of 1933 vintage. But I'd mislaid the letter of directions and we started too late, anyway.

I [hope] everything is well with you and mamma and the kids. Best to them and yrself.

Ted

Here's two poems for Michael

The Lamb[3]

The Lamb just says, "I AM!"
He frisks and whisks. *He* can.
He jumps all over. Who
Are *you?* You're jumping too!"

By God, this is
a masterpiece,
ain't it?

Gooses[4]

Their noise is louder than a quack;
Their beak can give an awful whack.
(You'd better leave without excuses
If you encounter any gooses.)

I *know* it's geese: my wits meander
I think I see a Papa Gander!

---

[2] From Mother Goose. Sometimes called "Dance, Thumbkin, Dance."
[3] *CP*, p. 182.
[4] Apparently unpublished.

To John Ciardi

[Saginaw, Michigan]
August 31, 1949

Dear John: Well, here it[1] is, and I hope you like it. I think I got around some tough problems,—considering the nature of these poems,—and I hope [I] am not undignified or puke-making in an I-love-me sense.

I think you'll find that just about all the points your questionnaire mentioned are brought up, one way or another.

You'll see that 1) I say some things about my method in general; 2) say some quite specific things about "The Lost Son," the text of which the readers will have; 3) speak about even later poems and the sequence as a whole,—which is necessary for any complete understanding of what I'm up to. (Incidentally, the poem about the very young child referred to on page 4 is entitled "Where Knock Is Open Wide" and will appear in *The Sewanee Review*. If you, as editor, think it necessary to note that fact in a footnote, that is all right with me. "Praise to the End!" elsewhere referred to, will also appear in *Sewanee*. In a way, I wish there were room for one more; but even if you were willing, it would be difficult because I don't want to approach John Palmer[2] about the matter: he's been long-suffering, indeed, about various matters. There is one,[3] as yet untitled, that's to appear in *Partisan* that represents a quite late phase. Maybe Delmore[4] will run it pretty soon.

One matter which the printer decides: I use a comma and a dash as ,— but just a dash's all right with me if that's what is preferred. The long blank after "dear ———" I should like left a blank.

One further thing: while I like this set of remarks, I'd *much prefer* that that they be put in the back of the book, *not* as a

---

[1] "Open Letter."

[2] Editor of *Sewanee Review*.

[3] Probably "Unfold! Unfold!" which appeared in *Partisan Review* (November, 1949). *CP*, pp. 89–91.

[4] Delmore Schwartz.

preface. The inference that poems need an introduction I find very odious. I feel very strongly about this, J.

All the best,
Ted

Let me know how you like it.
Last P.S.

It isn't clear—until perhaps the very end—whether the person addressed in the letter is a man or a woman. Again, that's deliberate, of course: a mild little dramatic ambiguity.

In the last weeks have talked to no one except some Saginaw richies (while on a week-end visit) and Allan Seager, one evening. Wish I could have a day of bullshit with you in Boston or elsewhere. Little chance, I think.

T.R.

To Kenneth Burke

Saginaw, Michigan
September 6, 1949

Dear Pa: Your post-natal letter received: forwarded from Washington.

I'm delighted, of course: and pleased that you've documented my pre-human history so extensively.[1] As to the *Sewanee*: they've announced the piece, don't forget. Palmer has been very decent: why shouldn't he be decenter? Tell him that some of the *zeit-geist*, ear-to-the-ground boys in England like John Lehmann[2] think I'm the only bard at present operating in the U. S. of A., that everybody is tired of Tiresome Tom, the Cautious Cardinal,[3] and wants to hear about the new jump-boy, the master of diddle-we-care-couldly. They have to be told, the goddamned sheep. Boomboom, you gotta believe. (I don't mean Palmer but the public.)

Sure, I'd love to see it, but that isn't necessary. Anything you say

---

[1] Refers to Burke's essay, "The Vegetal Radicalism of Theodore Roethke."
[2] English editor, publisher, critic, and poet.
[3] T. S. Eliot.

is Ho-Kay mit mich mir. Just so I ain't drummed out of Christendom, or that part of it called Academia. I had to do a loathesome solo job on me & poems for an anthology.[4] I made it in the form of a letter to make the tone less odious: lifted a page out of that letter I showed you (the one to the lady critic).[5] The whole thing ran to 5½ pages, but when I got done I had the sense of not really having come to grips with the subject. But some cracks seem pertinent and I hope I wasn't puke-making.

[scratched out]   What a bottomless Abyssh
                     The Navel Ish. Etc.

I would have sent you, only I thought you might think I was prodding you or trying to influence your remarks. Frankly, I don't think what the instrument says about his tune (or sperm) is v. important.

I did almost write asking: could I come over for an afternoon if I came to New York. It's about *the* new kick: the longer dramatic piece; but all of a sudden I start bursting with ideas in terms of *action,* by God. I think I got my design, my line, and is it ever pure, merciless: really Greek-like. Only six, maybe seven characters, and *one* set. I think I'm going to be able to build a tension that will make them wet their pants. Apart from anything having to do with language, it's going to be playable: a violent, not just plausible and inevitable, tragedy. Pa, I can't miss. If only I didn't have to bother about teaching.

Oh, about New York: I almost forgot to say that I probably won't get there at all. Caught a bad strep throat just before was going to take off for Maine & other points. Now my behind is full of penicillin. In bed about 5 days.

There are now eight pieces in all in the sequence; maybe one more kid's one. The last two are called:
                    Unfold! Unfold!— (from Vaughan)
                              and
                    Let Much Be Enough!
I wouldn't be surprised if I find I've taken up, by metaphorical

---

[4] *Mid-Century American Poets,* which was completed at the end of August.
[5] Letter to Babette Deutsch, January 22, 1948.

indirection or ironical aside, one or two of the points you make in the Great Screed.[6] But maybe not.

Hell, maybe the pernt to make to Palmer is that your piece ain't so much about ME as poesy in this time or some such crap. We'll see.

So I remain, bursting with pride, . . .
Yours, etc.
Ted

Best to ma & kids.

To JOHN CIARDI

Saginaw, Michigan
September 7, 1949

Dear John: I'm pleased you liked that pitch. If, later, anything seems vulnerable or stupid to you, let me know.

To answer:

1) O.K., put the remarks first and call it "Open Letter." Begin Dear ———, if you prefer. (I had it that way myself first)

2) I guess the spelling would be "cutesy."

3) Also on page 4, the line before the last would you fix the sentence to read, "I don't believe anyone else has been foolhardy enough to attempt a tragedy in this particular way."

4) Also on page 4, line 3 from top, read, "Sometimes one gets the feeling," etc. for "Sometimes you get" etc.

———————

Other matters:

1) It doesn't look like I'll make Boston, or N. Y., either, for that matter. Too bad.

2) It's very decent of you to inquire about my future publishing. Things are in a mess at the moment, and I'll probably have to get an agent to extricate me. Art (A. J. M. Smith) and others have been urging me to bring out a book with just the long ones (there are now 8 and probably will be 9 in all). It would make a beautiful

---

[6] Probably refers to Burke's essay on Roethke.

chaste small book, I say modestly. . . . I hear Kenneth Burke has done a 40–45 page essay on the first six of them: the "method." Ain't seen it.

3) Have ordered "L. A. D." [1] and asked the bookstore in Seattle to stock. Nice going. . . . Did I tell you I thought that prose piece on awarding medals in *Atlantic* very funny. . . . There's an English edition of "The Lost Son" out this fall, maybe an Italian later, but arrangements not completed yet.

4) Tell John A. H.[2] he's a gloob for not answering my silly note. I like his wife a good deal.

I'm dazed from lack of sleep: read all night.

I'm really glad you like the things, verse & prose, John. Hope, when they're all together, you'll think it's a sequence that breaks some ground; makes things jump around a bit.

Best,
T. R.

How's Harvard? . . . Did I pull a dumb one: Someone sent me a clipping of an interview with that "Big Sky" Guthrie man[3] in a Chicago paper. He praised Ted Morrison. I had it in a file, finally sent it to Morrison. No reply. Hell, now I notice Guthrie was on the staff at Breadloaf . . . I was just trying to do a friendly act, managed to look foolish, as usual.[4]

To John Ciardi

Saginaw, Michigan
September 13, 1949

Dear John: Delay has been due to fact that I haven't been able to get things typed from the first book.

You said four or five short poems. But since most of mine are very short, I've been so bold as to add more. You can lop off some if you like. But let me know, please. In making my list, I've been

---

[1] John Ciardi's book of poems, *Live Another Day* (1949).
[2] John A. Holmes.
[3] A. B. Guthrie.
[4] Theodore Morrison has been long associated with Breadloaf School.

guided by three considerations: 1) Picking those that are more *human* and often about people—since the longer ones are stark and terrifying to some; 2) Picking those that I know "go over" with a varied audience from experience in reading; 3) Picking those singled out by tough characters not always in sympathy with my kind of thing (Winters, J. V. Cunningham, Lowell, Auden, etc.)

Well, turn over, and here's the list, more or less in order of my preference

I   From *The Lost Son:*

Must poems (for me):

1. "My Papa's Waltz" p. 27. The best dramatic one. I think old Hardy looks down from heaven on this.

2. "The Cycle" p. 40. Cunningham, Winters, etc.

              (Put a comma after "ground," l. 16)

6. "The Return" Maybe this mood's in the long ones enough. But W. C. Wms. etc. have liked mostly. It's hard, I say.

From *Open House:* (all enclosed)

3. "The Heron" Cal Lowell, Winters, Cowley, etc.

4. "Academic" Even Grigson liked and printed in old *New Verse.* I've seen it in toilets—an improved version.

8. "The Adamant" Winters said "One of the best things in the book and in recent poetry" in *Kenyon.* I nearly fell dead.

7. "Night Journey" Winters, Kunitz, Cunningham, etc.

Then there are two v. short ones, *Vernal Sentiment,* beloved by Bogan, and I really think a little found type of simplicity; and *Child on Top of a Greenhouse.*

Forgive this name-waving: I'm just trying to let you in on my psychology, such as it is. And be as honest as possible!

If there's a press for space, maybe a smart move would be to bear down on those with the widest appeal:

"My Papa's Waltz"

"The Heron"

"Academic"

"Night Journey" Somehow *I* don't like it as well as "Interlude," which I've also put in, just for the hell of it.

"Vernal Sentiment"
"Child on Top Greenhouse"
                and (a new candidate)
"Big Wind" in *The Lost Son*
"Elegy for Jane"

But, God, "The Cycle" is one hell of a complete poem.

(You'll see I've had typed some from *The Lost Son* but not "The Cycle," "Big Wind.")

II On permissions. I've never asked Doubleday before. The copyright is in my name. I don't have a contract—lost it—they never sent another, though asked.

I have copyright transfer from *Knopf* on *Open House.*

III First line is

What's this? A dish for fat lips.

IV Don't have mss. of book as yet.

Much haste. Sister leaving for town.

Hell, I thought my sister was going right away.

V On adoption possibilities: Might be, but I don't call the tune. Why don't you get a tie-in with a book salesman (of college books) and make the approach that way? Then I can pull some strings. For my own courses, yes. I make the decision.

It might be swung—a big order. But not until book can be seen.

My mother has been quite ill. Hence the indecent haste, the addlement.

I'm getting more & more steamed up about the general plan of this book: that it will do something, as you say, for this generation of poets. The boys of the '20's have taken too many bows & Untermeyer, Benét & others have distorted the whole picture. . . . And so many of the academic crowd just hate anything alive, human, intense: bite it because it is human, because it's beyond 'em, etc. etc.

And I repeat: I really have been pleased that you, as a younger practitioner, get a charge out of the stuff.

More haste,
T.

To Kenneth Burke

Saginaw, Michigan
September 17, 1949

Dear Pa: Have read [1] several times and enclose answers to what you wished to know.

I can only say that I never expected during my own life, that close and perceptive a reading. I'm delighted, particularly, that you liked the short flower ones and "The Visitant" so much. I winced, on page 21, when you said "some of the short pieces come close to standard mag. verse." I'd agree about "Double Feature," and I'd also throw out "River Incident" and "The Waking." [2] But that leaves "The Return," which is one hell of a poem, in my book, and "The Cycle," which of its kind is far from mag. verse. (Police-Com. Winters and his henchman J. V. Cunningham care for this.) . . . Hell, I know you can't take up everything, and, furthermore, are calling them as you see 'em; *and* have been more than generous. But "The Return" I tot you cahed fah, suh.

The excerpt from the letter to the Lady Admirer will not be printed as you saw it, but a piece called "Open Letter" (probably "Wide-Open" would be better) using parts of it will appear in *Mid-Century American Poets,* published by Twayne, in December, 1949. The excerpt you quote will not be quite the same, so no harm done.

As to *Open House,* do whatever you think. But I am sending it so you'll have it at hand. I'd like to give you this one, but it isn't —literally,—mine. (I lent my mother's copy to someone and she claims this one.) The poems I still like in it are:

"Interlude" p. 10 "Prayer" p. 13 "The Adamant" p. 16 "The Heron" p. 28 "The Bat" (as a child's poem) "On the Road to

---

[1] Burke's essay.

[2] The poem of that title published in *The Lost Son* (*CP,* p. 51); not to be confused with the later poem which gave its title to *The Waking, Poems: 1933–1953* (*CP,* p. 108).

Woodlawn" p. 42 "Academic" p. 45 "For an Amorous Lady" (of its kind) p. 46 "Vernal Sentiment" "Night Journey." Maybe: "Epidermal Macabre" for that veil image. Winters liked "Reply to Censure" but I don't. He also liked "Adamant" "Heron" "Night Journey" and 2 or 3 others. Oh I guess you saw his remarks.

I shall probably be in Chicago either late Sunday, the 25th of September or Monday morning and early afternoon the 26th. I know you'll just have arrived, but if it's all possible to get together, let me know where you'll be. I'll probably call up *Poetry* (mag.) and you could leave your number with them. I'll be in Saginaw until Sat. morning the 24th, at least. I don't mean about *this:*[3] I'd just like to see you. In fact, I could arrive a day late, if necessary.

Back to the piece. I'd say that Palmer really would be nuts if he didn't take it. Don't *you* think it's one of your best jobs: most searching on a single guy, etc. . . . Never mind, I'm not trying to trap you.

I'd say anything in way of a letter you might want to get off (no need, except your Chi. address if you know it) would reach me if sent Wed. or even Thurs. air mail.

I'm sorry I crossed you up by revising that poem. I think of it as a kind of epilogue, or little comment-poem.[4]

Must run down to the sub-station.

All the best and a thanks that can never be said.

Yours,
Hates-Himself

1. p. 1 Line in poem should be *"When* sprouts break out," not *what.*

2. p. 5 Poem discussed has been revised and essayistic method abandoned except for very end. Revision is to appear in *The Kenyon Review,* probably Jan. 1950. (Revision enclosed.)

3. p. 18 "Caretaker" as applied to the male parent is a misleading term,—and I say this not for snob reasons, but in the interests of accuracy. Though the head of the company (a family corporation), he would have nothing to do with the *selling* of flowers: he was solely a florist, an experimenter, a grower of flowers. (This

[3] The essay.
[4] "A Light Breather." *CP,* p. 101.

might explain, in part, my lack of concern for flowers as a death-symbol. Instead, they were life-symbols; indeed, the little-blooming rare types (not for sale) were eternity symbols.)

Maybe a word more about the character of this greenhouse: While highly scientific in some ways,—pioneering in developing certain varieties of roses and types of fertilizer; some of the florists trained in European botanical gardens, etc.—it was also highly feudal in character: there were always six or eight people kept on the payroll for sentimental reasons; tramps were always fed and lodged in the boiler houses; neighbors took coal from the coal pile when they were broke. The whole idea was to be completely self-sufficient in everything. To this end, they had their own ice house; woods for moss; a small game preserve developed along German lines, with its "caretaker," specially stocked with pheasants, grouse, etc.; part of a coal mine.

I used to sneer at my father for not going into the machine and tool business or the brewery business, like most smart Germans, and making some real money. He'd laugh. Now I realize that what he did in creating the greenhouse (and *he* created [it], not the blood-sucking relatives) had more human significance than money-grubbing. I remember hearing S. S. Seridelsky, a Dutch bulb man visiting in the U. S., say it was the finest greenhouse in America; and others from Europe said this.

p. 28 By the *Ordnung! Ordnung!* I had also hoped to suggest the essentially Germanic character of the "Papa," the authority, whose Prussian love for order and discipline had been sublimated into a love for, and a creating of the beautiful (the flowers). . . . The child, a kind of sentry guarding the flowers, both lolling sleepily, guiltily; but jumping to attention at the *approach.*

p. 33 Your remark about the redistribution of the jingles,— which I don't think is right—may suggest to some readers that the piece is a kind of *collage.* The way I struggle for the "rightness" in feeling and phrase: they're not that, I think.

p. 41 Last line "A *King* of phallic pantheism" or *"kind"?* Me, I think the King is splendid! (In the very last poem, there's a line "I'm King of the Boops!"—having risen from being a mere "duke of eels" in "Praise to the End!")

Poem quoted at the end "Elegy for Jane" will appear, with "A

Light Breather," in *The Kenyon Review,* January 1950. That is, not this fall's issue, but *this* winter's.

p. 35 Lines should be "Once upon a tree / I came across a time" (not upon)

. . . .

To Princess Marguerite Caetani[1]

[circa 1949]

Dear Lady: I wrote a longish letter last summer but never sent it: too filled with self-pity and various howls. And now I write, harried by too many things to do; pressed for time. This, and the enclosed,[2] is simply a gesture, a letting you know I'm still alive. . . . Later, in a week or so, I'll write about the possibility of ever appearing in Europe. I am deeply touched by the repeated invitation.

The summer produced some work, but little that might be a possibility for your pages: one final piece in the sequence of longer [poems] (now 8) may get finished. There are some songs for children, which Douglas Moore[3] will set, eventually. In the meantime, there is this piece of prose, which may rouse or horrify you.

As you will see, it is written to be said aloud: an actual class harangue, beginning in outraged exasperation and ending in a kind of reluctant love. In this it is psychologically right, I *know.* A. J. M. Smith, the Canadian poet, says it brings back into the language the violent energy of the Elizabethan pamphleteers, the writers of the coney-catching tales, etc. I don't know: when I wrote it, I thought it really good,—funny, coarse, ribald and yet deeply serious. It may be, as another poet said, the best things in it *are* poetry of a high order and should be used in a long play. As I say, I don't know: and will be guided by your reaction. There are some topical references, but none difficult: "Tate-creeping," and things like "The old lion perisheth,"—which is from the bible, of course. ("for lack of prey" is the rest of it—as I remember). . . . I hope

[1] Founder and editor of the international literary periodical *Botteghe Oscure.*

[2] "Last Class," published first in *Botteghe Oscure* (1950). Reprinted in *On the Poet and His Craft.*

[3] American composer on the faculty of Columbia University.

the words like "bitches" and the references to Lesbianism don't offend you or seem too bald. There are so many lies about education; and there is so much idiotic tabby-cat prose written about it. I still think that this piece, *coarse and bludgeoning as it is,* says more, directly & by inference, about what actually happens in intense teaching than anything I know.

But this *isn't* a sales talk, and I shan't sulk or be cross if you think it isn't your sort of thing at all. But don't sell it short: there are many subtleties, not immediately apparent, I think, in spite of the God's-angry-man tone.

Enough! Enough! If I don't stop I'll never get this to the Post Office. But do let me say, in haste, that even if I don't write, you remain in my mind, actively, as a symbol of graciousness and another kind of ordered life—in which art matters. You *deserve* letters even better than Rilke wrote to his countesses (and how he loved to roll a title on his tongue) or than Yeats wrote to L. Gregory. I have *thought* such letters; but as a Prussian (by descent) I *can't* write them. Alas for me,—not you.

In some haste,
T. Roethke

Please let me know how you feel about the piece as quickly as possible? Air mail or even collect cable. I've several requests for work here, etc., etc.

Biography: Theodore Roethke

Born May 25, 1908, Saginaw, Michigan. At thirteen made speech used as Red Cross propaganda and translated into 26 languages (Better not say *this* for a European audience).

Educated University of Michigan and Harvard. Taught at Lafayette College, The Pennsylvania State College, Bennington College. Official job now is professor of English, University of Washington, Seattle.

Books:

Open House (Knopf) 1941
The Lost Son and Other Poems (Doubleday) 1948
——————————————— (Lehmann) 1949

New work to appear in *The Kenyon Review, Partisan Review,* and *The Sewanee Review.*

1950-53

To William Carlos Williams

To William Carlos Williams

Seattle, Washington
February 8, 1950

Dear Bill: This is just a hasty note to say that Paterson III has come and I've read it with a terrific sense of excitement, particularly the Beautiful Thing part, which I heard you read a long time ago. In fact the whole thing is so good, that I'm afraid to read it too much for fear it will louse up the longish sequence I'm finishing off at long last. (An *octet,* I've done, so help me.) Old T. S. E. can fall dead after this: We're both writing rings around him now, I say with the usual modesty. You might be amused, incidentally, to know that he is worrying that a satirical prose piece called *Last Class,* to appear in Europe, might get me into trouble unless I publish it under a pseudonym. He admires said prose "tremendously," says his distant cousin, M. Caetani.

I hope you got the smoked fish. As I said, somebody else ate one can.[1]

Léonie A.[2] wrote that she had seen you at the Library [of] Con-

---

[1] Roethke had sent Williams a box of tinned smoked salmon.
[2] Léonie Adams.

gress. Please say as little as possible to these complicated people about my being here.[3] It's a long story and has a happy ending.

To Elizabeth Ames

Seattle, Washington
February 24, 1950

Dear Elizabeth: Thanks so much for the card and the kind words about the work in *Sewanee!* Do tell me, I say greedily, what some of those other people said,—those who liked the poems.

Here is the important matter of business: Dr. William D. Horton, Director of the Pinel Foundation, says that I can be at Yaddo —arrive, that is,—on, or even a little before, April 1st. Both Dr. Horton and my lawyer, Max Nicolai, prefer that I arrive as soon as possible before the regular group so I can really concentrate on: finishing the entire sequence of long poems (there are now eight); really get the poetic play whipped into shape; and doing a few more children's poems. I would probably arrive even sooner,— if it were all right with your committee on admissions,[1]—if it were not for a bit of surgery that has to be done on my hammer toe! Don't be afraid that I will be any trouble: I won't be swinging from the chandeliers, sulking, or imagining I am the True Christ! I do, as you know, eat too much and I have grown a rather odious beard.

More seriously, Malcolm Cowley will undoubtedly write you

---

[3] That is, in the hospital.

---

[1] Elizabeth Ames's note: "On the return visit form T. R. submitted for his 1950 visit he listed as work he hoped to do:

'a) Complete the sequence of longish poems. There are now eight,—the last, "I Cry Love! Love!" will appear in The Hudson Review. But two earlier ones are yet to be done before the cycle of ten is finished. (Some elegaic poems are to appear in Kenyon Review this spring).'

'b) Complete the sequence of poems for children: a total of about fifteen. Four of these are appearing in Flair, and such musicians as John Verrall and Douglas Moore are writing settings for some of them. Jean George is doing illustrations.

'c) Work on a three-act poetic play: a playable intense tragedy based on experiences at Bennington. This has been blocked-out, act by act, and some model sets have been made. Many individual scenes of this play have been written.' "

and/or Mr. Hicks,[2] if he has not done so already. He, of course, has always been for my getting East as soon as possible. Even Bill Williams, bless him, asked me, all on his own, if I would go to Yaddo if *he* wrangled me an invite.

Be assured: there is no question at this end. I hope to see you before the month of March is done,—if that's ok with you and your committee.

All the best,
Ted

I'm getting pretty good on the piano: my own stuff, I mean. (This is a side you never saw, *Liebchen.*)

I meant Lieschen, but the girl who typed this made the mistake. I leave as is.

To Patricia Coombs[1]

[*Saratoga Springs, New York*]
[*May 3, 1950*]
Wednesday

Dear Patricia: I've loved the letters. Do keep them coming.

Not much production here.[2] But I'm not going to fret about forcing things. Why should I?

I've been somewhat prone to a sense of tiredness, or lassitude, that bothers me. But I'm getting over it.

Yesterday went for a wonderful walk by myself. Saw two geese, a fox (I *think*—just saw his tail going down a hollow); some spring flowers. It is so strange to walk down these roads and see no one. . . . There's a white skunk, but I haven't seen him (or *smelled* him).

The Guggenheim is not so fancy as it sounds: just for six months it is. But the local yokels don't need to know that. . . . They *did* give it, however, and they're so stingy with the poets. Only other

[2] The critic, Granville Hicks, who was a member of the Yaddo Corporation.

[1] A student of Roethke's at the University of Washington.
[2] At Yaddo.

one was Rosalie Moore, though Janet Lewis got a renewal for novels.

There are poets here in considerable plenty: Byron Vazakas, Hubert Creekmore, Phoebe Pierce, Ben Belitt (coming), Pauline Hanson (Eliz. Ames' secretary). Vazakas has my intense admiration on one score: he doesn't work, except for writing poetry. Lives in Cambridge & New York mostly. One of the few people who knows Stevens. A curious sly Levantine quality [. . . .]

Love,
T.

TO PATRICIA COOMBS

[*Saratoga Springs, New York*]
[*May 31, 1950*]

Dear Patty: Your grand letters were here when I came back from a week's romp in New York: mostly seeing Thomas.[1] . . . John Brinnin wrote me twice that he wanted to see me; so I came down for a May wine party given him. The party was a flop: dreadful movies of dancing, etc. But afterwards, Thomas and the inevitable dame for him (in this instance, Jean Garrigue), slipped away from Oscar Wms, José Garcia Villa & the other sycophants,—largely because I just stuffed Thomas & Garrigue in a cab & we left. . . . We drank bubbly all that evening. He was wonderfully funny, and we got along *very* well. . . . John Brinnin said that when he arrived in N. Y. from Europe they went to a 3rd Avenue bar and within the hour he had asked about two people: me & Shirley Jackson.[2] An odd combo, wouldn't you say?

. . . .

A good deal of the time was spent with Thomas in pub-crawling. He really does lick up the booze, consume quantities of pills, etc. His favorite bar: McSorley's. One night we got taken by some home town friends of his to a sort of Welsh Chowder & Marching Club. One night I met Cummings, with the Lloyd Frankenberg's. He and his wife came over especially, though he was at a dinner.

1 Dylan Thomas.
2 Short story writer and novelist.

As to here,[3] things are peaceful. I thought Fred Dupee[4] was going to be put in the Oratory across the hall from me,—which would have meant his sharing my bathroom. But he's been assigned elsewhere. . . . Still no tennis players; so yesterday played Phoebe Pierce some croquet singles; and some soft ball with the boys after supper.

I've been invited to stay until Sept. 1 if I want to,—for the season, in other words. *So I'm king of the cats* here.

I miss you: the small body, and black hair, and the wry twitches and other monkey shines. I really, really do.

You would love my suite, I think,—all the old wood and the busts and prints.

Much love, dear pet.

T.

To John Malcolm Brinnin[1]

June 22, 1951

Dear John: I have to write this down fast or I'll never get it said.

I was lying here, leafing through *Modern Poetry*,[2] and suddenly came on those lines beginning

Goodbye, god-father, sons go on their own, etc.

and I read through to the end with a real sense of excitement (not looking up for the author).[3] Then, of course, I read the whole piece[4] several times. I felt ashamed, ashamed that I'd never really got into the poem before: those evocative O's at the start seemed to throw me off. You're really with it in that piece; the true charge. It goes beyond your (almost excessive) skill with the language: breaks through the rhetoric.

Now, Jesus, don't take this amiss or think I'm condescending or

---

[3] Yaddo.

[4] F. W. Dupee, critic and professor at Columbia University.

---

[1] Poet and editor on the faculty of the University of Connecticut.

[2] Anthology edited by Brinnin and Kimon Friar.

[3] John Malcolm Brinnin.

[4] "The Worm in the Whirling Cross."

something. The list of contemporaries I can stand is so short that I feel impelled to praise as well (albeit clumsily) as I can.

Really all the best,
Ted

To Peter Viereck[1]

[*Probably 1951*]

Dear Peter: Forgive me for not having written and for not returning the *Atlantic* mss.[2] I guess I just wanted to keep the latter by me as something to hold against the devil. I am deeply touched, to say the least, by your confidence in me, and I hope I can go on to where you wish me to be.

About your poem:[3] It's a wonderful theme and through the whole there is a rare freshness and singing innocence. But once in a while it seems to me that you don't quite get the verbal felicity necessary in this kind of material: "I sleep-walked through my cycle"; and elsewhere in I. Likewise in "Here is my first, my fiercest consciousness" seems mannered. Does enough "happen" in II? From "I splashed" it seems a bit too static even though it's a period of waiting. (It may very well be that this is necessary to prepare for the élan of the last part.) I like the second ending the better.

Well, after your generous words, I feel a terrible stinker questioning anything. But you asked.

. . . .

The whole [*Atlantic*] piece carries the conviction of someone for whom poetry is a holy thing.

———————————

I'm a terrible letter writer, but I hope this conveys, clumsily, how much your belief in what I do has meant for me. . . . I have

[1] Poet and essayist; professor at Mount Holyoke College.

[2] Refers to an omnibus poetry review entitled "Technique and Inspiration: A Year of Poetry" which Viereck was preparing. It appeared in the *Atlantic Monthly* in January, 1952. Viereck singled out *Praise to the End!* and Yeats's *Collected Poems* for the highest compliments. He says of Roethke: "Any man who can write like this may well become a great poet of that same utter exaltation once sung by Rimbaud and Hölderlin."

[3] "Arethusa: The First Morning"; later included in *The First Morning* (1952).

Theodore Roethke, 1953
(Photo by John Deakin, London)

Theodore and Beatrice Roethke, San Francisco; 1959
(Photo by Imogen Cunningham)

a sense of great powers coming on, but it's scary to talk about such things.

Best,

T. R.

To Kenneth Burke

[Seattle, Washington]
January, 1952

Dear Kenneth: It was very nice to hear you over the long hook-up.

And thanks for letting me put you down again.[1]

But for God's sake, please get it where it will be postmarked before or on Jan. 19. There's seven grand at stake.

I was passed by the local committee in the face of numerous and (some) hot competition.

I've inserted a copy of my history (the autobiography the forms asked for) and (13b)—what I want to do with my time. Their big emphasis is on teaching, not writing,—so let fly or bear down on T. R. the ponderous pedagogue. You might be amused—and F. F.[2] too—that I've worked you both into the script.

Take a look at the current *Kenyon*. There's a piece (by me)[3] that may bear out your prophecy: about a person that is; oddly enough there are some terms via mystical literature too—used only incidentally. There's about seven lines I'd cut.

There was no chance to try to reach you earlier: the local committee has just made its decision. . . . You know how Academia is.

All best to Mamma, Mike, Fergie, Marion, etc.

Best,

Ted

Even Blackmur[4]

[1] For a letter of recommendation to the Ford Foundation. Roethke won a Ford Foundation Fellowship for 1952.

[2] Francis Fergusson.

[3] "Old Lady's Winter Words," *Kenyon Review* (Winter, 1952). The poem was later included in *The Waking* (1953). *CP*, pp. 103-4.

[4] R. P. Blackmur, American critic and poet.

I became a teacher against the wishes of a family that wanted me to enter the law. Where a very comfortable income awaited me if I chose that career. I did enter law school at Ann Arbor, but gave up in disgust. I did not wish to become a defender of property or a corporation lawyer as all my first cousins on one side of my family have done.

During the struggle and unhappiness involving this decision, I wrote my first verse. It was printed in magazines like *The Harp, The Commonweal,* and *The New Republic.* In the meantime, I tried to get an M.A. in English in a semester and a summer school at Ann Arbor (because of a technicality the degree was not awarded until 1936). In 1930–31, I went to Harvard, principally to work with I. A. Richards, the English critic.

From 1931–1935 I was an instructor in English at Lafayette College, in Easton, Pennsylvania. From March, 1934 until June 1935 I was also director of public relations, as well as tennis coach, proctor in the freshman dormitory, editor of the catalog, and a member of five committees. On the side, I was a public relations counsel for the J. Robert Crouse interests in Cleveland (National Lamp, Arctic Ice Cream, etc.). I lived on the Crouse estate in the summer; wrote editorials and reports.

The usual procedure at Lafayette was to keep an English instructor for two years at most. I was kept four—the longest anyone had remained in thirty years. When I left, the students petitioned for my retention—the first time they had done such a thing in fifteen years.

From 1936 until 1943 I taught at The Pennsylvania State College as an instructor and assistant professor. I was also varsity tennis coach from 1939 until 1943. The student paper *The Collegian* cited me as one of the eight best teachers in the college. In teaching polls, over 95% of my students put me in the highest possible category.

In 1943, Bennington College offered me its usual one-year contract. I went there, on leave from Penn State. My salary was increased each year as a major member of the faculty. (There are no ranks at Bennington.) In an article about Bennington in *Harper's Junior Bazaar,* the students were quoted as calling me "the best teacher they ever had."

The teaching situation at Bennington during the war was excellent. For the first time I saw what could be done when people like Kenneth Burke, Francis Fergusson, Erich Fromm, William Troy, and others worked intensively with students. I acted, often, as a "feeder" to Burke, a "breaker-inner" of material.

In 1946, I left Bennington to take a Guggenheim fellowship in creative writing. My first book *Open House* had had an excellent press, with extended reviews by Winters, Auden, Humphries, and others. But I was now working on some poems about my childhood and a sequence of longer poems. These appeared in 1948 in *The Lost Son and Other Poems,* shortly after I had come to Washington. The volume came out in England in 1949. The final sequence appeared in November 1951: *Praise to the End!* New poems of a more formal order are scheduled to appear in *The New Yorker, The Kenyon Review,* and in European magazines. The State Department is translating considerable work for its broadcasts and many poems have been translated into French by Bernard Citroen and others; into Italian by Henry Furst, etc.

The February issue of *Poetry: A Magazine of Verse* will be led by poems from the verse class at the University of Washington— the first time the magazine has done this with college work. There will also be an article on the teaching of verse.

Put succinctly, my situation is this: I have tried—and hard—to pursue a double career: teaching and writing. One complements the other. I am certain that I succeed most of the time as a teacher. (My last rating from the dean's office was 1.5%—which put me, I believe, in the upper 5%.) But I teach viscerally: I try to make up for ignorance by energy and enthusiasm. I do "know" a good bit about English poetry; I know it often by heart. It is part of my life. But there is much in philosophy and history and science which I wish to find out,—as a teacher and as a human being. In poetry, I have exploited the personal myth as far as I wish to at the present time. I want to make a greater use of the past. This means, for me, reading widely and deeply particularly in the Platonic tradition; in philosophers like Spinoza and Kant, Bradley and Bergson. I am not sure that I wish to take courses in these people. I wish to absorb them in my own way. I want to read—not write —at the present time. And I want the resources of big libraries like those at Columbia and New York Public. I am confident that I shall break into an entirely different style as a writer . . . and when this happens my teaching should be more balanced, more mature. As a teacher, I have taught what I learned as a writer. Any extension of my understanding, to judge from past experience, will be reflected in the classroom.

To Karl Shapiro[1]

May 23, 1952

Dear Karl: Here's this damned Thomas piece,[2] and I'm of a very divided mind about it: One minute I think it's a hot item that says things that should be said and effects a rough justice; another, it seems a damned impertinence to say such things in print about a contemporary. And of course I am v. fond of the little bugger.

So you call it, old chum. And I won't be sore if you say no. But I *don't* want to make changes—not any, except possibly to delete the sentence beginning "And there you have it, etc." on the grounds that it looks self-conscious and may be out of tone with the rest.

What I'd rather do—if you like the piece—is:

1) Have him clear it—and tell him I made that request.

2) Run it under the pseudonym I've indicated [3]—even if you want to say in the notes that the pseudonym is for Roethke, though I'd prefer to be completely anonymous. This may seem a little nutty, but you see the point: this is the vituperative or prose side speaking.

About the "snout" & "as if pigs could sing" references. These are not meant viciously, but make, as you'll see, a serious point: in the act of "wallowing," etc., deliberately he becomes purer in spirit,—or at least is trying to become purer in spirit. And in so doing he gives voice to the highest & lowest impulses, blah, blah, blah.

---

[1] Poet, critic, and professor of English at the University of Illinois; then editor of *Poetry*.

[2] "One Ring-tailed Roarer to Another," published in *Poetry* (December, 1952), is a review of Dylan Thomas' *In Country Sleep and Other Poems*. Reprinted in *On the Poet and His Craft*.

[3] Winterset Rothberg.

Forgive the explaining, which God knows isn't necessary with you & E.[4]

I'm on a Ford fellowship for next year. One idea was that you be approached to see whether you wanted to edit the mag.[5] from out here for a period and do some teaching. Were you ever approached by the Committee? The cozy boys never listen to my ideas,—of that you can be sure. Would you have been at all receptive to that notion? A private question, of course. (The dough would have been pretty good.)

All the best & love to E.
Ted

To KARL SHAPIRO

Edmonds, Washington
July 4, 1952

Dear Karl: Hot flash department:
A friend of mine, Harry Burns[1] (he appears, I guess, as a professor in one of the novels) was visiting Hemingway a while back, in Cuba. Was telling me E. H. showed him his poems—a combination, says he, of Eliot, Mother Goose & Hemingway.

It's occurred to me you might want to twist E. H.'s arm for some of these for the October number.[2] And I think he'd be likely to break down, since he published those early pieces in the magazine.

I don't have the address; could get it; but you can reach him probably via Wheelock[3] of Scribner's or maybe know it.

I'm not trying to be Mr. Nosey: just full of outgoing-ness.

Glad you liked Opening.[4]

Another matter for the business department: I have never sent

[4] Evalyn Shapiro.
[5] *Poetry* magazine.

---

[1] Member of the University of Washington English Department.

[2] A special fortieth-anniversary issue of *Poetry*.

[3] John Hall Wheelock.

[4] Roethke's poem "O, Thou Opening, O," contributed for the anniversary issue. *CP,* pp. 97–99.

that Hudgins girl [5] her check because she is in a looney-bin at present, in Pueblo, Colorado. My God, I've had the most heart-rending letter from her: Would-I-come-&-sign-her-out; the-doctors-would-listen-to-me, etc. They've slugged her, I have no doubt, with enough electric shock to kill six oxen. For why? She thinks in metaphor most of the time; therefore, of course, is "confused." Her relatives, or the institution, would just appropriate it.

Look at her stuff again, Karl. She's really good. Old Bill Wms. was genuinely cowed by it—and he's quite an egotist. And Wystan[6] was highly respectful.

Yrs. wordily,
Ted

To Richard Eberhart[1]

Edmonds, Washington
July 14, 1952

Dear Dick: I'm delighted—we all are—that you are seriously considering coming out here.

About a house with three bedrooms: it has just developed that Major Reid, from whom I leased a place this year, may not come back until next June. His wife was going to let me know today, or as soon after as possible.

This place has not three bedrooms but four, with a fireplace in the biggest. All are down stairs. Two bathrooms (one up, one down), a laundry; a utility room upstairs; big kitchen; and a huge front room with a fireplace. The house is set high on a hill, with a yard & woods behind it. One of the best views of the whole Sound I have seen—from any window, up or down or from the garage (two-car). Oil heat; construction of yellow brick and cedar.

Exactly what rent they might want I don't know. (I think they gave me a special break because I was alone.) But they are very fair people & I *know* they would ask less than what is usual for such a place.

[5] Elizabeth Hudgins, a former student of Roethke's.
[6] W. H. Auden.

[1] Poet, critic, and professor of English at Dartmouth College.

Frankly I've liked it better than any other place I've had. The people around (there are no close neighbors and you arrive at a dead-end road coming through a wooded area)—are very friendly but also mind their own business. Below about 75 or 100 feet (their roof is a good deal below the base of this house) lives an ex-general's wife and sister. Major Reid's father-in-law, Dr. Henry Burd, head of business administration, lives off to the left about 250 feet or 300. He's a very relaxed character; likes to sit around and have a drink on occasion.

Edmonds is about 16 miles from the University. It took me 25 minutes going in, usually. . . . This area is wonderful for kids because there are so many wooded areas, with pheasant, grouse, etc. No hunting allowed, of course. The grounds are pretty big: lots of trees & flowers.

If they decide this is available, I wouldn't hesitate to recommend it (and them) without reservation. I think you & yours would be very happy. It would be a kind of Northwestern year: I mean more Northwestern out here than in Seattle proper.

All this started, I guess, when you remarked on our trip from Yaddo to Boston that you might like to do some teaching again. To repeat, I certainly hope it does. The boys (the committee) put you No. 1 on the list; they particularly liked the fact you belong to no "school" or faction.

Enough of this gabble. As soon as I know for sure, I'll air-mail you.

What new poems? If you have copies, please send. I've done some in a more formal vein, coming out in *Atlantic, Partisan, Hudson.* Also some funny ones, Dirty Dinky, etc.[2]

> Love to Betty & best to yrself,
> Ted Roethke

Address me either care of the English Department or
> c/o Dr. Henry Burd
> Route 2, Box 2121
> Edmonds, Wash.

---

[2] Roethke enclosed the poem "Dinky" with this letter. *CP,* p. 114.

To Mrs. William Carlos Williams

Saginaw, Michigan
September 15, 1952

Dear Flossie: I've just heard, via Willis[1] and K. Burke, that Bill has been having a rough time. This is to hope he has been getting better fast. He must. He will.

If he's reading things, here's an item that may give him a laugh, may not.[2] My kids and some of my rowdy friends thought it v. funny; but Shapiro, Schwartz & the Princess[3] have rejected it with pious horror. Maybe it's too coarse; maybe money's a sacred subject, I don't know. . . . I send this also because once Bill urged me to do a piece on low-life in the twenties. This is all that's come out so far—the sole result of his exhortations, that is.

D. Thomas was out & cost me a pretty penny,—even a 30 buck traffic ticket—when somebody else was driving my heap in an effort to make a plane. I'm fond of him, but he does get a bit wearing when dames are around. But as one of the dames pointed out to me, "Dylan, you have to remember, is a child. . . ." From the lofty heights of adolescence, I make these observations.

No great news from my end to speak of. Someone wrote me I got two votes for the Nat'l Book Award; Moore got 3; she wins. Will be on a Ford Fellowship this year—am already on it, in fact. Hope I can see you both sometime during the year, all recovered & full of the usual beans.

Let me hear from one of you if it's at all convenient.

Much love,
Ted Roethke

[1] Leota Willis, a colleague and friend of Roethke's, now an advisor in the English Department, University of Washington.

[2] "Song for the Squeeze-Box"; later included in *Words for the Wind* (1958). *CP*, pp. 111–12.

[3] Karl Shapiro of *Poetry*; Delmore Schwartz of *Partisan Review*; Princess Marguerite Caetani of *Botteghe Oscure*.

To Babette Deutsch

Seattle, Washington
October 24, [1952]

Dear Babette: How nice to get your note. By now you should have a book,[1] since Doubleday said they'd send one a long time back. And, as I said, I hope the whole thing gives you a jolt, a bounce, a kick, a bang,—or whatever it is. Do let me know if you get, etc. As I said, I did some different things this summer, and one at least breaks through to something else, I think. I only wish I could read & work for about five years at this point, instead of having the hoorah & hullabaloo of teaching (as I try to teach, at any rate).

I've sub-let a biggish new house out in North Edmonds (four bedrooms); fireplace in my bedroom; in the living room—huge—looking out over the Sound. But oddly enough, it's lonely and I resent the 30 minutes drive each way. . . . Maybe, like old Willie,[2] I'll collapse into matrimony around 50. But there are no vivid prospects at the moment. "The parish of rich women" [3]—yeah, but to hell with them.

This time I don't even want to think about the damn book. It's done, and as good in that kind of thing as I can do, and I figure nobody else has dug into that particular vein—so that's that. I can't get "competitive" about it, or aggressive (I know you once thought I was, a bit, and I guess you were right). Forgive.

By the way, did you ever run across a prose piece in *Botteghe Oscure*, V, called "Last Class," p. 400—by Winterset Rothberg? That's me. It's had the damndest admirers—Eliot, Michaux,[4] Thomas, etc. Do look up. I promise you'll be amused.

Well, I wish you were whisking up the driveway to come to laugh & talk.

Love,

T.

---

1 *Praise to the End!*
2 William Butler Yeats.
3 From W. H. Auden's "In Memory of W. B. Yeats."
4 Henri Michaux, Belgian poet and painter.

Karl & family[5] are going to Europe in Jan. (maybe earlier) as you probably know.

Lousy as it is, this is the *longest* letter I've written in six months.

To John Malcolm Brinnin

Saginaw, Michigan
November 4, 1952

Dear John: I wrote out a long screed in answer to your letter of October 22, but have mislaid it.

Maybe it's just as well. The chief point is that I'm more interested, right now, in doing a really good show in December than in deciding about other engagements. However, why not say: pick up any possibilities *after* December 4 (following ten days) that are in the immediate area. I have long since decided that it's not worth while to open my trap for less than $100.00 *to me;* so maybe I'd be too hard to peddle. I take it that the 20% bit is not made on YMHA arrangements—the December 4 one, I mean.[1]

About that date: I'm taking my basic pattern from what I did at Reed College last spring—about forty or forty-five minutes reciting and palaver and gags *without* books and then some of my own things with books. I was loose, the kids reacted well, and they've already asked me back. But the chief thing that concerns me with your people is *what not to do* in a humorous way. I tend to get too rambunctious, start imitating contemporaries, etc. This, if people do not know you, I realize may be catastrophic. Maybe if you have a half hour the day before we could run over a few ideas in midtown somewhere. Understand: I'm not worried; I'm just trying to give the act some real polish.

Let's let the contract wait until I see you; arrange for any dates with a 20% bite understood, if any work out conveniently.

---

[5] Karl Shapiro.

[1] "My secretary at the [Young Men's Hebrew Association, New York] Poetry Center Elizabeth Reitell & I had begun an informal sort of lecture agency—mainly dealing with poets who hoped we would find engagements for them beyond commitments to the PC which we normally arranged" (John Malcolm Brinnin's note).

Needless to say, thanks very much for thinking of me in this matter.

Sincerely,

Ted

To Kenneth Burke

[*Saginaw, Michigan*]
November 5, 1952

Dear Kenneth:

. . . .

How come you never showed me any poems? Malcolm[1] wrote you were getting a book ready & he was trying to persuade you to leave out a lot of notes; that I should try to persuade you similarly. (This was quite a while back.) For whatever it may be worth to you: I'm agin elaborate notes, even when good. I don't like Moore's much & Empson's even less.[2] (By the way, I was told I got 2 votes on Nat'l Book Award; there were only five judges: Moore must have got three). . . .

I've done some poems on "dancing." One is in *Atlantic* for Nov.; one in *PR* (your favorite sheet), Sept.–Oct. . . .[3] The book[4] is still getting very fancy notices: Oct. *Harper's* & a recent *Hopkins Rev.* . . . A longish piece (of mine)[5] in Oct. *Poetry* had some ambiguities that would have interested you. At the end of a randy rant the lines occur

My fancy's white!
I am my faces,
Love.

And so on.

I'm to N. Y. in early December (Dec. 4) for a "single" or solo

1 Malcolm Cowley.

2 Refers to elaborate sections of notes appended to Marianne Moore's and William Empson's books of poetry.

3 "The Dance" and "The Partner," respectively. *CP*, pp. 105–6.

4 *Praise to the End!*

5 "O, Thou Opening, O." *CP*, pp. 97–99.

at YMHA. I've always hoped you'd catch my act some time. I'm much fancier than I used to be. Recite other people's poems without books, etc.

. . . .

Drop me a line. Several.

Ted

Love to mama & the young

To DYLAN THOMAS

Saginaw, Michigan
December 1, 1952

Dear Dylan: A guy in East Lansing, Michigan, showed me a copy of *The Listener,* with a comment by Martin Armstrong indicating you had read three poems of mine over the BBC. Naturally, I was pleased to hear this; and now the *Collected Poems* has come. Thank you very much. I am proud to have that book.

Not to be tiresome—but I am wondering whether it would be possible to get a copy of the recording made at the time. One is usually made, isn't it? If this is at all practicable, I'd be most grateful if you could put the proper wheels in motion to see that I get one, along with the date of the broadcast, which I need for the university files. Please ask whoever is responsible to send me a bill, for I am not trying to be a free-loader about this.

It is not vulgar or idle curiosity, or vanity, that prompts this request. I want very much to find out what you hear in those rhythms: I can be taught something by that, and maybe jogged into new effects later.

Karl Shapiro asked me for a piece on *In Country Sleep.* One afternoon I did a short up-boil: a prose-poem tribute in wild rhetoric which will either make you laugh or make you sore. I wanted K. S. to clear it with you first, but he said, in effect, Don't be naive. I did send the proof to John Brinnin, who thought there was nothing objectionable in it. I certainly hope it makes you laugh and pleases you, or else I never would have released it. At least it will be a change from the patty-cake Lowell and Jarrell play in print.

Here is the sequence about "dancing" [1] which you suggested I send on to you. Hope you like.

I curse myself because I write so slowly. A play idea keeps torturing me, but I can't get the thing going. I curse you for having got one done that is good. It isn't jealousy: exasperation. I envy you the BBC, and of course am really wistful about what you mean to your own people,—to say nothing of mine. (After rave reviews, hosannas, dancings in the street, *Praise to the End!* sold 550 copies. Me, I thought the book really did something new. Is it *too* far ahead or am I self-deceived?)

I hope we can poop around this spring, as we did in 1950. I'm tired of interruptions by jerks, well-meaning and/or pulchritudinous dames.

Break down and let me hear from. I do hope you like the poems.

Sincerely,
Ted

I wish I could make the long line roll the way you do.

To A. J. M. Smith

[New York, New York]
January 19, 1953

Dear Arthur: Items: 1) I got married—don't faint—on January 3 to Beatrice O'Connell of Winchester, Va., and N. Y. C. Auden was best man & Bogan the matron of honor (the only attendants except for her ma & pa & brother). She's v. pretty (26); Irish & German & no fool. You'll both like her, I know. I've known her for nearly ten years.

2) Auden has given us his place in Ischia until June 1 as a wedding present. We're sailing Feb. 24 for Naples.

3) Immediately before that our itinerary is as follows:
Week-end of 13–14–15 at Stanley Kunitz's in Lumberville, Pa.

a) & doing a reading Feb. 4 in New Hope, Pa.

b) on Tuesday, Feb. 17, am doing a pitch at Penna. State in the

evening. From there we're departing for Detroit & Saginaw from

---

[1] "Four for Sir John Davies." *CP*, pp. 105–7.

Altoona. I think John Brinnin or Eliz. Reitel has written Nye[1] or somebody asking whether Mich. State is interested in my electrifying presence. Feb. 19 or 20 are at least possibilities. Now don't think I'm twisting your arm about this because I ain't. I don't care a damn one way or the other,—except it would be a pleasant & painless way of getting to see you & Jeanie. . . . So don't feel embarrassed about this in any way; we're going to have too much to do as it is, etc., etc.

I think Brinnin or Reitel quoted a price. The rock-bottom is $150 and $200 if I have to give the agent a cut. This is about standard minimum for anybody any good, and my fellow bards in this dodge (even such characters as Viereck[2]) bitch if you work for less, so help me.

But I realize that if you wouldn't raise $150 for Thomas you might run into difficulty getting such a sum for T. Roethke.

[. . .] Twice I've given Arabel Porter & Victor Weybright of New Am. Library a sales pitch on how they ought to run a Canadian group of poems,[3] with you as ed., featuring Malcolm Lowry, P. K. Page, Patrick Anderson, etc. They said they've had it in mind. I'll prod her again. You'd get dough & line rates & big circulation 150,000—200,000.

Am doing a nutty show at Circle-on-the-Square Theatre (see enclosed ad). I go on the first part, just reciting. In the second part, there's night club songs, words & music by me, arranged by Ben Weber, with music by Pratt,[4] the Hobsons[5] & two hot trumpeters (names withheld because they're pro's); also a song "The Kitty-Cat Bird" done by Larry Pratt; a setting of "The Lady & the Bear" by Bernard Wolfman, which he does as a solo, with guitar. He's doing it Jan. 20 over WABS, and over TV on Jan. 22 on Channel 7, etc., etc.

[1] Russell B. Nye, professor of English, Michigan State University.
[2] Peter Viereck.
[3] In *New World Writing*.
[4] Larry Pratt, New York lawyer and musician.
[5] Wilder and Verna Hobson. He was a well-known music critic and musician, also movie critic for *Newsweek*.

Send me back this *Times* item, would you, it's the only one I have.

Let me hear from you. The phone is Butterfield 8-4000, Ext. 725 if you feel impelled to call.

Love,
Ted

To John Ciardi

[New York, New York]
February 2, 1953

Dear John: The lingo book I cherish, complete with inscription.[1] I'm reading it with a certain nostalgia: some of the terms I grew up with are now marked "rare." But I'm happy to know I could make some additions and modifications. Strictly speaking a "typewriter" is a mounted machine-gun, usually stuck in the rumble seat of a roadster, etc.

Yes, I do know one hell of a gifted poet under 30, and I'm prepared to go to great lengths in her behalf if your committee wants personal testimony. Her name is Elizabeth Hudgins, or as she sometimes signs it, Louise Hudgins Larson. (The "Larson" is some sort of legal fiction, I guess.) She led *Poetry* in February, 1952 with three poems which won their young poet's prize (Bess Hokin, I think it's called).

She has been having a very tough time in a personal way, and has since she's been born. (Her mother divorced her father *before* she was born; she was thoroughly exploited by some unscrupulous people for whom she worked while going to college in Seattle—a thing I found out after she'd left, etc., etc.)

Right now she is in a hospital in Pueblo, Colorado, but I think should be out soon.

Look up her three poems. Do. And I have some others. Shapiro wants more and so does *New World Writing.* . . . When I first showed her work to W. C. Williams he said, "Hell she can write better than I can." Granted W. C. W. is given to wild enthusiasms,

---

[1] *Dictionary of American Underworld Lingo*, comp. and ed. by Hyman E. Goldin, Frank O'Leary, and Morris Lipsius (1950). The book was published by Twayne Publishers, for whom Ciardi was working at the time.

off-the-record he is tough, usually. . . . And her stuff cowed old Wystan even.

My point is that such an award as the Lowell thing was designed just for such a kid. She needs to rest at a place like Yaddo and then get further away from her idiotic boy-friend and her shiftless (it would seem) family.

More anon on this subject.

Did I tell you Doubleday is doing a *Poems 1933–1953* next year? *Prays to the Tail!* (as Burke calls it) went out of stock in a month, it seems. But I don't rival Robt. Frost in sales as yet.

It was very good to hear from you, buster—a great relief from some of the elaborate frauds and fags I've encountered recently. It's fine to know more Ciardi's are on the way. Best to Blondie & yrself.

Hello to Morrison and Levin's when you see them.[2]

Ted

To Arabel Porter[1]

Forio d'Ischia, Italy
May 1, 1953

Dear Arabel: Thanks for the copies of the poems and the nice letter. I'm glad you had fun in the South.

Details:

(1) I am asking Barbara Zimmerman of Doubleday to get in touch with you about the publication date of *The Waking: Poems 1933–53*. I'm asking her to postpone publication until a time acceptable to you—which I would take to be some time in late October or early November. Her letter to me says, "If you (Roethke) still feel you'd prefer to put the book off until November (to appear after the *New Writing*),[2] I'm sure it can be done. . . . But

---

[2] Theodore Morrison; Harry Levin, critic and professor at Harvard.

[1] On the editorial staff of the New American Library, publishers.

[2] Refers to the selection "Five American Poets," edited by and including poems by Roethke, published in *New World Writing, Fourth Mentor Selection* (1953).

don't be too tough with us, for we want to catch the Christmas trade!"

I'd forgotten about any possible conflict in talking to Sargent (then my editor) just before I left—though I *had* ruled out Spring as a date, earlier, because of the *New World Writing* poems. Then I wrote him, later, but got no answer.

(2) I take it that you want to run the poems from our group of first choices, 4 Kunitz, 2 Roethke, 3 Garrigue, 1 Waggoner, 3 Kallmann.[3] Have these characters been informed about this? (I didn't want to say anything until it was finally official.) Please lemme know.

(3) Do you *really* want that short introduction? Somehow I got the feeling that reasons for not having a spiel in front might have developed,—matter of being inconsistent with previous issues, possible howls from other bards or what-not. I *have* been thinking about it and scratching down ideas, but the fact I'm in the group myself seems to inhibit me. Understand: I'll do it, if you want. I'm just trying to be honest and, possibly, even gentlemanly, for a change.

Please speak out about this.

Thanks for the Burke item. He had sent it, maybe prompted by a mild twinge of conscience. But he does love me dearly [. . . .]

For me, the impact of Italy has been considerable: the horror and the glory. I hate the filth, and the poverty distresses me, but I rejoice in the sea and the sky, and the sun, for the beautiful in these people. Today, for instance, the beach was magnificent: the water quiet, blue-green; a pure curve of sand cut off by high rocks on each end, and sometimes no other bathers but us. A couple of children came by, and a man with a horse,—that was all.

Beatrice sends her best to you and John, as I do. And also to Victor and Helen.

We depart from here about the 25th of May, my 45th birthday, damn it. So let me hear from you before then, if possible.

Much love,
Theodore

[3] Stanley Kunitz, Jean Garrigue, David Wagoner, Chester Kallman.

I-love-me-item: Thomas (Dylan) wrote me that he thought those dancing pieces "wonderfully good." . . . Yes, yes, Theodore, I can hear you say.

To J. F. Powers[1]

Forio d'Ischia, Italy
May 4, 1953

Dear Jim: It was very pleasant seeing you and Buck,[2]—in fact, for me one of the really good things that happened in a hectic two months in New York.

I got married in January, as you've probably heard by now,— to that dark-haired girl, Beatrice O'Connell, you saw me come into the reading with. Auden gave us his place for the winter and spring for a wedding present, and we've been here since early March; are departing about May 25th for other points, including Ireland. This leads me to ask:

(1) Do you know of anyone in Ireland from whom I could rent a smallish house for a month or so during latter half of June and July, say? Or is an inn a better bet?

(2) Are there any towns or hotels you'd care to recommend that are quiet and not too expensive?

———————

These are boring questions, I know, and don't knock yourself out answering them. But I thought since you'd cased the place, you might have an idea or two. About all I know is what Diarmuid Russell[3] told me: that the government has a list of approved hotels; that it rains a lot.

It's western Ireland that I'm most interested in.

Oh yes, if there are any Irish writers of the non-sullen and approachable variety that you think could endure my lardy charm, let me know.

———————

How are you? Well, I hope and the same by ma & the kids. Let me know about that, too.

[1] Short-story writer and novelist.
[2] Bucklin Moon.
[3] Well-known literary agent and editor.

I did some more (and better) readings later—one with a five-piece band behind me in which, so help me, I "sang" several songs, —settings of "children's" poems. This down at the Circle-in-the-Square Theatre. The management wanted a repeat, and the *N. Y. Times* reviewed the electrifying event in an off-hand way. You may have seen it, in David Dempsey's column.

What other triumphs? Doubleday is doing a semi-collected book *The Waking: Poems 1933–53*. I bullied a fantastic sum out of them for an advance, on the grounds that I was the hottest thing in "younger" American poesy, etc.

Italy has been rugged in some ways but pleasant. A magnificent beach here—and no tourists as yet.

If you write—and I hope you do—it better be air-mail, since we're leaving so soon. So invest 15¢ or 30¢ for old times' sake.

All best,
Ted Roethke

To Dylan Thomas

Rome, Italy
June 16, 1953

Dear Dylan: I was delighted immeasurably to get your note, and sorry that we couldn't get together in America: by the time you wrote, I (we,—how hard the plural comes!) were in Forio, Ischia in Wystan's nest, where we stayed until May 25. Since then we've been here or in Florence, and will go to Geneva, Paris, London, Ireland by slow stages, leaving for Geneva June 25. So I hope we can get together, in London or somewhere. (This is *not* fishing for an invitation, for I realize your household has children, etc., etc.)

But do let me know what you'll be up to in, say, early July, and maybe we can meet in London.

I'm touched you ask to see poems. Here are some, a sequence, of a more lyrical sort.[1] Hope they don't disappoint.

Did I tell you that Doubleday is going to bring out a semi-collected in the fall: *The Waking: Poems 1933–1953*. I've been brooding about an English edition: if you have any ideas, or guys

[1] "Words for the Wind." *CP*, pp. 123–26.

I should send the book to, let me know. Also: do you think the BBC would be interested in a pitch by me ever?

But don't fret about these matters unduly . . . I guess the English-publisher idea is the sensible one.

I hear the play[2] was a great success; and I must say the prose in *New World Writing III* [3] makes me jealous.

This is written before breakfast, and hence addled. Do let me know where you are, via the air-lanes.

Best to you and yours,
Ted

I took Oscar W.[4] to lunch when I was in N. Y. I must say he seemed quite sweet,—though his taste is still erratic, in my book, to my mind.

To Peter Viereck

Rome, Italy
June 21, 1953

Dear Peter: The books[1] came, and I was—and am—grateful; but I almost felt that I was taking them under false pretenses [. . . .]

"Hell, I'm not the guy to write about you: it takes one of those witty, hep characters who knows what's happening in the world, what has happened, and so on.

I *hate* writing prose: it kills me. A two-page piece has been hanging on my conscience for months. Believe me.

I *did* take up the cudgels, verbally, in your behalf at a gathering of the literarti (new word) just before I left New York. This was not so much about the poetry as about you as guy, phenomenon. I said you really cared about poetry, and were honest & specific about what you cared about: that any gaiety and gall was all to the good in these times, etc., etc. (Sounds very guarded, but it wasn't.)

---

[2] Undoubtedly *Under Milk Wood*.

[3] "Four Lost Souls," the last part of Thomas' unfinished novel, *Adventures in the Skin Trade*.

[4] Oscar Williams.

---

[1] Viereck's books *Terror and Decorum* (1948); *The First Morning* (1952); *Shame and Glory of the Intellectuals* (1952); *Conservatism Revisited* (1949).

In my advanced years I may hold forth on a few contemporaries. But not yet. I'd feel I wouldn't want to tell the young about things, anymore, in the classroom, if I wrote it all down. That's part of it, that, and plain incompetence.

You asked to see some copies of the bear poem.[2] So I have enclosed the sequence, "Four for Sir John Davies," and a villanelle,[3] which tail off *The Waking: Poems 1933–53*, out in Sept. '53.

In an odd way, I think you're responsible, for I am certain my unconscious was stirred by your linking my name with Yeats' in *The Atlantic* review.[4] Both consciously and unconsciously I set out to live up to your high praise. And I'm sure the muse, or whatever, helped me along.

I hoped they hit you hard. . . . Auden startled me by his enthusiasm for them; and Thomas, too.

All best, and apologies for being so slow.

> Sincerely,
> Ted Roethke

I can't seem to find the villanelle. But here's the Sir John Davies sequence, anyway. As you'll see, it goes back to the very plain style of the 16th century—Ralegh and Davies, himself, really not Willie Yeats.

To Dylan Thomas

Geneva, Switzerland
July 5, 1953

Dear Dylan: We stayed on in Rome later than we expected, and I just picked up your very welcome letter with the wonderful songs (of which I am jealous) yesterday.

We both think the idea of a trip to Ireland together absolutely splendid. Let's have only one precept: No fytinge except with

---

2 "The Dance," first poem of the sequence. *CP,* p. 105.

3 "The Waking." *CP,* p. 108.

4 Refers to Viereck's review of Roethke's *Praise to the End!* in *Atlantic Monthly* (January, 1952). See letter to Viereck, p. 170.

strangers. Do gather together a pile of cabbage; and I will, too. (I have waded through several piles the last six months.)

I'm sorry not to be in London when you were; but let's hope that can be effected, too, before we go back.

Now let's not get loused up on when and where. We'll be in Geneva about two more days and then are going to Paris, where we're trying to get a different passage. At present we have a 1st class on the *Ile de France*: couldn't get anything else. Address: American Express, Paris. By the time you are done with your Eistedfod—or a day or two later,—we *should* be taking off for London. But we may have to battle a bit longer about a return passage. Again, American Express, London is the best, I guess.

———————

My nameless wife was called Beatrice O'Connell and hence will be happy to see the Oulde Sod. She sends her warmest greetings to you both.

———————

Yes, there is nothing that would please me more than to sit around bellowing at each other and basking in mutual esteem *and* learning a thing or two: in my case, many a thing.

Incidentally, the fourth piece in that sequence[1] I have changed, and enclose it, along with a couple of rowdy numbers you may or may not have seen, "Song for the Squeeze-Box" and "Dinky," [2] hardly to be confused with The Divine Comedy, needless to say.

All best to you and yours from us both,
Ted

To Princess Marguerite Caetani

London, England
August 2, 1953

Dear Lady: I'm so sorry to hear you are in bed, and hope by now everything is all right. Do take care.

Thomas went back to Wales. He wanted us to stop off there on the way to Ireland, but the time is too short now, to attempt a trip. (I refuse to fly.)

[1] "The Vigil." *CP*, p. 107.
[2] *CP*, pp. 111–12, 114.

I also wrote Hemingway care the Biarritz P.O. But it may never have reached him. I gave him your Paris address.

The broadcast[1] has been recorded, but no time set as yet. The technical people professed to be mightily pleased, but I thought my voice sounded too blasty. This can be changed, I'm told.

John Hayward we met at a largish tea-party given by Edith Sitwell, who more or less plunked us down by him. He was cordial and witty: suggested we ring him up the next time we came to London. I did not mention his room-mate[2] in any way. Also present: Waley,[3] John Lehmann, Bonamy Dobrée,[4] Osbert,[5] Cecil Beaton[6] and various characters in feathers, tweed, silk, cotton. Earlier, E. S. had Thomas & wife, Beatrice & me, an agent named Hyam & wife & a cousin to lunch. This was fun, with stories about Hollywood, etc.: the lady with a pet canary that had learned to smoke reefers, etc.

And so on.

> Much love from us both.
> Ted
> Really much, queenie.

To T. S. Eliot

Saginaw, Michigan
August 25, 1953

My dear Sir: Thank you for your recent letter.

I have asked Doubleday & Co., Inc. to send you a copy of *The Waking: Poems 1933–53* by air express. Please understand that I do not cherish the jacket, which is inept and inaccurate.

I have always hoped that there might be an occasion for you to read at least the sequence of longer poems; and, more recently, I have come to include the more formal pieces at the end of the book.

[1] "An American Poet Introduces Himself and His Poems," made for the BBC. The text is printed in *On the Poet and His Craft.*
[2] T. S. Eliot.
[3] Arthur Waley.
[4] English scholar and critic.
[5] Sir Osbert Sitwell.
[6] Designer, photographer, essayist.

My only address after next week is Department of English, University of Washington, Seattle 5, Washington.

Permit me to extend every good wish for the new play.[1]

Yours truly,
Theodore Roethke

To Kenneth Burke

Seattle, Washington
September 10, 1953

Dear Pa: Heilman says you and he have been corresponding about once a week. And me you don't ever write saying happy marriage, I say ruefully.

Europe was fine. I lolled and smirked in fantastic waves and seas of appreciation "the best poet in America,"—La Princessa Marguerite Caetani di Bassiano of *Botteghe Oscure*; "the best younger poet in America" Dylan Thomas and Edith Sitwell; "these are great poems" (of the last ones) W. H. Auden—and so on. But my fat head was unturned: I went steadily through the restaurants and country houses (one) only to arrive home with a blood-pressure of 205–210 and landsickness. The latter has disappeared. But I still feel woozy from these wonder-drugs used to bring down the blood-pressure. And for the first time a wee bit concerned at the collapsing physical mechanism.

I asked Doubleday to send you a free book,[1] and by now you must have it. . . . I hope, of course, you are re-smitten by Theodore. In fact, this low scheme has occurred to me: Why don't you bring your vegetal piece up to date and publish it as a small monograph with one of the University Presses, say the Indiana? Or, what the hell, I'm a generous man, add [. . .] Moore and Dr. Bill Wms. A splendid scheme, Pop, a splendid scheme that will add new lustre to your Roethke Appreciation Club membership.

Marriage finds us in a motel trying to haggle a builder into selling a house at a reasonable figure, eating humble fare like hot dogs and hamburgs. Last winter and in Europe I was splen-

[1] *The Confidential Clerk.*

[1] *The Waking.*

didly solvent, thanks to your Ford fellowship and good old Doubleday, who plunked down 2 G's for the book of poems, so help me.
But now, no. But Mrs. Theodore has gone to work teaching art
& French in the Bellevue High School; so we should do better in
a few months.

If you want, I can send you copies, eventually, of a new, more
lyrical sequence called "Words for the Wind," much admired by
such diverse characters as Horace Gregory, Croce's daughter,[2] the
char-woman at the Hotel Berners, Stephen Spender. Also a broadcast I did for the B.B.C. 25 min. "An Am. Poet Introduces Himself & His Poetry." ("really wonderful, you know," etc.)

End of I-love-me items.

Do write. Love to ma & kids & yrself.

Shamelessly,
Theodore

(Actually, I'm a bit nervous. I've done little in the last four
months. But it is a beautiful book, don't you think?)

To Stanley Kunitz

Seattle, Washington
October 8, 1953

Dear Stanley: To say, hastily, thanks for the warm words and the
poems, which I have had duplicated, already, but haven't had time
to read properly.

I am "teaching" you like mad, in the appreciation course, and,
as always, the class (a small but very good one) is really sent. One
girl who had been in the Air Force in England said, "Why is a
poet like Spender so well known, when here is a poet so much
better and we've never heard of him before?" Etc., etc. But they
really care: that old gasp comes on the best ones.

About Ford Foundation: The best way in, as far as I know, is
via an institution. Have New School propose you. Then, once you
are selected from there, people can write. I'll be only too happy to,
of course.

[2] Elena Craveri.

However, I've just heard that Delmore Schwartz pulled off some fancy deal with them directly: for *three* years.

About *The Waking.* Why *not* review it somewhere, if you feel inclined? Who knows the pieces better? What about *Commentary* or *The Nation?* (I only mentioned Thomas to Lisa[1] incidentally, thinking he might like to work off a few aggressions on me, for a change.)

Yeah, Stanley, to be honest, it does seem a hell of a book: it startles me, looking at it. But I'm anything but pleased with myself. I did nothing all summer—and only these enclosed in Italy.[2] Maybe they're enough. Let's hope so.

We're living in a rented cottage-like place on Lake Washington in Bellevue, where Beatrice teaches art & French in the high school. (She's v. good, I'm sure, and works like hell.) But with only one car we're loused up. I get up to take her to school, then come back, sleep a while & go to classes myself.

Currently, we're plagued by the same thing we encountered at Ischia: fleas. They're in the damned grass or wood, outside. The bites make big ($\frac{1}{2}$ inch) red welts. Sounds comic; but ain't.

It's late & I'm pooped.

All best to Eleanor & the little one. And yrself.
Love,
Ted

Jesus,—did you see the blunder on my poem in *N. W. IV?* The world (instead of "the word") outleaps the world, and light is all? And I corrected it in the proof very clearly.[3]

---

[1] Lisa Dyer, a former Bennington student, was an editorial assistant on the *Hudson Review.* Roethke's reference to "aggressions" seems to suggest that Thomas might like to review *The Waking*—possibly for *Hudson Review*— as a kind of reply to Roethke's extravagant piece, "One Ring-tailed Roarer to Another," in *Poetry* (December, 1952), which is a review of Thomas' *In Country Sleep.*

[2] Probably "Words for the Wind." *CP,* pp. 123–26.

[3] Reference is to "The Vigil," the last of the "Four for Sir John Davies" sequence. *CP,* p. 107.

1954-59

January 7, 1954

Dear Mr. Ransom: Thanks so much for the note of October 4. I'm delighted you are using "Words for the Wind," of course.

But I was even more interested in those reactions of students. You might, if you felt inclined, some time trick them with this one—who did it, etc.

I'm *not* submitting it for editorial consideration. It's really an elegy about my Aunt Julia Roethke, who died shortly after Thomas did.

All best for the New Year.

Ted Roethke

THE STUMBLING[1]
(Julia Roethke d. Dec. 18, 1953)

I

Should every creature be as I have been,
There would be reason for essential sin;

---

[1] An early version of the poem later entitled "Elegy" and included in *Words for the Wind*. The dedication was also deleted. *CP*, p. 144.

I have myself an inner shelf of woe
That God himself can scarcely bear.

II
Each day the season brings the fond escheat;
You were, too, lonely for another fate;
I have myself an inner shelf of woe
That God himself can scarcely bear to bare.

III
Each fall[s] by seasons to a separate fate:
Man unto man you sheer heaven's gate;
I have myself an inner shelf of woe
That Christ, securely bound, could bear.

IV
Thus I; and should these reasons fly apart,
I know myself, my seasons, and I KNOW:
I have myself one crumbling skin to show;
God could believe I am here to fear.

V
What she survived I shall believe: the Heat,
Scars, Tempests, Floods, the Motion of Man's Fate;
I have myself an inner shelf of woe
That God that God leans down his heart to hear.

To WILLIAM WERNER[1]

Bellevue, Washington
February 2, 1954

Dear Bill: I was terribly touched to get your letter. And I find it characteristic, if you don't mind my being a little sentimental, that you should write as soon as you hear that there are troubles.

I was in hospital, as the limeys say, only 10 days: a mild hypertension, they call it, which is harder on my friends than anything else. When I got off the boat, I had a blood-pressure of 205, but now it's way down to 130–140. And my liver, kidneys, heart are all undamaged, I learn after a lot of fancy testing.

The book[2] has been getting fancy notices—or nothing at all. But

[1] Professor of American Literature at Pennsylvania State College.
[2] *The Waking.*

I shan't collect any rubber medals. At long last, I don't much care—well, not nearly so much, at any rate, for that kind of recognition.

Did a broadcast for the B.B.C. last summer—25 min. They claimed to be *enchaunted:* ran it twice: Sept. 30 & Oct. 1, but didn't print it in *The Listener.* (Thomas arranged this recording. We saw quite a lot of him in London, and it was his idea that we all—(Caitlin, Beatrice, he & I)—go to Ireland together. But in the end, the broadcasting took up too much time; he didn't get together enough dough, etc. . . . I was very fond of him, but I got disgusted with some of his antics anent his death. . . . Spender cabled for 800 words before I even knew he was dead; and I scratched out something one afternoon. I hear it was in *Encounter,*[3] but have not seen it. I thought Cyril Connolly's (sp.?) piece was v. good & I don't care for him usually.

———

Enough gabble. Hope it's well by you & Kitty. I did a long malediction against McCarthy[4] in which you are mentioned (a section lapses into garbled Platt-Deutsch). . . . But the tone is wrong: too shrill in spots & sometimes mawkish. Spender wanted invective, (on any subject) but his solicitor said the piece was libellous under English law.

All best,
Ted

To Princess Marguerite Caetani

Bellevue, Washington
March 10, 1954

Dear Marguerite: You may curse me for this, but I have turned against that poem "The Stumbling" [1] in its present form. I just don't think it advisable to print it. That shelf image seems wrong, somehow. It does have rhythmical drive and power, I suppose; but it seems the kind of poem that should be kept from the general public for a time.

[3] In January, 1954, issue; reprinted in *On the Poet and His Craft.*
[4] Unpublished poem called "Malediction."

———

[1] See letter to John Crowe Ransom, January 7, 1954.

Please understand! (I know I was trumpeting about it; but forgive me.)

On the other hand, that "Shimmer of Evil"[2] piece I think cuts the mustard—and (to change the stale metaphor) gets better as time goes on.

I might say your paragon of taste, *cortesia,* etc., Jackson M.[3] thinks likewise about "The Stumbling."

Me, I'm full of dolor and gloom about nearly all aspects of human existence: stomach flu, income tax, follies of the holidays, etc. Lonesome, sad, boring I am. I did manage to get to San Francisco State College for a "performance"—the opening of their new theatre, and even with a belly-ache, the audience was with the act all the way, so I'm told. (Also did a long tape on Station KPFA—half hour show at least.) About 300 kids, and I *was* loose and in control: most of the time no book at all. . . . Last week in Vancouver for two sessions: less funny but a touching kind of appreciation of the spoken word.

It was nice to see you in *Time,*—I just got another one for Beatrice,—even though I thought the article slip-shod and scarcely perceptive.

Such a stupid letter!—even worse than usual. But it's partly the weather, I think—the sun hardly ever gets out in these parts. (San Francisco and Berkeley were wonderfully warm & non-foggy the week I was there.)

But anyway, I send this with much love.
Hello to Raffredo, the Craveri's, the Tates.

T. R.

Do write.

I guess old Conrad A.[4] is going to win all the rubber medals this year.

----

[2] *CP,* p. 143.

[3] Jackson Mathews, translator, editor, and professor of Comparative Literature at the University of Washington.

[4] Conrad Aiken had won the National Book Award for his *Collected Poems* (1953); however, Roethke, not Aiken, won the Pulitzer Prize.

To Karl Shapiro

Edmonds, Washington
September 8, 1954

Dear Karl: Your letter of August 30 did not reach me right away because I have been living in Edmonds and not picking up my mail regularly.

I can come in October if *Poetry* wants to put up the dough: train fare on the Great Northern (with a roomette) plus $50 for expenses. This would probably run around $250 or $275 for a total. This may seem steep but as you know, I'd still lose money.

As to time: If you wanted a pitch on a Friday night, I could leave here on Wednesday afternoon and get in Friday afternoon, ready for Friday night or Saturday night. Or if you wanted it on a Monday night, I could travel to Chicago over the week-end, etc. But the mid-week dates aren't good for me.

As to kind of show: it could be a Mixed Grill with a warm-up on contemporaries & then Theodore; or Problems in Self-Love, or the Pure Roethke, undefiled. Maybe the first is more fun. I did a thing in S. F., which seemed to go over v. well, like that. Also in Vancouver, etc. I'd rather get at the tough college kids around Chicago (the City) than those tin-horn Aristotelean text-creepers. But maybe I'd like the latter, too, if I saw them. I certainly liked Olson (E.)[1] the one time I saw him.

This seems to give you the essential dope.

I hope I'm not too expensive. At first it seemed too far & too nutty an idea: but Heilman (the dept. head) likes the notion.

———————

Other items:

1) I was touched, really, by the wires about the rubber medal.[2] But it seemed idiotic to say thanks.

2) I may have a longish (about 100 line) poem later on.

We've leased Morris Graves'[3] house & the phone is not in yet. So wiring or phoning is difficult.

Love to Evalyn & Isabella.[4]

Ted

[1] Elder Olson.
[2] The Pulitzer Prize (1953), which Roethke received for *The Waking*.
[3] American painter.
[4] The poet Isabella Gardner, then on the *Poetry* staff.

To Princess Marguerite Caetani

Edmonds, Washington
March 9, 1955

Dearest Marguerite: I was much touched by your last letter and would have replied long ago, except for one event: my mother died, after an operation for cancer of the throat, some weeks ago. The event hit me very hard, and a great gloom is still in my mind. The world does not seem the same, somehow.

It's sweet of you to want pieces, but I have none. I have been poking away at a longish thing; but it will be some time before it's done. . . . You might be interested in this statement, which I relay shamelessly. Auden, when he was here, quoted his collaborator, Chester Kallman, to the effect that the sequence 'Words for the Wind" constituted "the finest love poems of our time." Said Auden, "I have great respect for Chester's judgment."

You ask about possible people for #15 & #16.[1] Jack Mathews and I went over some of James Wright's recent work, and agreed, together, on the enclosed three. So, if you want the authoritarian attitude—there it is, from two of us, no less! There is a minor roughness, or two, in these, but they have real quality, I,—we,—believe.

Also, I've seen some philosophical poems by Arnold Stein[2] which I quite liked. I asked him to re-type them & will send.

I'm sorry to be so gloomy.

Do write, anyway. *I* need cheering up, perhaps even more.

Love,
T. R.

Please say hello to Elena Craveri when you see her.

[1] Of *Botteghe Oscure*
[2] Critic and professor of English at the University of Washington.

To Dorothee Bowie[1]

Florence, Italy
November 24, 1955

Dear Dorothee: Thanks for the note, the check, the various forgeries, etc.

Here's some dough for mail forwarding. I haven't written out of negligence: just somehow the feeling I couldn't write anybody, even family, until *I Got-Something-Done,* after all the travelling.[2] So having sweated out two pieces,—exceedingly good, of course, —I take pen in hand. But in my next incarnation I'm going to take up something easy: baby-prodding, plain whoring, or some such. Instead of verse-making.

I'll write Miss G.[3] separately. I *may* have one book among my effects: the Novalis. The Untermeyer a kid was to take back, but apparently didn't.

The first class is tomorrow. There are only about 10 students eligible; so it won't be a mob I face.

Florence I—and we—like, as I may have said, though we're not being given the social rush we got in Rome or Madrid. Good thing, I guess.

We're on the top floor—seventh—right in the center of things. Someday I hope to find out whether I'm looking at the Pitti Palace, the Town Hall or whatever when I gaze from the terraces. It's "charming"—our nest, even centrally-heated, so they claim. (For this 30,000 lire extra a month)

I miss good old American efficiency—you gals & more of my colleagues than I'd admit; the A&P; American gin; my liver at 17, etc.

Later

Had my first class: about 40 or 45 showed up! This was con-

[1] Assistant to the chairman of the English Department, University of Washington.
[2] On a Fulbright grant in Florence. The Roethkes had traveled in Spain in the early fall of 1955, then gone by bus from Barcelona to Florence, with stops at LeLavendou, Marseilles, and Nice.
[3] Madeline Gilchrist, librarian at the English library at the University of Washington.

sidered remarkable, since an Englishman's course had none in one course the first day, and four in another. (Italians don't come around much when a course begins it seems.) It isn't expected that all 40 will stick around; there were some visitors, Americans, etc.

A batch of mail came today (26th). I was touched to get the testimonials from the students.

Best to Bob, Arnold, Stanley, Joe H., Porter, Jerry etc.[4]

Love,
Theodore

To Jackson and Marthiel Mathews[1]

Florence, Italy
December 14, 1955

Dear Jock-o & Marthiel: Here are some new poems[2] & hope you like. . . . Do let me know. *But please, for Jesus' sake, don't mention to Marguerite,*[3] that I'd sent them to you. I'm going to give her a slug of things pretty soon.

I guess I didn't write before because I felt I hadn't done enough work (guilt-before-Papa or Brother, it would seem).

The Christmas idea sounds grand, but the problem of dough still is with us, alas. If some fat check came in, maybe we could. In the meantime, don't let the possibility (not too strong) interfere with any other plans you might have. Certainly it would be wonderful to sit & mope & blab away and have some laughs. I (we) *have* missed you, individually, collectively, spontaneously, athletically, poetically, critically (end of adverbs).

I meet my class twice a week. So far attendance has been 45–17–25–15–17–18. The foreigners (there are usually 8 to 10 Irish, Eng-

---

[4] Robert B. Heilman, Arnold Stein, Stanley Kunitz (visiting poet), Joe Harrison, Porter Perrin, Leota Willis—Roethke's colleagues in the English Department at Washington.

[1] Editor, translator, and critic, then professor of Comparative Literature at the University of Washington. Mrs. Mathews is also an editor.

[2] Cannot identify.

[3] Princess Marguerite Caetani.

lish, Scotch) so help me, Germans, Americans, dig me gooder than the wops, I'm afraid. They *won't* talk back, sass you, or get into discussions. So I poop & fart away all by myself, mostly.

Liver Bulletin

1. One Dr. Gerbi, in N. Y., affirmed that said organ had gone up in size in September & I sh'd. drink only mild aperitifs & wine. This I did, for the most part.

2. His ex-colleague, Dr. John Fenwick in Florence said liver was not enlarged (as of Dec. 13, 1955); I sh'd. not drink wine but whisky or gin, diluted, and beer. So I return happily to my old ways, for the most part.

Blood-Pressure Bulletin

1. *Up. 162 over something.*

I'm sure you find these details fascinating. *Write.* Beatrice sends love, too.

Ted

Postscript:

. . . .

Florence is a frigging bore in a lot of ways.

Hope you like the poems.
All love,
T.

How was England? Did you see the Cardinal's room-mate? [4] Or his Eminence himself? [5]

Met any bright frog writers?

To A. J. M. Smith

Florence, Italy
January 14, 1956

Dear Arthur: Your letter of November 17 has just reached me here: for some reason there was a mix-up at Seattle.

---

[4] John Hayward.
[5] T. S. Eliot.

It is very nice to hear from you, however briefly. I'm here lecturing at the University of Florence, on a Fulbright, and won't be back until early September. Hope you and J. will still be around.

. . . .

Florence, as I expected, is something of a pain in the ass: a provincial town. (I applied for Rome—which also wanted me, it seems; but some gent here insisted—God only knows why.) My classes have been attended surprisingly well—sometimes as many as 40—an average of 20. But hell, I don't know Italian, and some of the poor dears are left out in the cold with my dazzle of verbalizing.

We have a nest, right in the center of town, top floor, central heating, two baths, two terraces—scarcely Italian at all. Belongs to a chi-chi character, one Baroness von Frauenberg, half Italian, half German & veddy easy to look at. . . . I've done some work here, but not enough. *The N. Yer* bought one of my Old Lady pieces[1] (100 lines) for a thumping sum. And dear old Stephen[2] printed a botched version of another sequence, "The Dying Man" —the fourth piece didn't get there on time; the proof came when we were in Spain, etc., etc.

We liked Spain, by the way. And the Spanish were most cordial: took us all over hell, wined, dined us—particularly a fine gent & his wife, Aurelio & Carmen Valls. He's in the Ministry of Information, a good poet; really cares about Am. poetry; educated in England; Franco's interpreter, of all things, among other things.

—————————————

My mother died in February—of cancer of the throat, after an operation. Or did I write you this? She had done a job at Christmas, pretending all was well. She was fond of you both; and of John Clark. It ain't fashionable, but I miss her.

Let me hear from you. Love to Jeannie.

All best,
Ted

. . . .

[1] "I'm Here," published in *New Yorker* (Dec. 15, 1956); later included in *Words for the Wind* as the second poem in the sequence "Meditations of an Old Woman." *CP*, pp. 161–64.

[2] Stephen Spender. The poems referred to appeared in *Encounter* (December, 1955). *CP*, pp. 153–56.

To Robert B. Heilman[1]

Florence, Italy
March 20, 1956

Dear Bob, I was delighted to get your letter, with its items of news [. . . .]

It happens that I was on the point of writing you on a professional matter:

Business

William and Mary College has asked me (for the second time) to be Phi Beta Kappa poet in Williamsburg on December 5, 1956. The pay: all expenses for me and wife, plus fifty bucks. I realize this comes at a hell of a time of the year, but since things like this have been arranged before, I thought I would ask. I still don't want to fly, and Beatrice probably would not go anyway, since she may be working half-time. If it all seems preposterous, unreasonable, or boring, please say so. I think I could pace things and arrange for someone to pinch-hit sufficient times so the customers would get their full due.

Personal Items

I think Beatrice wrote Ruth[2] about our adventures in Spain. In spite of the customary travel ailments, we had a wonderful time. The Spanish astonished us with their hospitality, particularly a guy (and his wife) named Aurelio Valls—who would be a fine Walker-Ames prospect, incidentally.

Florence, in some ways, has been non-wonderful, particularly this winter, when the heat went off, and the water froze during a siege of flu.

We seem to move (when I can be made to move) in a limited but fairly lively orbit of Americans and Americans married to Italians for the most part. [. . .] One of the nicest people around here is Mann's daughter, Elizabeth Borgese; and I've had a lot of fun going for walks with Peter Viereck, who is bright; has no

[1] Critic and chairman of the English Department, University of Washington.

[2] Mrs. Heilman.

delusions about what he is doing or has done; and is perceptive on people like Beddoes, Swinburne (the Vierecks live out in the country, where walking is possible). And the Jack Phillips, a Boston couple with six girls—sets of two by different marriages, have been jolly. . . . The feeding is quite splendid on occasion. For instance, the Phillips broke out with really good snails, squab—the works, since Beatrice had regaled them with chicken soup using a whole pressed chicken, tournedos, etc.

Speaking of feeding—the most cherished bit to come my way was a fruit cake the girls[3] sent. (I imagine Eleanor[4] baked it, since I doubt the admirable Dorothee would essay even a frozen Pillsbury biscuit.) Anyway, it was in beautiful shape and delicious. Fruit-cake is a thing the Italians simply don't do well, says our English secretary.

But for the most part I have been sweating away at verse—making, or putting together, notes for lectures. The dying-man sequence[5] is up to five pieces now, three of which were in *Encounter,* and four will be in *The Atlantic* in early summer. The editors have been startlingly receptive: "as fine as anything poetic we have seen in a long time," wrote Ted Weeks—and then sent me a check for a lousy hundred bucks. And Michael Straight took time off for a "not since Yeats" notey about a piece I don't like much. . . . And in England *The Times, London Mag., The New Statesman, Encounter* are running stuff, mostly that has appeared here already.

(I regale you with these loathsome items just to assure you I haven't changed.)

I can't claim, alas, any great burst of production: one hundred-line thing[6] which *The New Yorker* will run next winter, and four lyrics, one (enclosed) which is probably unprintable.[7] Love and death, the two themes I seem to be occupied with, I find are exhausting: you can't fool around, or just be "witty," once you are playing for keeps.

[3] Secretaries in the English Department at the University of Washington.

[4] Eleanor Hurka.

[5] *CP,* pp. 153–56.

[6] "I'm Here," the second of the "Meditations of an Old Woman." *CP,* pp. 161–64.

[7] Unable to identify this piece.

Teaching

Oddly enough, I have found the teaching no soft touch. During November and December the attendance, twice a week, averaged 21 people; during January, 14—considered very good, by European standards, even for a credit course—which mine isn't. But I kept trying to draw the Italians out: make them talk. I thought I was getting somewhere; but once right in the middle of the exam. period, during the flu-and-cold spell, only two people showed up. I got sore, knocked off classes for the duration of exams, and started over on a straight lecture basis: attendance has been good again.

Sometimes I think the fates brought me here for my own development: to see my contemporaries, and elders, in their true perspective. And some of the American biggies have dwindled a good deal in my sight. For instance, Hart Crane, whom I once thought had elements of greatness. Except for the early poems, he now seems hysterical, diffuse—a deficient language sense at work. Williams, for the most part, has become curiously thin, self-indulgent, unable to write a poem, most of the time, that is a coherent whole. (This last saddened me a good deal, since I'm really fond of Bill.) Etc. People who *have* held up are Bogan, Auden, and of course old Willie Yeats, whom I'm not lecturing on; and Tate, for instance, looks better all the time, as opposed to Winters, whose work is often dead, rhythmically, and so limited in range of subject-matter and feeling. . . . And this leaves out work by writers whose virtues are, as Auden would say, entirely imaginary. Make your own list.

End of high talk.

Next Moves

We go to Rome for the American Seminar (a captive audience) in April. Mizener[8] will be there, and that man Campbell[9] from Mississippi, also Rudolf Kirk.[10] Two lectures, two seminars a week. Marguerite Caetani is putting us up for the first two weeks

[8] Arthur Mizener, critic and biographer of F. Scott Fitzgerald.
[9] Harry M. Campbell, then professor of English at the University of Mississippi.
[10] Professor of English, Rutgers University.

—which should be a pleasant bit of free-loading. In May, to Austria for some lecture-readings.

Now what's all this about Minnesota's wooing you? Remember: you promised me, once, that if you left, you would let me know immediately of your decision. Of course we hope you don't go. I am deeply serious about this, for selfish and unselfish reasons.

I have heard not a word from Kunitz. . . . Our female friend —well, you know her as well as I do. That "groupy" pitch bores me.

Do let me know about that William and Mary date, since the man there has just written again.

Best love to you and yours,

To HOWARD MOSS[1]

Forio d'Ischia, Italia
June 19, 1956

Dear Howard: I've had the proof of "They Sing";[2] but I've been haunted lately by the possibility that I may be echoing someone in that last line—hell, I can't figure it out—maybe some bore like Wordsworth, or some obscure translation.

Anyway, I've lengthened the line out even more, into seven feet,—I think really better, and hope you and the others abide and agree with it. Let me know.

And here's the old lady, again, taking off like a big-assed bird.[3] If you don't love it, I'll weep.

Yrs.

The Weeper,
T. Roethke

P.S. Other proof around somewhere. Will send.

In the last part of "Third Meditation," she makes references,

---

[1] Poet, critic, and poetry editor of the *New Yorker*.

[2] "They Sing, They Sing," the fifth poem of "The Dying Man" sequence, was published in the *New Yorker* (Aug. 18, 1956), *CP*, p. 156. The line is "The immense, immeasurable emptiness of things."

[3] Refers to one or more of the poems in the sequence, "Meditations of an Old Woman," possibly "Her Becoming." However, the passages quoted later in this letter no longer appear in any of the poems. *CP*, pp. 157–73.

of course, to the bible: "My help is still in me"; and to old bore, Wordsworth, "Suffering may be permanent and obscure,"—of course, it's my mother talking; who went through the third grade, etc.

To Rolfe Humphries

Seattle, Washington
March 5, 1957

Dear Rolfe: Thanks for the notice of the new anthology and the notes.

With electrifying efficiency I am enclosing the entire mss. of a new volume, which is to be folded in to an English *Selected Poems*, along with *The Waking*, which Secker & Warburg is bringing out in the Fall.[1] Now the point is whether such practically simultaneous publication will bother you.[2] Hope not. As I remember, in one or two instances in the other volume, such a situation occurred.

Now if you want any of these, just let me know which ones & I'll have them copied for you here. Point is I need this set to go off to Italy shortly, since presumably Salvatore Rosati is doing the volume in translation. So I've enclosed an envelope to send the whole schmear back.

Of course I'd like to know how you felt about it as a book— whether it seems an integrated whole, has impact, etc. In an Am. ed. I'd put love poems first, then a few funny ones, then "Voices and Creatures," etc.) (Is that subtitle too fancy?)

Of the poems published before 1954,—ineligible, that is,—the light pieces and "Words for the Wind" are the only ones, I believe.

It's been a tough grind this year. Among other thing, Beatrice has been in Firland Sanitarium for the last six weeks with T.B. She's coming along very well, however; and even came home for a day last week. But it's not easy with complete bed-rest the first

---

[1] The book appeared as *Words for the Wind*.

[2] Roethke refers here to new poems which might be included in Humphries' anthology, *New Poems by American Poets Number 2* (1957), and which would also appear in the forthcoming English edition of *Words for the Wind* (1957).

six weeks, etc. If you feel inclined to send her a postcard or note, her address is

Firland Sanitarium
150th & 15th
Seattle, Washington

I tried to call you when we were in New York in August, but got no answer, twice, at the Newton number.

The "teaching" in Florence was tough: the students' English inadequate for my pitch, and a split audience—Italian kids (who gradually disappeared), and a group of ultra-sophisticates—writers, travelling scholars, etc. But the Am. Seminar[3] was really good: a picked bunch of kids, who said my "lessons" were the hardest & the best. Competition with Arthur Mizener, Campbell (from Miss.), etc. And the Austrians were v. generous, enthusiastic, hospitable. . . . For six weeks we were at Ischia—Wystan & Chester[4] were there. I worked hard, boozed & swam with the aforementioned & an Irish character name of Harry Craig. Then we went to Nice, to Paris & London, where I did a 15 min. broadcast for the limeys, which they ran Dec. 30 & New Year's day, ultimately.

Enough prattle. Hope you like the book.

All best,
Ted

TO LÉONIE ADAMS

Seattle, Washington
October 14, 1957

Dearest Léonie & (Bill): First one tiny irritation, one little irritation I must get off my chest.

[3] In May, 1956, after their stay in Florence, the Roethkes traveled to Austria, where he gave readings at Innsbruck and Vienna. Later in the month, they went to Rome; Roethke took part in the seminar at the American Academy. In June and for most of July, they were in Ischia; then followed the visits to several cities mentioned in the letter. They docked in New York on August 22.

[4] W. H. Auden and Chester Kallman.

I was a bit cross with you, and deservedly so (I thought for a time) when I said in that bistro something about "The buds now stretch into the light," being one of the finest poems you ever wrote,[1] and *you,* at least for a split second or so—or longer—took my clumsy teasing seriously. For I remember saying, "Yes, I agree with you absolutely," to your sharp rebuke, "That only you could write your poems."

Enough of that.

But you should have been a mouse in the wall when I took off about you & Louise, before a French Institute (only high school level, alas)—but for one hour we rocked & rolled until even I was jabbering French. Let me tell you there are about 30 characters who know, now, about Mees Bogán and Mees Addóoms until eternity breaks.

For I got hot, baby, I got hot: even you, old cynic, would have dropped a briney tear about it all; and regretted all the mean (and deserved, usually) things you ever said about me.

Just twice this year have I broken loose that way: then, and at a do up at Lewis Jones' old stamping ground, Reed College, last May. That time I gave them mixed grill without a book from Wystan, Louise, Rolfe, Janet Lewis, your "It was my life, and so I said,

> And I did well forsaking it,
> To go as quickly as the dead,

that hurry one, and two others, as I remember. And some Hardy, old Frost, etc. Then I stopped for a break, drank a cup of coffee & went into my own tiny triumphs.

Enough of sloshing egomania. Write me one of those squiggly letters with news—or, better yet, write on the typewriter so I can read it. Tell me the news. I shan't be in town till Christmas, when I'm going to do a thing with Rolfe & bully Doubleday into an enormous advance of some kind. (I hope.) My God, I have to

[1] Roethke refers to an early poem of his bearing heavy influences of Miss Adams' verse. See also his essay "How to Write Like Somebody Else," *Yale Review* (March, 1959). Reprinted in *On the Poet and His Craft.*

we've had nothing but bills, what with buying a new house,[2] with Beatrice long in the hospital, etc.

Love to you both
Ted Roethke

Who's the one to vote for on the poetry medal?
Louise
You
Cal Lowell
Rolfe?
Hope no old guy gets it.   T.

To Alain Bosquet[1]

Seattle, Washington
October 24, 1957

My dear Alain Bosquet, I am honoured to know that you have been re-reading the poems and have translated three further pieces. I'll be delighted to see them in print.

And I'm happy indeed to be included in the group of poets to be published by Seghers, and would be glad to receive any of the works of the people you quoted, in case they exist in French or in English. Please let me know of any charges which you might incur, personally, in such matters.

As to poets in Spanish, the three younger men who interested me most were Dionysius Ridreujo (sp.?), Aurelio Valls, and Lorca's great friend, Rosales or Rojes—a great hulk of a man who could drink brandy like tapwater and was wonderful singing gypsy ballads. Valls is now first secretary of the Spanish Embassy in London; Ridreujo was in jail (put there by Franco) but must be out by now.

You ask about new poems. I had already written my English publisher, Secker & Warburg, to send you the new comprehensive English edition that is coming out in early November, with the title *Words for the Wind*. This volume includes *The Waking,*

---

[2] In the spring of 1957 the Roethkes bought the house at 3802 East John Street, in which they lived until the poet's death in August, 1963.

---

[1] French poet, critic, translator, and editor.

which I believe you have in your library, as well as an entirely new volume—including about twenty love poems; some poems of flight and terror; a sequence dedicated to Yeats called "The Dying Man"; a sequence of longer poems entitled "Meditations of an Old Woman." It is these last—in addition to some of the rougher love poems—that I hope will interest you most. "Third Meditation" contains a soliloquy beginning "What is it to be a woman? ——" that should interest the French, I think. Also the poem "The Sensualists" and "I Knew a Woman" are the ones I'd most like to see you do next—if you would be so kind.

But in all this I shall be happy to have your advice and guidance. I do hope the total effect of the new work will be strong—will hit you where you live, as we Americans say.

> In the meantime, my best regards.
> Yours faithfully,
> Theodore Roethke

To Lillian Hellman[1]

[*circa December, 1957*]

Dearest Lillian: Grand to hear from you, and nice to have the suggestion about a play.

I've got not one but three plays that I've been taking notes on & writing down lines for, & casting situations for, etc. One, a farce or maybe a tragi-comedy (whatever that is); one a long-haired yammer play in blank verse that only English actors could do or an English audience endure. And what's the third, a play laid in a nut-house (out of my rich experiences of same).

But not one nickel advance would I ever take because that would be catastrophic in my case. When I get one done, or close to done, then I'll come to you, maestress (a new word, the feminine of *maestro*), and offer you 30% & not a nickel more for the final touches. I can see it all now, in lights:

THE VIRGIN
(A Period Piece)
Rothberg—Hellman Smash

[1] American dramatist and writer.

I'm serious. That's my title & my sub-title. You want in on this? It might be too puke-making for your austere attentions, lovey.

Did I told you the limeys made me their Christmas cherce? The *book*. Poetry Book Society over there, that is. I probably did. It's my one Tiny Triumph of this year. On the strength of this, old Doubleday & Co., Inc., want to bring out a *Collected Verse* in the fall of '58.

I'll probably take on a lectureship at the Univ. of Michigan for second semester and let things cool off here. Maybe you should come out to Dee-troit and we could pub-crawl, etc. . . . But I'll probably be in N. Y. C. before then, in some form or shape. . . . I do want to do some plays, but don't want to talk them away.

Love,
Ted

To John Holmes[1]

Seattle, Washington
April 7, 1958

Dear John: This is at once a word of greeting and a cry for help.

The greetings carry the hope that you and yours are well, and that you are productive. (I read some of your poems in class— those in the Auden anthology, and they went over very well.)

The cry for help is this: my act in verse form is getting rusty. I mostly work things on a line-basis: studying four-foot, five-foot, three-foot, etc. Then other gimmicks like imitating people. (Humphries & Adams are very good in this respect). Writing a passage in prose & then doing it in verse, etc.

What do you do? Have you any special gimmicks that seem to get results? Have you any old exams or mimeographed material you could send me? I'd be very grateful.

You might even, I say slyly, want to write me one of your famous long gabby letters about what you do and later turn it into an article.

Sometimes, some of the simplest and dumbest devices get startling results, What is poetry? for instance. Tell me what you do in your summer workshops, for instance.

---

[1] Poet, critic, and professor of English at Tufts University.

I'm very serious in all this and hope I'm not being a bore. And I ask you humbly, as my oldest poetic friend, or poet I knew first, and hope you will feel inclined and have the time for an answer.

Personal: It's been a rough year, what with crawling in and out of hospitals, etc. Professionally, it's been all right. The English edition was the Christmas Choice of the Poetry Book Society, and has been getting, on whole, fantastically generous reviews. Exception: The Times Lit. Sup. which was an example of English knifemanship.

I had hoped I might see you, since I was scheduled to read at Harvard, but the doctors advised cancelling the whole tour. Was going to Loyola, Harvard, YMHA & Walker Art Gallery in Minneapolis.

Doubleday is bringing out a Collected Verse in the fall. I'll see you get one, and hope you might want to hold forth in a large way on it. . . . Ach, hell, that isn't necessary. Nobody, damn it, has ever worked out those long poems, Praise to the End! But that would take an article, not a review.

But all this doesn't make me dance in the streets. I've written nothing in three months. And my ego is a lowly worm.

Hope yours is otherwise.

The best,

Ted

To James Wright[1]

Seattle, Washington

June 3, 1958

Dear Jim: I had Beatrice mail you off a copy of *Words for the Wind* (I got a new batch), and I hope by now it has reached you, and that you like the whole thing as a book, mightily.

I'm in the clink (hospital) again, as you may have heard. It's a neurosis and hell to break, but the doctor thinks it can be broken, once and for all, but it's going to be a long and very expensive

---

[1] Poet and former student of Roethke's at the University of Washington.

process. Just where the dough is going to come from I don't know.

Oddly enough, I'm writing some, but not much. The great Stein[2] liked only one piece out of three. They were all short . . . so don't tell me about the sixty poems you've done since I heard from you last.

Been reading Graves and Stevens[3] lately, and damned if I don't think both are over-rated. I get so tired of Stevens' doodling with a subject-matter—the same subject-matter. And Graves, while at least he's specific, is usually *thin,* I think.

Find I like reading history, particularly Roman history: today did Sol Katz's book[4] and some Seutonius (sp.?) in translation.

Well, write me a jolly better when you have time.

Best to Libby, Allen, O'Connor,[5] and all the rest.

Love,

Ted

I noticed you were at the do at Wayne. Congratulations.

To Marianne Moore

Seattle, Washington
July 26, 1958

Dear Marianne Moore: Let me be, for once, unabashed:

When I got your letter I wept, not once but several times. (I'm in "deep therapy"—see the doctor six times a week, and really scraping bedrock; so perhaps I weep easy.) But anyway, I had always thought you thought me a lump, a nothing. To realize the poem[1] hit you, well, it shook me up, as the boys say. Alas, I'm afraid there are some (perhaps many) in the book you *won't* like

---

2 Arnold Stein.

3 Robert Graves and Wallace Stevens.

4 Solomon Katz, *The Decline of Rome and the Rise of Mediaeval Europe* (1955).

5 Allen Tate and William Van O'Connor. Wright was teaching at the University of Minnesota, where they were on the faculty.

---

1 "Her Becoming" (part 3 of "Meditations of an Old Woman"), published in *Botteghe Oscure* (Spring, 1958). *CP,* pp. 165–67.

—coarse, sensual pieces, and the Praise to the End! sequence; but maybe not. I hope a totality, an evolution, is apparent.

You will indeed see me in October; in fact, we want very much that you stay with us. We have a big old house over-looking the lake, rather sparsely furnished, but Ruth Witt-Diamant[2] says you would love it. (This is not just a recent idea, you see.) My wife is seventeen years younger; Wystan is very fond of her, etc., etc. Do say yes. There wouldn't be any elaborate entertaining because the doctors keep us too poor; but I daresay you're not interested in that, anyway.

You're a dear to say "Be well." I *am*, at long last, getting to the causes of the damned neurosis with someone who is careful and whom I respect. But what *work* it is, and what an expense.

Forgive the personal details.

Yes, I suppose I was referring to desperation when I wrote *The Renewal*.[3] Certainly I was in a desperate state.

Not to over-do things, but here's one I just wrote this week;[4] and I hope you think it has the real finality.

What else can I say but—
Love,
T. R.

To Henry Rago[1]

Seattle, Washington
August 6, 1958

Dear Mr. Rago: It has been on my mind for some time to congratulate you on your poem on light[2] that appeared in *Poetry*. It is very beautiful.

Recently, when in the hospital, I read through a whole year's issue[s] of the magazine. Your piece and Nemerov's narrative about

---

[2] Professor of English and founder and Director of the Poetry Center, San Francisco State College.

[3] *CP*, p. 135.

[4] "In a Dark Time." *CP*, p. 239.

---

[1] Poet and present editor of *Poetry* magazine.

[2] "The Knowledge of Light," published in *Poetry* (October, 1957).

poker-playing[3] stick in my mind best. I copied the whole thing out—yours, I mean—so help me.

Sincerely,
Theodore Roethke

To James Wright

Seattle, Washington
August 16, 1958

Dear Jim: Thanks for the letter and the staggering compliments.[1] You probably got carried away, out of generosity of mind. Anyway, the general word has not got around as yet. I *did* have some terrific fan letters, from, of all people, Marianne Moore believe it or not. . . . And congrats on the child. Many.

Now to you. I hope you won't take it amiss: I worry; I worry my can off, practically. And I've spent nearly the whole of three sessions with my doctor yacking about you. Apparently you're more of an emotional symbol to me than I realized: a combination of student-younger brother—something like that. (I even shed a tear or two.)

But the chief point now, as I see it, is you. I've been through all this before, through the wringer, bud, so please respect my advice. Once you become too hyper-active and lose too much sleep, you'll cross a threshold where chaos (and terror) ensues. And believe me, chum, it's always a chancey thing whether you get back or not. When I was 27, I thought I was made of rubber; I skipped, habitually, a night of sleep a week. I held three or four jobs, etc., etc. I was, probably, in better physical shape than you (the tennis, etc.) . . . And yet I just gave out, at last.

To come to the point: it would set my mind at rest if you would go to see some professional (yes, a psychiatrist) and tell him what's been going on in the past two weeks. If you aren't sleeping, there are drugs. Sure, it's expensive—20 bucks, anyway, but it may save you 5 or 10 thousand—his advice at the right time.

---

[3] Howard Nemerov's "A Day on the Big Branch," published in *Poetry* (November, 1957).

[1] On *Words for the Wind*.

Here's one last point: those closest to you don't usually recognize the "signs" of a manic, or any other phase.

Please do this, Jim, just as a kind of insurance. Don't be pigheaded or arrogant: don't think I'm trying to interfere in your life. I write this out of real concern and love.—Besides, I want you to stay intact so you can write that piece.[2]

Love,
and love to Lib!
Ted

To William Carlos Williams

Seattle, Washington
September 10, 1958

Dear Bill (and Flossie): I never said Thank-you for the edition of you letters.[1] Of course I have enjoyed them enormously, and I regret that I did not make more haste in sending on some of yours to me, for they would have enlivened the collection, added to it, I believe.

Shan't bore you with an account of my troubles, about which you no doubt have heard. Suffice to say I'm out—have been since June 26—and am going to teach in the Fall. I see a head-shrinker five times a week—was seeing him six—and already am so far in debt that it no longer matters. It's tough going, but I'll make it, I daresay. This guy is careful, conscientious, and bright.

Haven't done much work, but *some,* at least, and one piece really hot, a great lyric, I say modestly.

This is not blarney: one reason I don't write oftener is that you're such a father-figure to me (God knows, I have others: Burke, even Heilman) I'm afraid I'll slobber over or bawl you out for not mentioning *me* in some connection or other, in general be silly or unseemly. So please understand.

I took your advice about making my old lady less lit'ry. (See enclosed.)[2] And I hope you get a boot out of the whole sequence of

2 A piece on Roethke's poetry.

---

1 *The Selected Letters of William Carlos Williams,* ed. by John C. Thirlwall (1957).
2 Evidently encloses some portion of the sequence, "Meditations of an Old Woman." *CP,* pp. 157–73.

five, which ends up the *Collected* (yeah, I'm that old—50), coming out this Fall. Doubleday will send you one.

In England I got either raves or very strong reviews (about 80%), or almost complete rejection. I'd rather have it this way. Was the Christmas Choice of the Poetry Book Society (833 copies); so Secker & Warburg did not lose money on me, at least.

It was nice to see your puss in *Newsweek* and the *Times* looking so benign and distinguished.

The only literary news around here is that Marianne Moore is coming October 10 and Babette Deutsch the 20th. We asked M² to stay with us, but she'd rather follow the book & stay at the Men's Dormitory (Good God). However, she's on a very tight schedule, and I can see her point. . . . She's written me some v. sweet and startlingly enthusiastic letters about recent work.

Had some scraps of news of you & F. from my ex-student, John Pearce.

Love to you both. Do write when you feel like it.

Ted

And Beatrice joins me in this last.
P.S. Do you have Jay Laughlin's³ private address? I did, but lost my address book. He's been v. nice, and I wanted to send him a volume.

To Princess Marguerite Caetani

November 7, 1958

Dearest Marguerite: Don't think me an oaf. I did get your sweet letter with the checks and thank you very much. And also the second one with the check from your sister. I'm now going through a great moral struggle as to whether I should accept this last. Beatrice thinks I shouldn't, but my doctor says, "Yes. It was given to you for the poetry you have written and will write." Whatever I do, I certainly am touched.

Now let me tell you an extraordinary thing. In the verse appreciation class we have been ranging around following associations and somehow René Char's name came up. I talked about

³ James Laughlin of New Directions.

him briefly as a poet and told one story that I knew to be true about his heroism. Then the next day in my session with the doctor I began relating this and suddenly without my seeming to understand it a great flood of emotion burst loose. I kept talking about him and his poetry and quite literally weeping, in a sense tears of joy, during the whole hour. I said to the doctor, "I suddenly realize that René Char is an older brother symbol for me." I am always looking for a father, it would seem, but this is the first time I realized that emotionally I've always wanted an older brother. Someone who's strong and powerful yet gentle and innocent and gifted. Bound up with all this, I suppose, is a kind of obscure guilt that I never fought in the war, though this feeling has never been very strong with me. The point is Char, to me, is a real hero and, I suddenly realize, a great poet, as good as Camus says. When I was younger I tested my courage running around with mobsters and telling off thugs—sheer idiocy, of course. I really feel I'm a nothing beside him.

Well, I went right from the doctor's office to a class, carrying René's book,[1] and I started reading at random and commenting and in some cases elaborating on the aphorisms and some of the war diary. I can say honestly that the class was literally stunned by the depth, profundity, power, and wisdom of these translations. A mature woman taking the course waited an hour while I taught another class to tell me very simply that it was the most exciting classroom experience she had ever had.

Then, oddly enough, today I found a letter René wrote me some time ago on getting *The Waking*. I was startled to notice that his underlined very first sentence emphasized the fraternal.

Well, that's that. I don't mean to overdo this but the whole thing has been a staggering psychic experience for me and one which has unloosed a whole flood of pent-up emotions that I never realized existed. You can tell René this or show him this letter if you wish. I don't mean to put him under any spiritual obligation. I have deliberately dictated this letter to someone I trust because I was afraid I'd get far too slobbery if I tried writing it in long hand.

Don't worry about me, I'm out of the woods at last.

Love,

[1] *Hypnos Waking*, ed. by Jackson Mathews (1956).

To Howard Nemerov[1]

Seattle, Washington
January 21, 1959

Dear Howard Nemerov: Thanks for the warm note; you and Lowell, I guess, were the only ones* to read the damn book[2] until the rubber medals started descending. *(I mean of those I sent out.)

Say, tell Ben Belitt some time that his translation of Lorca,[3] has become practically a holy text with my kids: god, it is a beautiful job, if my old tin ear is still functioning—better than Humphries' even.

Have you got an extra off-print of the Sewanee Review article on you,[4] by any chance?

Hello to old Hornberger[5] & the rest of the menagerie.

Best,
Ted Roethke

To the Ford Foundation

[January 22, 1959]

Confidential Inquiry Form—Part I

1. If I were given a grant-in-aid [1] freeing me from other occupations, I would complete, not endeavor to complete, the following works (listed in their order of importance):

   I A sequence of serious poems beginning with a long dirge which will express through suggestive and highly charged symbolical language the guilts we as Americans feel as a

---

[1] Poet, novelist, and critic, on the faculty of Bennington College.

[2] *Words for the Wind.*

[3] *Poet in New York* (1955).

[4] Review of Nemerov's *Mirrors and Windows,* included in James Wright's "Some Recent Poetry," *Sewanee Review* (Autumn, 1958).

[5] Theodore Hornberger, professor of American Literature at the University of Minnesota and the University of Pennsylvania.

---

[1] Roethke was awarded a two-year grant by the Ford Foundation in 1959.

people for our mistakes and misdeeds in history and in time. I believe, in other words, that it behooves us to be humble before the eye of history.

Obviously such an attempt would, indeed, must bring into play great boldness of imagination, poetic and spiritual wisdom, in order to reveal some of the secrets of our enigmatic, vast, shrill, confused and often childish nation. Obviously, this would not be chronological, yet would expose some of the lies of history; our triumphs of rage and cunning; our manias, our despairs; our furtive joys. And it would attempt to expiate some of our collective mistakes.

General Design of this Proposed Long Poem:

   I Three dirges of increasing line length (two already partly written).

  II A lament and two songs (possibly more).

 III A sudden break into a kind of euphoric, pure joy.

II To finish and publish a book of songs and rhymes for children, with illustrations by Robert Leydenfrost. Musical settings already composed by Ben Webber, Gail Kubik, and others may be included in a slip-case in the back of this book. These poems have been widely published in America and England, danced to all over this country and broadcast (without payment) over all major networks.

III (For Second Year). Help European translators with editions or sections of anthologies in progress:

    a. Italian: to be first in a new series; editors, Salvatore Rosati, University of Rome, and Agostino Lombardo of University of Bari.

    b. German: Hans Sahl. Mr. Sahl is incomparably better as a translator of my work, at least, than any that appeared in *Perspectiven*. Three poems of mine have been read by him over at least a dozen German radio stations, and he has done the best critical article in German.

    c. German-Swiss: Elizabeth Schnack. (This may be abandoned since she is ill.) She has done a good deal of work, and has a publisher in Zurich "most" interested.

d. French: Alain Bosquet, René Char, perhaps Henri Michaux.

TO ISABELLA GARDNER[1]

Seattle, Washington
January 28, 1959

Dear Isabella Gardner: Thanks for the nice wire about the Bollingen. I'm beginning to feel aged 85.

You, know, I think you are the only person living who has that very bad thing I did on McCarthy[2]—for choral singing it was. I wonder if I may not borrow it back for a time. I'm poking around with some autobiographical chapters, and this might be funny, in a different perspective. Grisly funny, maybe.

Do give my love to Bob.[3] His house present is in the living room of our modest stash, along with a picture by Graves[4] of two geese we owned when living out at his place. Marianne & Louise they were called. The latter turned out to be a gander.[5]

This summer we intend to get East. Maybe we will meet, after all.[6]

Love, love,

Ted R.

&

(Beatrice)

[EDITOR'S NOTE: *This unpublished poem, sent to Ben Belitt on February 23, 1959, was written by Roethke during a period of hospitalization, which accounts for certain excesses evident in it.*]

To Ben Belitt

(February 23, 1959)

THE OLD FLORIST'S LAMENT

"The times have past me by, he said,
The times have past me by.

---

[1] Poet and one-time associate editor of *Poetry* magazine.
[2] Refers to unpublished poem, "Malediction."
[3] Robert Gardner, anthropologist and brother of Isabella Gardner.
[4] Morris Graves.
[5] Named, of course, after Marianne Moore and Louise Bogan. Mrs. Roethke notes that the former, not the latter, turned out to be a gander.
[6] Isabella Gardner tells me that she and Roethke never did meet.

There's nothing whole that's torn or rent,
    But a pig's eye.
And since I am myself, I know:
    Pork's in good supply."

"Who but a Prussian hog could know,
    Or a sleek Polish ham,

Where Roethke's
("poop-arse
aristocrats")
came from
*Stettin's a place so cold and wet,
    Pork keeps in good supply.
A cold-eyed drunken Prussian man
    Taught Jews new ways to die."

"What was his name, the drunken one,
    Who had no drunken ways;
He taught himself; he loved the sun;
    All things the sun would praise.
Therefore, I say this holy man
    Became both good and wise."

"A roaring man's a careless man;
    As Willie Yeats might say;
But such a one *he* never saw
    Under the light of day;
An Irishman's no candid man
    Come to the sexual play."

"They think it is Danae's gold,
    The splatter of the spray,—
When Otto Roethke went to bed,   (My old man)
    That was the end of day.   died 1922
I think my song's run on enough—   of cancer
    Easter's a holy day."

"I never did so well so fast,—
    That's what the old men say;
I think again, I think again:
    Easter's a holy day."

            For B²
            Ted Roethke

Are the allusions *too* multiple? I figure to dazzle even Pa Burke
here. Anyway, they're fancy for me.

To Roy Harvey Pearce

Seattle, Washington
February 26, 1959

My dear Pearce: I trust you will excuse the oddish paper and ink. I am away from secretaries, at the moment.

Let me say, first, that I was enormously pleased that you should call "A Rouse for Stevens" [1] a "wonderful piece." I'm sure you're the only person in the world that does, for it came out after Stevens had died, and even I felt embarrassed. It *was* written out of love, and I thought it really funny. Nobody else did—not even my wife —except possibly Ferdinand Puma, editor of *The Seven Arts,* who asked for material and paid $20 for it. Dare I print it in a subsequent *Collected,* do you think? Of course there is some invented Pennsylvania Dutch in it that would escape most people.

Last spring I read an MLA piece of yours on Stevens [2] at least three times. . . . And I learned a good deal, in so far as a dope like me can learn to follow conceptual thinking.

It has been a great source of regret to me that I never met the old elephant. He was most kind, and flattering in a letter, once, when I was quite young. But I felt I never dared approach him. And now he is dead, damn him anyway. He loved the martini; and all that went with it, I gather.

A central figure, a great poet, yes; but in final terms, *except* at the very last, wrong. One can, and must learn to whistle in any dark.

Yours,

Theodore Roethke

To Marianne Moore

Seattle, Washington
April 6, 1959

Dearest Marianne: I've sent you many "mental" letters, but they're not much good, are they?—or maybe the best of all.

---

[1] *CP,* p. 266.

[2] "Wallace Stevens: The Life of the Imagination," *PMLA* (September, 1951).

Your fables[1] were a kind of holy book in the hospital. A nurse, Mrs. Helen Norton, often read from them to me, and a French boy, an attendant from the Canadian air-borne, did too. And I lent it to people, on occasion. If they were especially nice, only.

It would be so pleasant to sit and gabble about a variety of matters: mostly poesy & gossip.

I seem to be up to a variety of things: some very savage in mood, some not. . . . By you, is the enclosed ballad[2] "authentic"? I did it about a year ago & put it aside, worrying whether it was too "pat"—the thing sort of wrote itself. But the (or my) analyst or therapist (who has high standards) thinks it the real thing—and not an arrangement of archetypal symbols. . . . Hope it seems all right, to you,—of its kind, which is special, of course.

Please don't think I'm trying to bully a comment from you, dear Marianne. I quite realize that many of the things I do must seem quite horrid to you—and are.

I send the poems to indicate I am alive, out of the hospital.

Forgive the enclosed envelope. In some cases I have only the one copy. Just stuff them in if you're not in the mood for Bleak Roethke.

Love, love,

T.

To Ralph J. Mills, Jr.

Seattle, Washington

June 12, 1959

Dear Ralph: (To reply in kind—for Ted it shall be, must be.) And Ralph Roister-Doister.

Of course, I am very pleased that you are mulling over the idea of a short book—hell, why not a long book, says that Beast, my Super-Ego. Knowing to some degree how you work, I'm sure you wouldn't fall to the ground with it. I'd be honored; and I'm shameless enough to be willing to provide any dope you might want, if it happens to be needed. For instance some of those titles in (*Praise*

---

[1] Miss Moore's translation, *The Fables of La Fontaine* (1954).
[2] Cannot identify.

to the End!) are little quotes from those I think of as ancestors. "Praise to the End!" from Wordsworth, for instance: and then of course there's Blake ("I cry Love, Love"). He cries Love three times, but I decided to be modest. And others I've forgotten Herrick, I think; C. Smart, etc. . . . Not a great point, but one which in a book would have interest, if developed.

Actually, old Snodgrass[1] (for whom I have beaten the drum long ago with editors like M. Caetani—irrelevance) was stumbling on a point that interested *me* a lot—the prosey style; for I began (at eleven & twelve) as a great admirer of the familiar essayists (Stevenson, Repplier, Tomlinson,[2] etc. . . .). I subscribed to the *Dial* in the seventh grade, honored their ideal of "chiselled prose". . . . But when I got to the University all this fell apart: I got B+ in freshman "Rhetoric" and decided I could not possibly be a writer if I couldn't get A. (I'm oversimplifying: what I want to say is that *early,* when it really matters, I read, and really read, Emerson (prose mostly), Thoreau, Whitman, Blake, and Wordsworth; Vaughan and real slugs of dramatic literature—Jacobeans, Congreve, & W. S., of course.) My point is this: I came to some of Eliot's and Yeats's ancestors long before I came to them; in fact, for a long time, I rejected both of them. . . . So what in the looser line may seem in the first old lady poem[3] to be close to Eliot may actually be out of Whitman, who influenced Eliot *plenty,* technically (See S. Musgrove T. S. Eliot and Walt Whitman, U. of New Zealand Press—again not the whole truth, but a sensible book.)—and Eliot, as far as I know, has never acknowledged this —oh no, he's always chi-chi as hell: only Dante, the French, the Jacobeans, etc. My point: for all his great gifts, particularly of the ear, Eliot is not honest, in final terms, even about purely technical matters. It's here I guess your point about the *parody* element comes in[4]—though I hate to call such beautiful (to my mind) poems mere parodies.

---

[1] See W. D. Snodgrass' review of *Words for the Wind* in "Spring Verse Chronicle," *Hudson Review* (Spring, 1959), pp. 114–17.

[2] Robert Louis Stevenson, Agnes Rippler, and H. M. Tomlinson.

[3] "First Meditation," from *Meditations of an Old Woman. CP,* pp. 157–60.

[4] I had mentioned to Roethke that certain parts of "Meditations of an Old Woman" seemed to contain parodies of Eliot; however, I did not mean to be understood as thinking the individual poems or the group of them constituted mere parodies.

Oh Christ, let's before the eye of God, try to wipe away the bullshit about both Willie & Tiresome Tom & say this:

In both instances, I was animated in considerable part by arrogance: I thought: I can take this god damned high style of W. B. Y. or this Whitmanesque meditative thing of T. S. E. and use it for other ends, use it as well or better. Sure, a tough assignment. But while Yeats' historical lyrics seem beyond me at the moment, I'm damned if I haven't outdone him in the more personal or love lyric. Why Snodgrass is a damned earless ass when he sees Yeats in those love-poems: look at that fart beat in "Words for the Wind," the 4-part poem—is that a Yeats cadence? or the tone in those love lyrics (I do agree they get a little monotonous).

As for the old lady poems, I wanted (1) to create a character for whom such rhythms are indigenous; that she be a dramatic character, not just me. Christ, Eliot in the Quartets is tired, spiritually tired, old-man. Rhythm, Tiresome Tom. Is my old lady tired? The hell she is: she's tough, she's brave, she's aware of life and she would take a congeries of eels over a hassle of bishops any day. (2) Not only is Eliot tired, he's a [. . .] fraud as a mystic —all his moments in the rose-garden and the wind up his ass in the draughty-smoke-fall-church yard.

Ach, how vulgar I become—perhaps.

But let me become more vulgar—*entre nous*. Teckla Bianchini, one of W. H. Auden's closest friends and a woman of unimpeachable verity, told me on the beach at Ischia that Wystan had said that at one point he was worried that I was getting too close to Yeats, but now he no longer did because I had out-done him, surpassed him, gone beyond him. Well, let's say *this* is too much, in its way. . . . But I think it, sometimes. Who wouldn't.

It's time the Pound-Eliot cult and the Yeats cult, too, got nudged and bumped, no? I'm glad [you] worked on W. C. W. and am particularly interested in what you'll say of Aiken—I never got close to him as poet—slackness in rhythm bothers me; lit. diction.[5]

I sure have let my hair down. Needless to say, the whole truth is a good deal less crude than my violence.

Yes! do the book. Hurray, hurray!

T.

[5] At the time, I must have been reading Williams or thinking of an essay about him, but I never did write anything on him or Aiken.

You see the *Am. Scholar* for summer? Will send tear sheet of the "Dirge" [6] when I get them. I hope you like the thing.

[EDITOR'S NOTE: *The following poems were sent to the editor on June 2, 1960, as examples of new work which might later be included in a collection. These poems, of course, do not appear in* The Far Field.]

DIRGE[1]

O what I say, and without end,
Burns me the true cigar,—
A kiss as cold as my best friend,
A smoke without a tar;
I wrote a book, "Words for the Wind,"—
My whole undoing's there.

When last is first, my final fiend,
Old Jupiter's least tear
Becomes a wave, engulfing who
Cries for the right true end.

Last night I lay alone and cold,
Cold, cold my sweetheart's toes,
I was alone, old, old, old,—
For I was one of those
Who thought that promises, once told,
Were pure as Joseph's clothes.

Which way, which way, my dear friend cried,
Cold on my sweetheart's toes,—
And all his random cries in vain,
For he was one of those:
        Only the empty air did hear
        That howling, so obscene.

THE EARLY FLOWER[2]

When the long root, the tensile stem disturb
The air with its fixed flower, a single bloom
Triumphant in the rain, a piece of sun
Beyond this time, this sensual ebb and flow,—

---

[6] Reprinted below.

[1] Sent to Ralph J. Mills, Jr., June 2, 1960. Unpublished.
[2] Sent to Ralph J. Mills, Jr., June 2, 1960. Published in the *New Yorker* (April 25, 1959).

A spire of bloom expands on the mind's eye
To hold and heal, shimmer and stay
Despite the moment's spare diminishing:
Then true beginnings move the mind,
And steal through all our hearts like direst spring.

DIRGE[3]

I would praise:

> —Those who will be compelled to dance
> Through a final flame;

> —The pathetic, with their flaccid
> Beauty;

> —Compilers of lines, inert
> In their own paltriness;

> —Their streets streaming with
> Ice, their immobile children staring
> > On far stars,
> Their tears welling out of
> A cradle of naphtha.

I would praise:

> —The Holy Korean dead,
> Aging their bodies in
> Straw, in the slime
> Of deliberate napalm;

> —That coolest trickling,
> cooler than wind—
> Than wind-divided streams tumbling
> Down from glaciers
> (Easy as the cobra's stare)

> —The last scream
> Of the dying,
> The dying
> Young.

II

And I would praise the interdictory bombers, at night sleeping in the
Korean straw houses—and their watching doctors:

[3] Sent to Ralph J. Mills, Jr., June 2, 1960. Published in *The American Scholar* (Summer, 1959).

The eternal waiting before the 100th mission;
The steady-eyed mixers of the jellied petroleum, those clear-eyed pilots;
The guardians of the Pyongtaek pipeline from the raging seacoast,
Bringing, in convoy, their supplies, the final candy for children;
And I would praise the *keloids,* the loose leathery saddles on the bodies
    of limping children,
(What a sweet shrinking away, an inexorable shrinking!)
For I remember, I recollect, I have been told:
One single splatter equals a *keloid.*
                     Father of us all,
                     For this I would have us forgiven.

III

And I have been delighted, vicariously, thinking of the sweet smells
    rising from dying bodies;
Those retreating armies, who left their own dead for the flies on the
    African desert—
The sweet effluvia ascending from the gradually distending bellies:
That surest of clues, that friend to the animal nostril,
Telling him truly friend or enemy no longer was lurking,
But lay in his own lovely bones, his flesh unlovely;

            And lonely in space,
            A fighting man,
            An hyena
            In habit,
            Eating.
            Some times:

            In the drifting mists,
            In the raw wintry morning.

IV

            And I would praise the looped bootlace,
            That surest of weapons:
            With the sleeping—
            Or sleepless—
            Sentry.

THE DANCING MAN[4]

In Memoriam: Denis Devlin, poet and Irish Minister to the Italian Republic,
    after an evening in which he outdanced everyone . . .

4 Sent to Ralph J. Mills, Jr., June 2, 1960. Published in *Atlantic Monthly*
(October, 1960).

The wine was old, the talk was new
   That Devlin plied each guest,
When who should step into the room,
   But a One in formal dress:
His tail popped out when he made his bow,
   And O! we knew the worst.

He said, 'Devlin's no roaring man,
   But he's a dancing fool,
I can't abide a dancing man,
   And I would have his soul:
I'll dance the bones out of his skin,—
   Would the Devlin wager all?'

The Devlin bowed, 'O Prince of Sin,
   I'm honoured in my home,
The bargain is, I call the tune,
   But should you fail the theme,
You'll never plague a dancing man,
   And that till Kingdom Come.'

Then he began a Connaught step,
   The like we'd never seen,
He altered with a triple dip,
   And a double bounce between;—
The sweat stood on the Devil's lip;
   He blanched like a colleen.

They heard the reel round Innisfree,
   From Dublin to New York;
The noble Irish peasantry
   Put down the spade and fork;
The ghoulies and the ghosties they
   Paused in their impish work.

'I am the Irish Minister,'
   Cried Devlin from the ceiling,
O, he was dancing on the air,
   And with prodigious feeling.
One foot performed an Irish jig,
   One went Virginia-reeling.

He twirled upon a single leg:
   O he went fast and faster!
The Devil's face began to sag:

He knew he'd met his master;
From County Down to Inishbeg
   They sensed Ould Nick's disaster.

The Devlin, a good Christian man,
   Knew where his Foe was weak:
He crossed himself, then jumped across
   The left foot of Ould Nick.
'Ochone! Ochone!' the Old One cried,
   'My back's about to break!'

He sighed in Scots, 'Ae gae it oup,
   Ae canna stand the pace.'
His clothes, they fell into a heap;
   As he limped from that gay place,
And all His minions howled in Hell,
   For He was Hell's disgrace!

Reflection:

The Irish know a thing or two
   About the ways of hate;
They either beat you black and blue,
   Or dance you off your feet:
When a dancing man turns on his toe,
   He makes his soul complete.
—*And the Devil, O, the Devil, O,*
   The Devil don't like that!

1960-63

To Dorothee Bowie

Inishbofin, Ireland
[circa September, 1960]

Dear Sweetie: Would you, could you possibly root around my second-class mail & then send *air express* to me the following:

(1) *Michigan Alumnus* with my piece on Bogan,[1] summer issue.

(2) *Inventario,* with my fourteen poems, including the first-time printing of the "Elegy to my Aunt Tilly." [2] Poggioli[3] of Harvard sent this I think.

(3) The copy of Bosquet's anthology into the French[4] that I sent the Old Man.[5] Apparently he got it—for Doubleday sent it him. But see he sees (a) the *amount* of stuff translated and (b) what Bosquet says about Theodore at the end. (Pa thinks Bosquet is no good because Jackson Mathews, that lovely but not infallible man says so. But the point is this is the best collection yet of Am. verse

[1] "The Poetry of Louise Bogan." It was originally delivered as a Hopwood lecture at the University of Michigan. Reprinted in *On the Poet and His Craft.*

[2] Later simply called "Elegy," *CP,* p. 144.

[3] Renato Poggioli, professor of Comparative Literature at Harvard.

[4] *Trente-cinq Jeunes Poètes Américains,* ed. by Alain Bosquet (1960).

[5] Robert Heilman.

in trans. yet & is selling to beat hell (relatively) in France & the
French aren't easy to impress. Bosquet is going to approach Gallimard about a separate volume & now I'm faced with the problem
of whether to let him. My instinct is to say yes. Hell, the English
text will be *there,* anyway. Look at Eliot's translation of *The
Anabasis,* St.-J. Perse. At least 80 major boo-boos.

But have the chicks gather this together & *air express* it to me

> Fox's Hotel
> 14 Upper Leesom Street
> Dublin, Ireland

We're both splendid & will be permanently so.

> Love, love,
> Theodore

To Lillian Hellman

> *Ballinisloe, Ireland*[1]
> *September 1, 1960*

> *Am resting here for 10 more days before doing a single
> shot 20 min. on BBC. And will probably also do one TV
> show for David Jones of BBC. TV.*

Dearest Lillian: Will you co-produce a show with me on a 60–40
basis?—me 60, you 40%—in a word own it lock and barrel—except:

I give one of my 10% to my favorite charity: O'Toole's Bug-
house—a fund that is just beginning.

Here's the nice part of this pitch: 1) we don't have to use one
goddamned Broadway character *or* musician: in a word, no Bernstein.

2) The material is absolutely fresh and new, can be expanded or
contracted at will, adapted to special or local conditions.—Who
wrote the words *and* music?

I did. And if you think Dick[2] was good in the syphilis song[3]—

---

[1] Written from St. Brigid's Hospital.

[2] Richard Wilbur.

[3] "Pangloss' Song" from the comic opera *Candide,* on which Wilbur col-
laborated with Lillian Hellman and Leonard Bernstein.

and he was—wait until you get a load of this stuff—which I deliver; and I guarantee I'll stop the show more than once every night.

You want in on a dry run?

Come to Inishbofin, Eire for Christmas: Fly to the Shannon Airport, then take train to Galway and I'll do the rest, i.e. get you to the Island. The room *and* board is 1 £ a day: finest lobster in the world, fresh mackerel, curlew, brown trout, turkey, geese, wild duck, etc.

There, during the Christmas season sometime we'll give the show it's 3rd performance. (We've already had two.)

The characters—principals

1. Me, as M. C., etc.
2. Two—no three pub singers
   a. Young Desmond O'Halloran: a very shy boy with an absolutely beautiful heart-piercing Gaelic voice.
   b. James Coyne: an older man, with a fine head but punk teeth (like many western Irish). But this is being fixed up.
   c. Bernard Tierney: a comic pub-singer: absolutely uninhibited, who has his own variation of "MacNamara's Band" that he brays at the drop of a hat.

5. About five little Boffin kids—we can cut to four who do Irish jigs absolutely deadpan. Their leader is 16, very pretty—they all are—and bright.

6. A "baby priest." Now this takes some doing. We have to carry him because the whole cast except me—and La Beatrice, whom I may use if she "cooperates" (ugh) are Catholics, v. devout. The priest need not come on stage. But we need a special dispensation from the Bishop for him to travel: and he must find his own substitute.

7. One accordion, also from Boffin.

B. We could have a further dry run at YMHA—using just one or two pub singers to test the material—and make Lizzie Kray[4] pay for their travel expenses. I'm on the committee & I think she'd jump at the chance. Call her up, read any of this you want to her, and get her to write or cable me how much she

4 Elizabeth Kray of the YMHA Poetry Center.

can give for a three-night stand at the YMHA in March: tickets $5 & $10.

. . . .

Cable or call me, not if "interested" but a) whether you'll get here Christmas b) how many blue chips of your own you'll gamble, "blue chips"—being ten grand apiece to open in N. Y. *after* YMHA.

. . . .

Get going, sweetie.

Love,
Theo

. . . .

To Katherine S. White[1]

September 7, 1960

Dear Mrs. White: I can't get a typist—so resort to this.

It's a kind of companion piece to "Sequence." Hence, the deliberate use of the phrase "in this evening air." A kind of theme-refrain, as it were.

. . . .

Did I send my gutty poem, the anti-Nixon one.[2] It's completely beyond the pale, for you; but a noble sentiment.

Best,
T. R.

The Knowing[3]

In Ballinisloe,
The gull's a crow,
The wren's betwixt-between.
                    —O'Toole's Refrain

Colours deepen the Eye.
I am Here, But O! I am Here!

[1] An editor of the *New Yorker*.
[2] Refers to a still unpublished political poem written in the spring of 1960.
[3] Unpublished.

Lark, how you tell the Ear!
When you lift up to the Sky,
The God[s] themselves Cheer,
Knowing Eternity's Near.

Symbols enshrine, consume
The Selfless utterly:
A Prick-Song wipes the Eye
With the slow, the sad salt Tear;
We sit in the humblest Chair,
Knowing Eternity's Near.

The Brave, they do not die;
And the Gracious sing good cheer
To the Dead Man slumped in his Chair,
His pure Soul fled Elsewhere,
His self consumed utterly,
Knowing Eternity's Near.

Sad Soul, poised for a while
Above the radiant Stair,
Embrace, given without guile,
The Kiss, the heavenly smile,
And dream, in this evening air,
Knowing eternity's near.

> —Theodore Roethke
> Fox's Hotel
> 14 Lower Leesom Street
> Dublin Eire

> (Cut those silly capitals

TO DOROTHEE BOWIE

London, England
January 12, 1961

Dear Dorothee: You are an absolute darling to send all those
Christmas cards along with the addresses, you really are.

About the royalties—deposit them wherever you have been de-
positing things before. Incidentally, are there any addresses on
Glyn Mills & Co. and Windmill Press—and any indication of the

work they were paying for? I ask this since I would like to include this in the bibliography which I am desperately trying to assemble.

I think I should say something about text books. For the Verse Course:

The English Galaxy   edited by Bullet, in the Everyman edition
Robert Graves Poems   chosen by himself in the Anchor edition
Yvor Winters collected poems   Swallow Press

Then Louis Untermeyer's combined anthology of British and American poetry. The earlier edition that they always ordered *not* the last one. I am sorry I cannot give you the exact number of this edition. Earlier order sheets should show which one this is.

The Appreciation Course: There is a big anthology published by Row, Peterson of Evanston of British and American Poetry.[1] Jacob Korg[2] can tell you the exact title. There are 16 British poets and 16 American, of which I am one (natch). Also I would like the selected poems of William Carlos Williams, the paper-back of Hart Crane's collected poems, and the paper-back edition of Louise Bogan, Noonday Press.

You asked about those Bogan reprints.[3] You might send one to Professor Harry Levin, Department of Comparative Literature, Harvard University, Cambridge, Mass., and one to Mr. Elliott Coleman, The Johns Hopkins University, Baltimore, Maryland— if you have time.

I will write you a decent newsy letter later. My broadcast—25 minutes in length—is scheduled for February 8th. I sing a song at the end.*

Yours,

Ted

* Incidentally, the Library can obtain a tape of this if it agrees not to release it "commercially." They could write Anthony Thwaite, Esq. BBC, Broadcasting House, Portland Sq. London.

Is there any chance of getting part of an assistant—to do leg-

[1] *The College Book of Modern Verse,* ed. by Walter Rideout and James Robinson (1958).

[2] Critic and professor of English at the University of Washington.

[3] Reprints of "The Poetry of Louise Bogan" from *Critical Quarterly* (Summer, 1961).

Theodore Roethke, 1963
(Photo by Mary Randlett)

Theodore Roethke at home, 3802 East John Street, Seattle; 1963
(Photo by Mary Randlett)

work—like the one I had—the little Catholic girl. It was a much more efficient system.

And how will I live without you there?

Love, love,
Butch

Hello to Arnold, Boss, Frank, Fitzgerald, etc.[4]

To Louis Untermeyer

London, England
February 27, 1961

Dear Louis: I loved your letter—all the warmth, taste, & generosity of spirit. Thanks. Thanks. Of course, if you don't use "Oyster River" [1] you are totally mad: I've had the most extraordinary set of letters from various people on this. "Not since Whitman and Yeats have I been so moved," etc. Tough guys like Frank Jones.[2]

But do you have the *last* collected book "Words for the Wind"? I suspect not, or you would have seized on one of the old lady poems. Ask Ken McCormick for a copy.

But are you still playing *Ein fluss?* Shame on you. The interval theme is as old as literature. I got it from reading the bible aloud in The First Presbyterian Sunday School, Saginaw, Michigan, and *also* from having to learn at an early age Longfellow's

> Between the dark and the daylight
> When the night is beginning to lour
> Comes a pause in the day's occupation
> That is known as the children's hour.

Actually once I wrote a bad poem on that theme, sent it to someone else who promptly wrote *another* poem on the same theme; so

---

[4] Arnold Stein, Edward E. Bostetter, and Frank Jones were colleagues of Roethke's in the English Department at Washington. Robert Fitzgerald, who later held the Poetry Chair at Harvard, was then teaching Roethke's classes at Washington.

---

[1] "Meditation at Oyster River," *CP*, pp. 190–92.

[2] Critic and professor of Comparative Literature at the University of Washington.

I said to hell with it until this passage. . . . Look what's *done* in the imagery: no more like Eliot than a cow's tail.

Hell, we miss each other again. We fly to New York next Sunday and I do turns at Williams, Trinity, Connecticut, Yale, YMHA.

Was on *live* telly-vision Sunday along with Peter Ustinov, Trevor-Roper. But tough work. The announcer gave me, little me, the blast "this remarkable poet," "a steadily growing international reputation." Lovely stuff to listen to.

Best,
Ted

To Dorothee Bowie

[London, England]
[February, 1961]

Dearest Dorothee:

. . . .

Here's the bibliography—about ⅔ complete, I should say and particularly incomplete on translations. Look, I had Robert[1] sent a copy of a Gallimard anthology of Am. poetry done by Bosquet[2] —in which I had the biggest representation. *Could* you borrow it from him & put down the dope? It's a v. important entry. There is also stuff from Swedish, Bengali, etc. I can't get.

My ego is booming, also. Ransom, Kunitz, & Deutsch have done a symposium on "In a Dark Time." All three are "brilliant," but Ransom's really knocks the ball out of the lot. Of the sequence of love lyrics: "It is a great triumph." First he had wound up comparing my piece with Yeats' "Sailing to Byzantium," my being more "sinewy," of equal gravity, etc., *then* he changed & compares it with a passage in Krishna & there he is really right. But this is incomprehensible unless you have the *stuff*—poem, the essays.[3]

[1] Robert Heilman.

[2] *Trente-cinq Jeunes Poètes Américains,* ed. by Alain Bosquet (1960).

[3] This symposium was first published in *New World Writing 19* (1961), and reprinted in *The Contemporary Poet as Artist and Critic,* ed. by Anthony Ostroff (1964).

Sunday on the live T.V. show with Peter Ustinov & Trevor-Roper, the announcer wound up giving *me* the blast "this remarkable poet" "a steadily growing international reputation"—all to a mass audience.

Every damn English mag. of intellectual importance is running two or three poems, or have run—*Encounter, Spectator, The Listener, The Observer, London Mag., New Statesman.* And the *Critical Quarterly* is going to do the Bogan piece.

Blah, blah, blah,
T.

To John Frederick Nims[1]

Seattle, Washington
May 6, 1961

Dear John Frederick Nims: Thanks for inquiring around.[2] There was no time anyway. My plane from the Coast was delayed & there was but ten minutes the other way. Hence no telephone call.

Now about the enclosed.[3] I hope you like them, of course, but if you think they'll offend readers, do send them back. I really did write them for three pub-singers in Western Ireland, and they're a reaction against the sugar-tit Betjeman[4] (the second and the Saginaw Song) & some of Cal Lowell's Irish-maid effects. I think it's time poetry got coarse and rude again. Whether these are the answer, I don't know. People are either mad for them or hesitant. Merwin (W.S.) much taken by them, for instance.

All are written to be sung; all have tunes (airs, as the Irish say). They, incidentally, thought these foine, very foine & "Fonny."

"Gob Music" is mouth music: the noise the old fellers make when there's no fiddle or concertina—and they want to dance.

---

1 Poet, translator, critic, and professor of English at the University of Illinois; then visiting editor of *Poetry.*

2 To see if Roethke might read in the Chicago area.

3 A group of pub songs. "The Saginaw Song," *CP,* pp. 267–68; "Gob Music," *CP,* pp. 269–70; :"The Shy Man," *CP,* p. 216. The last two were published in *Poetry* (August, 1961).

4 The English poet, John Betjeman.

It must be understood that the pub-song is a form where a degree of ribaldry is expected. It ain't for ladies.

Best,
Ted Roethke

To Anthony Ostroff[1]

Seattle, Washington
July 15, 1961

Dear Anthony: My (part-time) secretary read me the substance over the telephone when I was in the San Juan Islands, from where I have just returned, with hay-fever and a hellish arthritis in both knees and one shoulder.

About doing an essay on "Father and Son":[2]

(1) I don't see how in God's name I'm going to get the time to do a decent job by October! I'm supposed to go to New York, to California (for some nutty "award"[3]), and to British Columbia, maybe Alaska before that time. . . . I want to do a piece on Stanley, eventually, since I feel I know his work as well as anyone; but the project means so much to me that I don't want to do a hasty and sloppy job on it. I do *not* write well under pressure.

(2) It seems to me *a real tactical blunder, if one is thinking of a series or a book, to have the same persons writing on each other.* Frankly, I think it lies upon you as editor to take a firm stand on this matter. It's bound to weaken the whole effect of a book, raise eyebrows, sneers, particularly among the English. There are some people, like Auden, who feel that contemporaries never should write about each other: this I think nonsense, but I do feel very strongly about things in this instance.

Now obviously I'm in a box, since I've already been written

---

[1] Poet, editor, and professor in the department of speech at the University of California, Berkeley.

[2] Anthony Ostroff had invited Roethke to contribute an essay to a symposium on Stanley Kunitz' poem "Father and Son." Ostroff had edited a similar symposium on Roethke's "In a Dark Time." Roethke did not, as the letter indicates, write the piece.

[3] Golden Plate Award of the Academy of Achievement, San Diego. See letter to Isabella Gardner, February 17, 1963.

about, and beautifully. And it would ease my mind if you, in thinking things over, would come to the same conclusion and tell Stanley just that. Hell, there are plenty of people who could write better on him than I—though I think I probably *teach* him as well as anyone else.

I'm sorry to hear about your operation: it sounds quite a seige. Hope you're O.K. now

Well, put me down for a "maybe," but a most doubtful one.

I hope I haven't done you in here. I do feel I am absolutely right; and I am sure Stanley will too, eventually.

This is a hell of an envelope your secretary enclosed. But here are the forms.

Best,

Ted

I cherished your letter about the piece v. much.[4]

Galleys received & will be sent off shortly.

Let me know your reaction to all this if you have time.

To LOUIS UNTERMEYER

Seattle, Washington
August 18, 1961

Dear Louis:

. . . .

Sure, send me the list,[1] but don't count on me until I send in something. It's just the kind of thing I don't do with three fingers or a cork up my bum. But I'd love to try. My secretary (who's a professional reader, reciter of stories to children) has already brought me a whole box of examples. I've been reading "Johnny Crow's Party," "Little Bear," etc.—some several times. Never realized how close my affinities are to the dribblenoses. As Cal Lowell [2] says, just a child of the moment with no knowledge of evil.

[4] Refers to an appreciative letter Ostroff wrote after he had received Roethke's contribution to the symposium on "In a Dark Time."

---

[1] A word list to be used in writing a children's book. Untermeyer was general editor for the series. Roethke did write the book, which appeared as *The Party at the Zoo* (1963).

[2] Robert Lowell.

Look, as a personal favor would you look over these three "pub songs." I did them in Ireland, literally for three singers of Inishbofin, James Coyne, Bernard Tierney, and Dennis O'Halloran. The last[3] I never finished in time to sing to them—but I did it because they always wanted to know about Saginaw, Sheechargo, Il Paso, New York—(but *not* Hollywood).

Is the Saginaw one *too* vulgar—I ask you as one of the last of the real belly-laughers. Auden has said he could endure those meetings (Institute)[4] because of your japes.

I *thought* I was bringing back something lost, in part, in the language in these, particularly the last, which is in part a reaction against Betjeman's treacle and Cal's We-love ourselves us Yankees prose.[5] Merwin, W. S. & wife loved it; my wife hates it; my sister will suffer from it, alas; the N. Yorker was horrified; *Poetry* turned it down but printed the other two in the August number. Louise B. said it should be re-written (out of love)—my God that's what it was written out of: Saginaw was a tough rich nutty town—and my old man & I moved with the bloods (I say this because Nims said I was too "angry").

On I jabber like a tyro. But I would like to have your judgment in this particular interest. Hell, you know I woo no more.

All best,
Ted

I've just done a longish (100 lines) one that I *am* really sure about:[6] underworld lingo in part with (I think) wonderful & exact shifts in association & tone. It damned near killed me to do. This duelling with God gets exhausting.

To Stephen Spender

Seattle, Washington
September 16, 1961

Dear Stephen: Here's a comic poem[1] which I hope very much you

---

[3] "The Saginaw Song." *CP*, pp. 267–68.

[4] National Institute of Arts and Letters.

[5] Probably refers to Lowell's *Life Studies* (1959), which includes the autobiographical essay "91 Revere Street."

[6] "The Abyss." *CP*, pp. 219–22. Here Roethke is speaking of a version of the poem different from the published one.

---

[1] "Saginaw Song." *CP*, pp. 267–68.

will like. It's earthy, as you will see, the kind of poem that makes ordinary people laugh, vulgar in the original sense of the word. You need not fear libel, because Burrows Morley[2] is perhaps my best friend, and I am sure he'd laugh like hell over this piece. The poem is also written as a reply to the Laurie Lee and John Betjeman kind of sentimentality. Saginaw was a terribly rich town: 200 millionaires in a town of 40,000, a tough town where money was no distinction. End of explanations.

O yes, I meant to thank you for the extraordinarily perceptive review in the New Republic, and I was deeply touched of course by the last sentence.[3] I'm just back from California, from the damndest clambake in human history which went beyond anything Hollywood might have thought up. (Hollywood was there in the person of Willie Wyler.) There was a very nice Englishman, Douglas Harding—do you know him?—he and I and Thomas Hart Benton were about the only people to stand up for the arts and the interior life. The whole thing nearly blew up during the speech by [. . .] Teller,[4] [. . .] who "fathered" the hydrogen bomb. I'm thinking about doing a piece about the whole business; would you be interested? Maybe it would be better to have it appear in the Observer, with whom I'm going on contract.

The second piece[5]—I hope you feel that the imaginative jumps work, that they are right. There is a lapse into underworld diction at the end of section I, but I don't think that it is necessary for the reader to know exactly what the words mean, but here's a glossary:

> foon—the stuff, the drug
> get the nail in—get the needle in
> taking it man—taking it in the veins
> Miss Emma—morphine
> gunsel—a homosexual killer
> to break a cap—to fire a gun

I do hope you like both these pieces, and feel that they represent again a genuine growth. Do give my love to your wife.

All the best,

---

2 Mentioned in the poem.

3 "Words for the Wind," *New Republic* (Aug. 10, 1959).

4 Edward Teller.

5 Refers to an early version of "The Abyss." The poem was published in its final version in *Encounter* (October, 1962). *CP*, pp. 219–22.

To Stephen Spender

Seattle, Washington
September 25, 1961

Dear Stephen: I'm delighted that you like all three poems,[1] and you can have first rights on all of them: they have not appeared and will not appear in America until you print them first. I'm hoping, of course, that you will want to put the whole bunch in the 100th number; I'd like to stand comparison with old Wystan (best man at our marriage) and so forth. Do let me know how and when you are going to run them.

I can honestly give you first rights in this instance because I sent you these pieces *before* my arrangement with the Observer was completed.

I hope I can see some slugs of the very very very long poem. I envy the energy that can drive through on a piece that long. Me, I rarely last more than a hundred lines.

Oh, but I do want to send you the little funny book for children,[2] for your children. Faber turned it down (I own all English rights) much to my astonishment. It saddens me that Mr. Eliot seems to think me a thug. He's right of course, but I am convinced I can write rings around some of those punks on his list. I guess Marguerite Caetani, his second cousin, badgered him so much about me that he's just tired of the subject.

In this country four out of five notices are raves, and some are long and solemn considerations of what was simply planned as a nutty Christmas item. The fifth guy always wants to drum me out of Christendom. I *know* kids like these when they hear them— even as young as two (I'm carrying on so long, I suppose, because I feel Eliot and du Sautoy[3] have treated me very shabbily, alas!*)

love,

Ted

---

[1] "Saginaw Song," "The Abyss," "Once More, the Round." *CP*, pp. 219–22, 251, 267–68. The poems appeared in *Encounter* in the issues of January, 1962, October, 1962, and May, 1962, respectively.

[2] *I Am! Says the Lamb* (1961).

[3] Peter du Sautoy of the Faber and Faber editorial staff.

* I'm always grumbling about Eliot: it's the old love-hate business. He can't stand anyone who will duel with God.

To Ralph J. Mills, Jr.

[*December 15, 1961*]

Dear Ralph: Sorry I haven't written.
Delighted you're going back to the *project*.[1]

"Ideas": (which you ask for:

1. It's the middle poems (Praise to the End!) that need the most explication, I'd say. What the symbols mean are what they usually mean, I always say.

2. Much of the style (in these pieces) and elsewhere is based on shifts in association. Now, either these are imaginatively right or they're not. Plenty of times chances are taken,—but I'd change nothing in that middle sequence. . . . I don't say this is the only way to write, but it does seem to me to be one of the ways really to break ground (It's a civilization of objects and nutty juxtapositions—certainly the surrealists have exploited that). But think: it is one thing to make amazing metaphors as opposites on a string;—this Thomas does, but rarely does he go in for real *jumps* in association. . . . Eliot does, bastard that he is, and so does Crane; but Crane's sense for language sometimes betrays him & also his sense for a total unity.

More anon. Love,
I-love-me
Theodore

To Ralph J. Mills, Jr.

Seattle, Washington
March 23, 1962

Dear Ralph: I have enclosed some brief notes about the green-

---

[1] The "project" was to be some kind of critical monograph on Roethke's poetry. It finally took the form of an essay in the University of Minnesota series of Pamphlets on American Writers, but did not appear until three months after Roethke's death in 1963.

house. If there is anything more you want to know about it, let me know.

I think I have mentioned some of the titles of the long pieces. Sometimes they are simply a tribute to ancestors whom I have admired, but not necessarily been heavily influenced by. For instance, one fairly obscure one, "O Lull Me, Lull Me."

> O lull me, lull me, charming air!
> My senses rock with wonder sweet;
> Like snow on wool thy fallings are;
> Soft like a spirit's are thy feet.
> Grief who needs fear
> That hath an ear?
> Down let him lie
> And slumbering die,
> And change his soul for harmony.
>
> —William Strode

"Praise to the End!" is, of course, from Wordsworth, exactly where I have forgotten.[1] "I Cry Love! Love!" is, of course, from Blake, but his line carries three Loves I believe.[2] (I thought I would be modest and cry only twice.) Another title comes from Vaughan's "The Revival"—I have forgotten just which one at the moment.[3] "Where Knock Is Open Wide" is from Christopher Smart,[4] and so on. I'll try to put down any others that come to my mind.

Do you have the bibliography compiled by William Matheson[5] of the University of Washington? I can get it from the University Library for about $1.50. I can send you any supplementary items which the department puts out.

About the new book,[6] I am still fiddling with the order and composition of certain final poems but I should be able to send you a carbon before too long.

Do you have the enclosed piece from College English?[7] If you

[1] From *The Prelude,* Book I, line 350.

[2] From "Visions of the Daughters of Albion": "I cry: Love! Love! Love! happy happy Love! free as the mountain wind!" line 191.

[3] "Unfold! Unfold!" *CP,* pp. 89–91.

[4] From "Song to David," LXXVII.

[5] John William Matheson.

[6] Roethke refers here to the manuscript of *The Far Field.*

[7] James G. Southworth, "The Poetry of Theodore Roethke," *College English* (March, 1960).

do have it already, please send this one back since they are hard for me to obtain. Not that you need to know what other people say; I just thought you would be interested.

Sincerely yours,
Ted
Theodore Roethke

About the greenhouse.

It was originally started in the very early 1870's by my grandfather, William Roethke, who had been Bismarck's sister's *hauptfoerster* sp.? (head forester) and for a time I think Bismarck's also. At any rate it seems he got in a row with the old man (Bismarck) about pacificism and the family was virtually kicked out of Germany. The Roethke's were what my father called "poop arse" aristocrats. The great grandfather had had I guess a couple of sandy villages in East Prussia but they got out of his hands one way or another. The maternal grandmother was a peasant type. She kept the keys to the Bismarck wine cellar. There were five children in all: Emil, Anna, Elise, Charles and Otto. All helped with the business and owned part of it for a time. At the end, it was owned by my father, the youngest son who was president, and my Uncle Charlie.

My father's chief interest was the growing of flowers. When the firm was at its height, around 1920, it took up twenty-five acres within the city of Saginaw with a quarter of a million feet under glass. We lived in a frame house* which was in front of the greenhouse and my Uncle Charlie lived in a stone house which was next door. At one time the firm had three retail outlets, but a good deal of its business was wholesale. Its advertising carried the slogan "The largest and most complete floral establishment in Michigan," and undoubtedly it was, for it had its own ice-house, a small game preserve, and the last stand of virgin timber in the Saginaw valley (mostly walnut and oak—not pine). In spite of the fact that it was a working commercial greenhouse, a good deal of space, time and money were spent in experiment. Not only in flowers but also in determining what kinds of wild game could be stocked in the game preserve which was seven miles outside the city, a plot of only

---

* My sister, June Roethke, still lives there [Roethke's note].

one hundred sixty acres but completely fenced and very good natural cover for pheasant and partridge.

As a child I heard Europeans, Dutchmen and Belgians, say repeatedly that it was the most beautiful greenhouse in America. My father specialized in roses and orchids particularly. A good many of the items were never put on sale.

Some of the florists were wonderful men, trained in botanical gardens, an absolute law unto themselves and whom my father let alone, but the working crew usually included half a dozen misfits, old punchy animal trainers, or people my father just liked to have around. The whole atmosphere was feudal and the bookkeeping frequently chaotic. At one point my Uncle Charlie, the treasurer, was paying bills on the basis of a fifty-fifty split between my father and himself and declared profits of fifty-four percent for himself and forty-six percent for my father—a real Bonzi, who finally committed suicide after my father rejected him. It was a family tragedy and I don't like to go into it. Some of the names of the workers are actually incorporated in the shorter poems. Frau Bauman, Frau Schmidt, and Frau Schwartze[8] are actual people for instance, and Max Laurisch, who appears in a poem about my father which you haven't seen,[9] was a great florist and still alive. (If you don't mind I'd rather you didn't quote me directly. Just use the information in any way you wish.) Sometime I hope to do some prose of my own on that early childhood.

To Anthony Ostroff

Seattle, Washington
June 23, 1962

Dear Tony: Thanks very much for the two jolly letters.

Let me brood further about the cummings poem.[1] I had rather hoped to do nothing but purely creative stuff this summer.

You ask about the courses I teach. Here they are:

[8] Refers to the poem of that title to be found in *The Waking* and in *Words for the Wind,* p. 47.
[9] "Otto." *CP,* pp. 224–25.

---

[1] Ostroff had asked Roethke to contribute to a symposium on one of e. e. cummings' poems. Roethke did accept, but the project was canceled by cummings' death that summer.

1. *Types of Poetry,* or *Contemporary Poetry.* This is not a lecture course but (is) run like a seminar with usually about twenty-five students, undergraduate and graduate. Usually I use complete texts of two or three people and a couple or three anthologies for general background reading. The whole idea is to get the student to hear the language, to develop sensibility. The people I usually concentrate on are, say, Yeats and Hopkins one quarter; Kunitz, Auden and Tate in another; or in another, Bogan, Adams, Marianne Moore and other women poets. The method is eclectic and intensive. A student is supposed to have a very intimate knowledge of the texts we use and there are *always* spot questions on a pretty tough exam, and there is always a paper on a particular poet not taken up in class or some special aspect of poetry. I get very bright kids and they tell me repeatedly that the course is the best thing they ever had, or that my course and Heilman's are the best in the department.

2. *The writing of verse,* called for juniors, seniors and graduate students *Advanced writing of verse.* This course has been drawing students from other parts of the country and Europe for some considerable time. Twice in the last ten years a student from this course has won *Poetry's* Young Poet's Prize, and James Wright, Auden said, had the best Yale Series volume under his editorship,[2] and graduates from the course have printed poems in practically every good magazine in the English language as well as the Scribners' Series and the Indiana Series of poets. There are no scholarships or fellowships and no effort is made to recruit candidates, as Iowa does. The February 1952 issue of *Poetry* had a statement which explained the aims and methods of the course.[3] I had a copy but cannot lay my hands on it at the moment—I'll try to get one to send you. Also I'm including a couple of typical exams which give some notion of how I go about things. In one instance I take some material on words from one of Josephine Miles' books. I was going to send her this but finally thought it inadvisable.

I am beginning to find this course a real exhaustion and would not want to teach it as a regular thing. Perhaps once a year or once every other year I could run one semester.

[2] *The Green Wall* (1957).
[3] "The Teaching Poet." Reprinted in *On the Poet and His Craft.*

You can use your own judgment, of course, about whether to present any of this or not. I don't want to seem a too eager beaver.

You can add on the poop sheet about prizes and honors one more item: last week I was given an honorary degree, Doctor of Letters, from the University of Michigan, along with Frost, Cantinflas, and MacNamara.

The University of Washington has just announced in today's papers that it is giving me its first honorary title; in addition to Professor of English it has been added: Poet in Residence. This may not seem very earthshaking, but it represents a departure in policy by the University and according to my department head it is its way of giving an honorary degree. In addition the Regents raised my salary above the figure I mentioned to you. While this may make things even a bit more difficult please understand that I am still interested.

Mondadori, the Italian publisher, is going to do an Italian selected edition in its same series with Ungaretti, Montale, and Quasimodo.[4] There is supposed also to be an edition in Polish, in Japanese, and possibly one by Gallimard in French. In all, some work has been translated into about twenty languages.

Your saga about the fishing trip is hilarious. Me, I stopped at Glacier Park this week and saw my first mountain goat and a golden eagle, among other things.

If there is anything else you'd like to know, or any other material you'd like, just give me the word. I have some critical opinions I may send along which could be presented to the big brass.

To Isabella Gardner

Seattle, Washington
February 17, 1963

Dear Isabella: I feel a terrible toad for not writing sooner to say thanks for the wire: It bucked me up a good deal—really. . . . In the end, everything went swimmingly: a sell-out, with people offering as high as $15 for a seat! Even the president (Odegaard)[1]

---

[4] Giuseppe Ungaretti, Eugenio Montale, and Salvatore Quasimodo, three of the most important contemporary Italian poets.

[1] Charles E. Odegaard, president of the University of Washington. Roethke is referring here to a reading given in connection with the Seattle World's Fair.

professed to be highly pleased—and he doesn't please easy. But I'd never do it again for such heels (the Fair publicity boobs).

Did Louis U. ever write about the children's book? He said he was going to. Also I'm dying of curiosity as to whether Hy Peskin[2] [. . .] ever wrote Allen[3] about coming to its second annual meeting in December. He (Peskin) asked me to recommend someone, preferably on the West Coast because his funds were running low. I told Peskin the nearest poets of the stature he was thinking about were Allen & John Ransom [. . .]; gave him a longish supporting set of facts in each case. But Peskin has never written what he did. . . . Beatrice & I were going, but finally didn't for a number of reasons. . . . Last year this outfit had $125,000 to spend in Monterey, and the hilarity was splendid: champagne like tapwater, even wild boar at one party, police escorts at times; a lovely chick to drive you about—the damndest shindig I ever attended. And the people, for the most part, warm, generous-minded.

The affair had its sinister sides: Dr. Edward Teller was the main speaker, and there were [others] like Louis Johnson of Lockheed, and the guy that designed that spy aeroplane, U2 is it? Etc. . . . I, poor I, and a wonderful Englishman named Harding were practically the only people to stand up for the arts. . . . There was *one* painter, that old guy from Kansas;[4] and a Hungarian photographer. All the rest people saluted by *Time, Life,* etc. We all got a golden plate with our names fired on it. On mine they had misspelled, not "Roethke," but "Theodore." Ah, California.

Continued on Tuesday

(I'm in bed with Asian flu *and* a cold; so is Beatrice—but in her case it's more dangerous. She has a T.B. history, and for that matter I've had pneumonia twice, and have been told if I get it again, I'll die. Apparently it's that mixed type I get which the damned drugs don't get at, or something.) . . . So if this letter sounds nutty, put it down to that.

Anyway, I'm trying to find out whether Peskin asked either Allen and/or John Ransom, because if he didn't, I'd be inclined to resign from his silly National Board, unless he simply didn't

---

[2] Of the Academy of Achievement in San Diego.
[3] Allen Tate, who was then married to Isabella Gardner.
[4] Thomas Hart Benton.

have the travel expenses to offer. . . . But at least he could have written to me what he did.

My idea was: The four of us might have had real fun deflating phonies & getting some sun & getting to know each other. (The University was prepared to underwrite any travel expenses, but not Beatrice's of course.)

This brings me to another embarrassing question or point. Over the 'phone Allen said Minnesota could dig up $500 flat for my electrifying services, but I haven't heard anything further,—maybe he was just in a euphoric state of good will, or maybe he just plumb forgot—as *I* have, alas, in such matters.

But here's the pernt: I'm labouring at Illinois for the *Speech* people there, largely because a former student, Chester Long, wants me to: two days for $550, and no expense money god-damn it. So I can't take Beatrice (without earning money),—which Bob H.[5] and the doctors prefer I do. . . . All this on April 26–27.

Well, to wrap it all up, if Allen still has $500 in his kitty for a reading, I could come on, say, Tuesday or Wednesday *before* the Illinois do, and then proceed to Urbana. . . . But *don't* think I am trying to twist Allen's arm. Matter of fact, out of the blue, Wisconsin wrote hoping I could make a side trip sometime with a fee that would have insulted a snake oil vendor. Haven't even answered them. . . . And who the hell is at Wisconsin? I thought it a stodgy place in 1925.

My God, this is the longest "letter" I've written in years. . . .

And I guess the real reason (deep in my heart of hearts, where there is nothing but wormy ambition) is that I would so much like both of you to take a gander at *Dance On, Dance On, Dance On,* the mss. of the new book.[6] (I've got old Cal [7] beat, but really); and if you don't think it's one hell of a book, I'll turn in my suit. I say this, I suppose, because I always have the terror that I won't-write-another, etc. Ach Gott, you know.

Enough of slobbering egomania and four *I's* in one sentence.

What set me off on all this, I guess, is Andrew Lytle's[8] writing

[5] Robert Heilman.

[6] Not published until after Roethke's death, and then under the title *The Far Field* (1964).

[7] Robert Lowell.

[8] Editor of *Sewanee Review,* to which Roethke had sent, among other poems, "The Far Field." *CP,* pp. 199–201.

me that Allen had written saying he liked "The Far Field," particularly. Since Arnold Stein had told me, rather loftily, that there were "things wrong with that poem," or something like that,—I was especially heartened. It's a vulnerable piece, and part of a sequence of six; but I'm damned if I can find a *lousy* passage.

Dear love, if all this sounds nutty, put it down to the fever. And don't bother Allen with any of this if he is harried unduly about things.

But it would be grand to see you (pl.), John the Berryman, & Gentleman Jim Wright.

Love, love,
Ted R.

THE MOMENT[9]

We passed the ice of pain,
And came to a dark ravine,
And there we sang with the sea;
The wide, the bleak abyss
Shifted with our slow kiss.

Space struggled with time;
The gong of midnight struck
The naked absolute.
Sound, silence sang as one.

All flowed: without, within;
Body met body, we
Created what's to be:

What else to say?—
We end in joy.

My last piece. I'd like to think it has some of the bleak terribleness that Allen gets in "The Cross" (and others)—a piece, incidentally, that knocked my kids down. (I put it on an exam last quarter.)

---

[9] *CP*, p. 238.

To Judith Gerber[1]

February 28, 1963

Dear Miss Gerber: Please accept my apologies for not answering sooner your letter of January 13, 1963. I have been laid up with the flu part of the time.

I am afraid I can't help you very much. I can honestly say I have read very little Freud, not even the basic writings. On the other hand, some of my fancy friends went through analysis with some of the Viennese people and I dare say I picked up some notions from their babbling about their therapy. I am thinking particularly of the late Professor Harold Chidsey, who had the chair of philosophy at Lafayette College when I first began teaching. On the other hand I have known such distinguished analysts as Eisler of New York and Hoffer of London and much of their talk has been at least influenced by Freud.[2] But I met these men a good deal after the writing of the poems that you would probably consider "Freudian."

I have read part of Jung's *Modern Man in Search of a Soul*, but again, rather recently. Officially I am a Presbyterian, but a most indifferent one, I'm afraid. Stanley Kunitz says I am the best Jewish poet in the language. I am really not trying to be witty or flippant—all this happens to be the truth.

Thanks for your kind remarks about "The Waking" and the other pieces. With all good wishes,

Sincerely yours,
Theodore Roethke

---

[1] Miss Gerber, who was preparing a master's thesis at Columbia on the "Blending of Freudian and Christian Sensibilities" in Roethke's verse, wrote him (January 13, 1963) for "a statement about the influence of Freud's writings or ideas" on his poetry.

[2] Dr. Kurt Eisler and Dr. William Hoffer are noted Freudian psychiatrists.

To Ludmila Marjańska[1]

Seattle, Washington
March 29, 1963

My dear Ludmila Marjańska: It was a great pleasure for me to hear from you, particularly since I had been thinking about you recently and had been intending to send on a recording[2]—not really good, but overpraised by the reviews—and some other items that might interest you.

Beatrice and I both loved your card and the sense it gave of what Poland is like. We have been thinking that we would like to visit there. As you may not know, my family originally came from Stettin—my grandfather having been Bismarck's head forester. So in a sense I feel I am a sort of Pole, rather than a German (my grandfather, incidentally, had a terrible row with old Bismarck and was virtually kicked out of Germany in 1870. My grandmother, equally hot-tempered, was the keeper of the keys to the Bismarck wine cellar, and I am sure that she too was never afraid of telling the old man off, so it may be that it is only the Roethkes and the Rothschilds who really faced old Bismarck down. The Rothschilds came off somewhat better, since my grandfather worked for a year for a barrel of flour when he first came over).

So I am delighted and honored that you are going to do the translations, and I hope you go on and do even more than the one or two other poems you mention. As a matter of fact, I had heard of it indirectly from a presumably reliable source (the wife of a man in the Canadian embassy) who said there was a sort of underground entire edition of my works being translated into Polish. If that is the case I think there should be some gesture of payment —even if the money has to remain in Poland. It would give me great pleasure to come over and spend some more, or to be invited by the government to do some readings and lectures in English. But this is a matter which goes beyond your present charming and witty letter.

---

[1] Graduate student in literature at the University of Warsaw, who did some work at the University of Washington. She had translated into Polish work by several English and American poets.

[2] *Words for the Wind* (selections), read by Roethke, Folkways Records FL 9736 (1962).

As to your particular questions:

(1) "Elegy for Jane." [3] Yes, it is Jane who is scraping her cheek against straw—presumably lying down as a child would, feeling an emotion that is a kind of cross between humility and exaltation—something like that. She, too, is stirring the clear water. I hope the gesture isn't insurmountable.

(2) "Nor the moss, wound with the last light." Definitely I mean the last light to imply sunset. (The final ultimate light,   )

(3) "I wake to sleep." To wake here means to be awakened into full awareness: a paradox that this wakening does partake of the nature of an eternal wakening.

(4) "I hear my being dance from ear to ear." As far as I know this is not an idiomatic expression. It means that the being of the speaker does its own internal dance within the mind, within the brain.

Please do not hesitate to ask me anything else, and if you really want the manuscript of the entire new book, to be called *Dance on, Dance On, Dance On,* which will be published first in Ireland, then in England,[4] and a good bit of it in Italian, let me know.

I assure you that I am overly fond of straight Russian vodka—I think I like it and the Russian zubrovka (the kind flavored with European buffalo grass) the best of all dry drinks.

Sincerely yours,
Theodore Roethke

To JUDITH BAILEY JONES[1]

Seattle, Washington
June 10, 1963

Dear Judy: I am delighted that you are printing John Logan's poetry and I'll do what I can to talk the volume[2] up. He was out here some weeks back and we had a splendid time.

---

[3] *CP,* p. 102.

[4] This publishing scheme did not work out as mentioned here. *The Far Field* was not published in Ireland, and appeared in England (Faber and Faber) in 1965, a year after its American publication.

---

[1] Former Bennington student, then an editor at Alfred A. Knopf.

[2] *Spring of the Thief* (1963).

You asked me some time back to keep thinking about possibilities for paperbacks, and so on. One beautiful one, I think, would be Rolfe Humphries' collected poems. I wanted to use it as a text last year and found it was out of print. Also, have you ever considered Caroline Gordon's short stories? Some of them, like "Big Red," are very good indeed, to my mind.

That beautiful Greek anthology you sent me some student swiped.

Douglas Moore was in town a while back and we had news of you. Let me hear if you have any reaction to any of this.

> Love,
> Theodore Roethke

To John Frederick Nims

Bainbridge Island, Washington
July 4, 1963

John old matador: New poems[1] smashin': I mean it: we're going down the same road: witty, bawdy, tender.

Knock 'em dead at Harvard.[2] If you get panicky, wire and I'll send you a bale of crap-tricks, gimmicks, I've used. . . . And tell them if they want *me* it's $35,000 (thirty-five) and not a penny less.

T. R.

New documentary movie (on me) supposed to be a smash—better than any so far[3] . . . Ralph Mills' pamphlet on sweet myself (Minnesota Press) also out in the Fall. . . . Love to mamma & the chickies.

> Graf von Roethke

---

[1] Refers to some poems which Nims had given Roethke.

[2] John Nims was invited to Harvard as a visiting professor in the coming year.

[3] *In a Dark Time,* a film by David Myers, produced by the Poetry Center and Associated Students of San Francisco State College, was made in January, 1963; much of the film was shot in Seattle and on Bainbridge Island (where Roethke died suddenly on August 1, 1963).

Index

Correspondents

Persons Mentioned

Works